The Impact of Academic Research

William Schweiker | Michael Welker | John Witte
Stephen Pickard (Eds.)

The Impact of Academic Research

On Character Formation, Ethical Education,
and the Communication of Values
in Late Modern Pluralistic Societies

WIPF & STOCK · Eugene, Oregon

Wipf and Stock Publishers
199 W 8th Ave, Suite 3
Eugene, OR 97401

The Impact of Academic Research
On Character Formation, Ethical Education, and the Communication
of Values in Late Modern Pluralistic Societies
By Schweiker, William and Welker, Michael
Copyright © 2021 Evangelische Verlagsanstalt GmbH All rights reserved.
Softcover ISBN-13: 978-1-6667-5056-0
Hardcover ISBN-13: 978-1-6667-5057-7
Publication date 6/14/2022
Previously published by Evangelische Verlagsanstalt GmbH, 2021

Inhalt

Acknowledgments 7

Preface to the Series 9
Character Formation and Moral Education in Late Modern Pluralistic Societies: An Interdisciplinary and International Research Project

William Schweiker
Introduction to the Present Volume 13

Part One Academic Work and Ethical Concerns in Research Universities?

William Schweiker
The Idea of a Research University 23

Andreas Glaeser
Analyzing Actually Existing Ethics 39
A Hermeneutic-Institutionalist Approach

Bernold Fiedler
Absolute Truth—A Toxic Chimera? 65

Rüdiger Bittner
Can Academic Research Be a Moral Guide? 89

Michael Welker
Joy of Discovery—Respect for the Search for Truth—Honesty .. 99
The Blessings of a Global Network of Research Universities

Part Two Character and Ethics at the Intersection of Disciplines

Jörg Hüfner
The Impact of Science on Ethics 109

Michael Kirschfink
Ethical Considerations in Biomedical Research 119
Welcome Guidance or Unwanted Restrictions to Scientific
Progress?

Gary S. Hauk
Academic Bondage and Social Transformation 131
The Case of American Universities and Slavery

John Witte Jr.
The Educational Values of Studying Law and Religion 153

Andreas Schüle
Emergence of Truth 169
The Interplay of Science and Theology in Genesis 1 and
Psalm 104

Stefan Alkier
Forming Identity by Scripture 179

Celia Deane-Drummond
Forming Research Scientists? 197
Developing Practical Wisdom and Virtue in Multidisciplinary
Academic Frameworks

Contributors 211

Acknowledgments

In this book, twelve scholars from different academic fields in the natural sciences, humanities, social sciences, theology, and mathematics explore the impact of academic research on character formation, ethical education, and the communication of values in late modern pluralistic societies. The focus on research naturally requires special attention to the variety of tensions inherent in the modern research university as it has developed over the past two centuries.

The book began with a consultation in Heidelberg in the spring of 2019 and is part of a larger project that includes volumes on the impact of the market, the impact of law, and the impact of religion on character formation, ethical education, and the communication of values in late modern pluralistic societies. Six more consultations are in the planning phase.

The Heidelberg consultation and this publication were made possible by a generous grant by the Alonzo McDonald Agape Foundation and the University of Heidelberg. We thank the late Ambassador Dr. Alonzo McDonald for his initial support and his son Peter McDonald, now president of the foundation. Thanks go to the Internationales Wissenschaftsforum Heidelberg (IWH) and its staff for hosting the consultations. David Reissmann, Christine Böckmann, Hans-Joachim Kenkel, Viola von Boehn, and Daniel Stil helped us organize the consultations and prepare this publication. Dr. Gary Hauk, of Emory University, kindly agreed to support the editorial process. Finally, we are grateful to the publisher, Evangelische Verlagsanstalt (Leipzig), and Dr. Annette Weidhas for their cooperation in this ambitious project.

Chicago, Heidelberg, Atlanta, Canberra, October 2020
W.S., M.W., J.W., S.P.

Preface to the Series
Character Formation and Moral Education in Late Modern Pluralistic Societies: An Interdisciplinary and International Research Project

Five hundred years ago, Protestant reformer Martin Luther argued that "three estates" (*drei Stände*) lie at the foundation of a just and orderly society—marital families, religious communities, and political authorities. Parents in the home; pastors in the church; magistrates in the state—these, said Luther, are the three authorities whom God appointed to represent divine justice and mercy in the world, to protect peace and liberty in earthly life. Household, church, and state —these are the three institutional pillars on which to build social systems of education and schooling, charity and social welfare, economy and architecture, art and publication. Family, faith, and freedom—these are the three things that people will die for.

In the half millennium since Luther, historians have uncovered various classical and Christian antecedents to these early Protestant views. And numerous later theorists have propounded all manner of variations and applications of this three-estates theory, many increasingly abstracted from Luther's overtly Christian worldview. Early modern covenant theologians, both Christian and Jewish, described the marital, confessional, and political covenants that God calls human beings to form, each directed to interrelated personal and public ends. Social-contract theorists differentiated the three contracts that humans enter as they move from the state of nature to an organized society protective of their natural rights— the marital contract of husband and wife; the government contract of rulers and citizens; and, for some, the religious contracts of preachers and parishioners. Early anthropologists posited three stages of development of civilization—from family-based tribes and clans, to priest-run theocracies, to fully organized states that embraced all three institutions. Sociologists distinguished three main forms of authority in an organized community: "traditional" authority that begins in the home, "charismatic" authority that is exemplified in the church, and "legal" authority that is rooted in the state. Legal historians outlined three stages of development of legal norms—from the habits and rules of the family, to the customs and canons of religion, to the statutes and codes of the state.

Already a century ago, however, scholars in different fields began to flatten out this hierarchical theory of social institutions and to emphasize the foundational role of other social institutions alongside the family, church, and state in shaping private and public life and character. Sociologists like Max Weber and Talcott Parsons emphasized the shaping powers of "technical rationality" exemplified especially in new industry, scientific education, and market economies. Legal scholars like Otto von Gierke and F. W. Maitland emphasized the critical roles of non-state legal associations (*Genossenschaften*) in maintaining a just social, political, and legal order historically and today. Catholic subsidiarity theories of Popes Leo XIII and Pius XI emphasized the essential task of mediating social units between the individual and the state to cater the full range of needs, interests, rights, and duties of individuals. Protestant theories of sphere sovereignty, inspired by Abraham Kuyper, argued that not only churches, states, and families but also the social spheres of art, labor, education, economics, agriculture, recreation, and more should enjoy a level of independence from others, especially an overreaching church or state. Various theories of social or structural pluralism, civil society, voluntary associations, the independent sector, multiculturalism, multinormativity, and other such labels have now come to the fore in the ensuing decades—both liberal and conservative, religious and secular, and featuring all manner of methods and logics.

Pluralism of all sorts is now a commonplace of late modern societies. At minimum, this means a multitude of free and equal individuals and a multitude of groups and institutions, each with very different political, moral, religious, and professional interests and orientations. It includes the sundry associations, interest groups, parties, lobbies, and social movements that often rapidly flourish and fade around a common cause, especially when aided by modern technology and various social media. Some see in this texture of plurality an enormous potential for colorful and creative development and a robust expression of human and cultural freedom. Others see a chaotic individualism and radical relativism, which endangers normative education, moral character formation, and effective cultivation of enduring values or virtues.

Pluralism viewed as vague plurality, however, focuses on only one aspect of late modern societies—the equality of individuals, and their almost unlimited freedom to participate peaceably at any time as a respected voice in the moral reasoning and civil interactions of a society. But this view does not adequately recognize that, beneath the shifting cacophony of social forms and norms that constitute modernity, pluralistic societies have heavy normative codes that shape their individual and collective values and morals, preferences and prejudices.

The sources of much of this normative coding and moral education in late modern pluralistic societies are the deep and powerful social systems that are the pillars of every advanced culture. The most powerful and pervasive of these are the social systems of law, religion, politics, science/academy, market, media, family, education, medicine, and national defense. The actual empirical forms of each of these powerful social systems can and do vary greatly, even in the relatively homogeneous societies of the late modern West. But these deeper social systems in one form or another are structurally essential and often normatively decisive in individual and communal lives.

Every advanced society has a comprehensive legal system of justice and order, religious systems of ritual and doctrine, a family system of procreation and love, an economic system of trade and value, a media system of communication and dissemination of news and information, and an educational system of preservation, application, and creation of knowledge and scientific advance. Many advanced societies also have massive systems of science, technology, healthcare, and national defense that exert vast influence over and through all of these other social systems. These pervasive social systems lie at the foundation of modern advanced societies, and they anchor the vast pluralities of associations and social interactions that might happen to exist at any given time.

Each of these social systems has internal value systems, institutionalized rationalities, and normative expectations that together help to shape each individual's morality and character. Each of these social spheres, moreover, has its own professionals and experts who shape and implement its internal structures and processes. The normative network created by these social spheres is often harder to grasp today, since late modern pluralistic societies usually do not bring these different value systems to light under the dominance of just one organization, institution, and power. And this normative network has also become more shifting and fragile, especially since traditional social systems like religion and the family have eroded in their durability and power, and other social systems like science, the market, healthcare, defense, and the media have become more powerful.

The aim of this project on "Character Formation and Moral Education in Late Modern Pluralistic Societies" is to identify the realities and potentials of these core social systems to provide moral orientation and character formation in our day. What can and should these social spheres, separately and together, do in shaping the moral character of late modern individuals who, by nature, culture, and constitutional norms, are free and equal in dignity and rights? What are and should be the core educational functions and moral responsibilities of each of these social spheres? How can we better understand and better influence the complex interactions among individualism, the normative binding powers of these social systems, and the creativity of civil groups and institutions? How can we map and measure the different hierarchies of values that govern each of these social systems, and that are also interwoven and interconnected in various ways in shaping late modern understandings of the common good? How do we negotiate the boundaries and conflicts between and among these social systems when one encroaches on the other, or imposes its values and rationalities on individuals at the cost of the other social spheres or of the common good? What and where are the intrinsic strengths of each social sphere that should be made more overt in character formation, public education, and the shaping of minds and mentalities?

These are some of the guiding questions at work in this project and in this volume. Our project aims to provide a systematic account of the role of these powerful normative codes operating in the social spheres of law, religion, the family, the market, the media, science and technology, the academy, healthcare, and defense in the late modern liberal West. Our focus is on selected examples and case studies drawn from Western Europe, North America, South Africa, and Australia, which together provide just enough diversity to test out broader theories of character formation and moral education. Our scholars are drawn from across the academy, with representative voices from the humanities, social sciences, and natural sciences as well as the professions of theology, law, business, medicine, and more. While most of our scholars come from the Protestant and Catholic worlds, our endeavor is to offer comparative insights that will help scholars from any profession or confession. While our laboratory is principally Western liberal societies, the modern forces of globalization will soon make these issues of moral character formation a concern for every culture and region of the world—given the power of global social media, entertainment, and sports; the pervasiveness of global finance, business, trade, and law; and the perennial global worries over food, healthcare, environmental degradation, and natural disasters.

In this volume, we focus on the role of academic research in shaping character development, ethical education, and the communication of values in late modern pluralistic societies.

William Schweiker, the University of Chicago
Michael Welker, the University of Heidelberg
John Witte Jr., Emory University
Stephen Pickard, Charles Sturt University

Introduction to the Present Volume
William Schweiker

Reflection on contemporary Western societies and cultures by scholars in various fields has noted that while they are indeed "secular" in many respects, they are also home to a variety of religious forms and practices. Whether one speaks of a postsecular age or late modernity, previous convictions about the withering away of religion and the triumph of secularism in the West have simply proven false. That is true as well on the global scene. Not only have virulent forms of religious fundamentalism risen to dot the global landscape, but so, too, Christianity, Islam, Buddhism, and other traditions have experienced worldwide growth. Furthermore, late modern societies are characterized by differentiated but interacting social spheres or systems rather than a hierarchical structure. Educational systems interact in complex ways with economies, political institutions, media, and even the military. The purpose of this volume is to explore the formation of character and the communication of values within the sphere of the contemporary research university. This introduction aims to provide orientation to the volume as a whole and also to specific contributions.

Reasons for the Inquiry

Education and academic research are complex topics that have, for several reasons, preoccupied people and communities throughout history. First, insofar as human beings do not come into the world fully formed, they must be morally and socially shaped and educated, a conjunction captured in the German idea of *Bildung*, or self-cultivation. Of course, the idea of self-cultivation is ambiguous. Does it mean the self is cultivating itself in some act of freedom, desire, and will? Discourse about the formation of the virtues and character has been important in Western thought at least since the time of the ancient Greek philosophers. Any account of the formation of humans must make sense of the ways in which people through their actions and relations carry on the process on self-cultivation. Conversely, thinkers, especially modern thinkers, have explored the ways in which the self is cultivated or shaped by social, cultural, and religious forces. The great social theorists of the past two centuries—Karl Marx, Emile Durkheim, Max Weber, and Friedrich Nietzsche, to name a few—examined how social processes—language use, economic exchanges, collective experience, and the like—form distinctive types of human life and character. Of course, the formation of character must be some combination of these two perspectives. Human beings seemingly individuate through socialization.[1]

Interestingly, authors contributing to this volume disagree on this point. Some contributors place greater, if not exclusive, emphasis on social spheres that shape character, while others are much more concerned with individual agency. Of course, this is a distinction without a separation: the dynamics of self-cultivation are deeply woven together. Nevertheless, matters of emphasis do make a difference, no matter what social sphere one is examining. How, then, to understand, to analyze, and even to direct the dynamics of self-cultivation? Again, the series that includes this book explores that question with respect to the various social systems or value spheres that characterize late modern society. The present volume does so with respect to that social sphere concerned with the interaction of character formation, education (in the broadest sense), and research. The reader is encouraged to isolate and explore the difference that an author's perspective on the topic makes in understanding character formation and, with it, the communication of values.

The second reason that people have been preoccupied with education and research throughout history is also rooted in a characteristic of human life. Not only do people come into the world unformed, but they also enter at birth and exit at death a world—a culture and society—that they must come to understand, help to shape and to transmit, and alter under particular conditions, doing so in collectives.[2] This raises the philosophical question of what we mean by a "world" and how we understand the ways in which worlds are made.[3] Worlds are determinate domains or spheres of meaning and value, such that to be human is to live in and move among many worlds.

On one hand, human beings are world-creating creatures driven by want, anxiety, and fear, and with amazing curiosity about their communities, themselves, and the widest extent of reality, physical and nonphysical. Their social worlds have to answer for those basic needs and the many other challenges that cluster around them. On the other hand, those basic needs are the roots of education, insofar as humans must answer the problems that finite life presents to

---

[1] On this point about human sociality, see Jürgen Habermas, *Moral Consciousness and Communicative Action* (Cambridge, MA: MIT Press, 1990).

[2] See John Rawls, *Political Liberalism* (New York: Columbia University Press, 1971).

[3] On the idea of worldmaking, see Nelson Goodman, *Ways of Worldmaking* (Indianapolis, IN: Hackett, 1978).

them and yet also wonder about their existence and place in reality. History is, then, the dialectic of structures to meet basic needs and the adventure of creative responses to them driven by human imagination and industry.[4] In this respect, to be human is to seek and to create knowledge, because we are problem solvers and also questioners. Education and research are, then, fundamental to human life, insofar as people are knowers and doers fashioning their various worlds. Here, too, the reader of this book will find agreement and disagreement among authors on the point and purposes of education. Not only on the work and ethical concern of education and research in general (Part One), but also with respect to specific disciplines and research agendas (Part Two).

The reasons just enumerated for interest in character formation and the communication of value in academic research intersect with some challenges. One challenge is that world making and self-formation are matters of collective action. It is true that, often enough, a researcher works alone in her laboratory or engages in solitary research in archives, libraries, and offices. Nevertheless, at profound levels, especially in validating hypotheses and claims, research is a social practice. And that is true of every form of education in ways that open reflection on the nature of human individual and social life. That is, within families, small communities, cultures, and even global social dynamics, human beings are profoundly, and sometimes troublingly, social creatures who must fashion lives together. People face the challenge of creating and sustaining some measure of functional social cooperation provoked by the facts of finite existence. How do pluralistic societies do so? This series of books, and especially this one about academic research, seek to address that question.

Collective action demands reflection on the aims and values of social and personal lives as well as the development of norms, legal and moral, that guide and structure human interaction as well as self-development. How are norms and values defined, authorized, ranked, applied, and lived? And who does the defining, authorizing, ranking, applying, and living? This second challenge is not the practical one of collective action and how to foster and sustain it, but an ideological challenge, in a nonpejorative sense of the word. That is, academic research, like any individual and social practice, must have some aim in view or purpose, norms for the practice of a specific form of research, criteria of evaluation and validation of claims and results, and patterns of authority and certification. To be sure, these are "ideological" elements of social practice. They express human ideas that can be distorted and used to legitimate—as Marx, Nietzsche, and others have noted—false and destructive practices and authorities. One task of the modern research university, then, has been to engage in the self-criticism and critique of social practices and the ideologies that drive them. Even the longstanding and much

---

[4] Alfred North Whitehead makes this argument in *Adventures of Ideas* (New York: Free Press, 1967).

disputed cry for "value neutral" research is, in fact, a plea that ends in the view that the criteria and norms that guide research must be validated in public ways rather than by simple appeals to authority.

All of these issues and challenges (self-formation in its various forms, world making, collective action, and creation and critique of norms and values) intersect with each other in exceedingly complex ways around the themes of education and research. The intersections have given rise to diverse theories of culture, sociologies, moral theories, and philosophical positions. As noted below, this volume is apt testimony to this diversity of theory, as becomes evident in reading the various authors and chapters. However, before noting the specifics of this text, one more dimension to the book's inquiry must be noted, and that is religion.

Religion and Education?

Not only the topic of this book but also the issues and challenges noted above are configured in specific ways by the world's religions. Religions have always been profoundly concerned with the establishment of norms and values as well as character formation and collective action. They have also presented many domains of meaning, that is, many worlds, which human beings, whether in body and/or soul, can inhabit and traverse.[5] Religions have also defined and enacted worlds in profoundly different ways (for example, karmic cycles, heavenly realms, gods and demons, divine judgment) that often stretch the imagination and credulity of modern peoples. What contribution, if any, might religions make to reflection on academic research in our time?

For most of human history and for most religions, universal formal education has not been the norm, nor has it been compulsory. Education was often reserved for men and boys and for members of religious orders or social elites. Confucianism, for example, was institutionalized through the imperial examination systems in various Chinese dynasties. The Greek philosophers developed their own schools, but this was more to practice a way of life than to educate the populace. Aristotle, after all, was tutor to Alexander the Great. In Judaism, the yeshiva for some Jews supposedly predates even the giving of the Torah, but flourished during the Second Temple period (516 BCE to 70 CE). With the destruction of the Second Temple by the Romans in 70 CE, rabbinical Judaism and its school began and developed its exceedingly complex forms of interpreting Torah and engaging in argumentation.[6]

---

[5] See William Schweiker, *Theological Ethics and Global Dynamics: In the Time of Many Worlds* (New York: Wiley-Blackwell, 2004).

[6] For an incisive account, see Michael Fishbane, *Biblical Myth and Rabbinic Mythmaking* (Oxford: Oxford University Press, 2003).

One more example is in order. The modern Western university, beginning with the University of Bologna in 1088, evolved out of the Christian cathedral schools as well as monastic schools instituted by various Christian religious orders. This was due in part to the growth of towns within the Holy Roman Empire and, with them, increased trade and degrees of political autonomy for princes and lords. There also arose guilds for training people in a range of trades from merchants to various crafts. Flourishing from the eleventh to the sixteenth centuries, the guilds were intrinsic to the economic and political structure of society. Reaching their height in the thirteenth century, they lasted into the nineteenth century in Germany. They were often associated with fraternities that flourished in the universities. In a word, the social order of medieval Europe was becoming increasingly differentiated into elements of civil society (for example, guilds and fraternities) that were increasingly important for social order.

During the same centuries, one sees a shift in the meaning and task of theology and, so, different ideas for the aim of education. The background of these developments is found in Saint Augustine's *De Doctrina Christiana*, which set the educational agenda well into the Middle Ages.[7] In the monastic schools from the early Middle Ages to the twelfth century, theological labor focused scriptural commentary and even philosophical reflection on holy writ. Theology was spurred on by the quest for wisdom (*sapientia*). Yet in the context of the monastery, Saint Anselm of Canterbury (d. 1109) sought to prove the existence of God in his famous *Proslogion* (1077-78) with the so-called ontological proof. Called the most important theologian between Augustine and Thomas Aquinas, Anselm has been seen as the "father of scholasticism," that is, theologies in the schools. Yet it ought not be forgotten than even the complex and abstract *Proslogion* begins in prayer and is, at it were, a commentary on the psalmist's claim that the fool says in his heart that there is no God.[8] In a word, reason and not just revelation can grasp the human highest good. Yet the meaning of theology shifts with the founding of the great universities (Paris, Oxford, etc.). Thomas Aquinas (1225-74), in his *Summa Theologiae*, argued that theology is both a form of wisdom (*sapientia*) and a kind of knowledge (*scientia*). This meant, for Thomas, blending the forms of argument and analysis found in so-called pagan authors, especially Aristotle, with Christian exegetical and doctrinal concerns. Yet Aquinas was also certain that the reason to

---

[7] On Augustine and education, see William Schweiker, "The Saint and the Humanities," in *Augustine Our Contemporary: Examining the Self in Past and Present*, ed. W. Otten and S. Schreiner (Notre Dame, IN: University of Notre Dame Press, 2018): 249-66.

[8] See Philip Clayton, "The Otherness of Anselm," in *The Otherness of God*, ed. O. F. Summerell (Charlottesville: University Press of Virginia, 1998): 14-34.

engage in theological reflection—its end in view—was, given grace, human salvation and the ultimate blessing of the vision of God.[9]

Most of these factors—social, economic, and theological—were at play during the period of the Protestant Reformation and Catholic Counter-Reformation. The Council of Trent (1545–63) addressed not only doctrinal issues but also the education of priests. Likewise, the Protestant reformers recovered the work of *sacred page*, theology as commentary on the Bible, but they also established schools that included women students.[10] Additionally, with the rise of humanistic thinkers like Erasmus and many others, classic texts and the recovery of rhetoric altered the face of education. Phillip Melanchthon, Martin Luther's collaborator, set the curricula for schools, making him not only the first Protestant systematic theologian but also the "teacher of Germany." The institutions established by reformers, Catholic and Protestant, endure today.

In a word, the medieval and Reformation-era universities explored the scope and kinds of knowledge that should be their special purview. But it was not until the founding of the Friedrich-Wilhelms-Universität (1810–1954, now Humboldt University of Berlin), that the modern research university was established with a research component as well as teaching requirements. The idea was to create an institution dedicated to research and the creation of knowledge that found, in the United States, institutional expression in the University of Chicago and Johns Hopkins University. But Hopkins and Chicago were decidedly different than Humboldt in one crucial respect. Unlike their German forerunner and the many land-grant universities in the United States, Chicago and Hopkins were not beholden to the state. In the United States, Germany, and elsewhere, universities became part of state-run compulsory education, in which students were to be admitted and educated under state-legislated forms. Thankfully, there was also a movement to include girls and women in the educational system. In this respect, the current volume assumes decidedly late modern societies and does not and cannot address other forms of society. However, it is also the case that even late modern societies have, as part of their history and cultural background, premodern religious forms and practices.

Structure of the Book

The remarks above noted some of the reasons for concern for education and the communication of values in different social contexts, and sketched the rise of the

---

[9] Most recently, Denys Turner, *Thomas Aquinas: A Portrait* (New Haven, CT: Yale University Press, 2013).

[10] For an excellent discussion of this point, see *Europa Reformata: European Cities and the Reformers*, ed. M. Welker et.al. (Leipzig: Evangelishe Verlagsanstalt, 2017).

modern research university in the West. The various authors represented in this volume will, in different ways, address these issues as well as note other conceptual, social, and historical factors important for reflection on the formation of character and the communication of values in research universities. It is the reader's task to engage these authors, so a comprehensive review of their arguments is not needed in this introduction. Nevertheless, a few words by way of introduction are in order, thereby to orient the reader.

As noted, the volume is divided into two parts: "Part One: Academic Work and Ethical Concerns in Research Universities?" and "Part Two: Character and Ethics at the Intersection of Disciplines." The two parts of the book are obviously deeply interrelated, but, in general, Part One explores general issues about character formation and ethical communication within the research university, while Part Two picks up the question with attention to specific disciplines. Given the focus of the book as a whole and, indeed, this entire series of books, religious questions and religious texts and forms of thought are found in both parts of the volume. This organization of the book, while seemingly simple, does allow the reader to see how deeply intertwined are general issues about the relation between character and ethical communication within a research university and the work and intersection of specific scholarly disciplines.

Part One of the book opens with historical and sociological analyses and constructive proposals for ethics and the modern research university. *William Schweiker*, in chapter 1, explores various shifts from the medieval to the modern university and what these mean for the ethical purpose of research itself. The sociologist *Andreas Glaeser* explores, in chapter 2, the interdependence between ethics and other institutions, including the modern university. He notes that to grasp "the diversity, fragmentation, and transformation of actually existing ethics, including dramatic episodes of apparent ethical breakdown or, conversely, of ethical flourishing, it is key to understand ethics in relation to a wider range of other institutional formations and their development." Part One of the book then explores, in a moment of dialectical tension, whether or not ideas of absolute truth are in fact toxic for the moral life and research (see *Bernold Fiedler*, in chapter 3), and then Rüdiger Bittner questions, in chapter 4, the very idea that the university could or should be a moral guide. Part One of the book concludes with *Michael Welker's* account in chapter 5 of research in relation to differentiated truth claims and, in this respect, his response to skeptical arguments about the ethical task of the modern university.

The volume then turns, in Part Two, to inquiries into the formation of character and ethical communication in specific disciplines. Part Two begins, in parallel to Part One, with two general inquiries—first into the impact of science on ethics (chapter 6, by *Jörg Hüfner*) and then into the extent to which ethics can guide but also restrict biomedical research (chapter 7, by *Michael Kirschfink*). Part Two then moves from those general inquiries into specific disciplines, specifically history (chapter 8, by *Gary Hauk*), law (chapter 9, by *John Witte*) and biblical studies (chapter 10, by *Andreas Schüle*). These chapters, in their own ways, not only probe the questions of this book within specific disciplines but also exemplify the topic by working within those disciplines. If Part Two started with basic questions about the place of ethics and moral values in scientific (that is, *wissenschaftliche*) research, then the final two chapters explore the formation of the "scientists" in biblical studies (chapter 11, by *Stefan Alkier*) and in the natural sciences (chapter 12, by *Celia Deane-Drummond*). In this way, the reader can ponder the impact of science on ethics at the level of lived experience.

All told, each part of the book has its internal logic, while the volume as a whole enables reflection on the general topic as well as on exemplary disciplines. To be sure, much more work can and must be done on this topic. It is the hope of the authors that their reflections will spur such inquiry into the contributions and dangers of academic research to character formation and ethical communication in highly pluralistic societies.

For the Future

This introduction began with the observation that research, education, and moral formation are rooted in some basic human needs and challenges. Cultures will understand, assess, and respond to these needs and challenges in exceedingly different ways. Given this, as the volume shows, current research in the natural and social sciences as well as in the humanities must engage a welter of topics and resources, even as research, while living off the past in the present, pushes into the future. In this respect, the book is not only a snapshot and assessment of current realities. It also is a charge to researchers and all interested people to work on how to forge the future in ways that rightly form human character and communicate the ethical values needed for the flourishing of life, both human and nonhuman. This is not, as some rightly worry, a moralistic agenda that could curtail or warp research. It is, rather, an aim needed to sustain the ongoing labor of careful, serious, and truthful inquiry.

Part One
Academic Work and Ethical Concerns in Research Universities?

Part One

The Idea of a Research University

William Schweiker[1]

Task and Approach

The connection between education, broadly conceived, and the formation of character has been known but also debated from the distant past to the present and in virtually every known human society. There is ample reason for this knowledge and the debate. It is hard to imagine the transmission, reformation, and continuation of human institutions without education in some form.[2] Equally difficult to conceive is a form of personal life that is not shaped by the person herself or himself and by social institutions, and that does not entail in some way the transmission of knowledge, routine actions, and habitual modes of interaction. And in each case, some things, actions, and relations are deemed more important than others, and thus objects of human care and value. Little wonder, then, that the dynamics of education and character formation would, in virtually every society, ascend to some form of reflection on those dynamics—call it philosophy, law, theology, or what have you. In this respect, the topic of this book is neither remarkable nor novel, and it is tempting to leave the topic to those specialists who develop educational theories and to the public policy makers who try to implement them. Such, at least, would seem to be the case. Yet that is not the case. Reflection on this topic is still needed for reasons I hope to explain and then answer in this essay.

My strategy of reflection approaches our topic on different but intersecting levels or planes of reflection. I begin with some brief historical comments on the origin and demise of the idea of the university. That will be followed, on another plane of reflection, by isolating interacting forces that gave rise to the possibilities

---

[1] I want to thank Michael Welker and Sara-Jo Swiatek for helpful comments on this essay; all errors remain mine alone. I am also mindful that among others, authors represented in this book might very well disagree with the history I tell, the analysis I give, and the constructive conclusions that I propose. Yet recall that intellectual collaboration and disagreement is the engine that drives the research university.

[2] See the essays by Rüdiger Bittner and Andreas Glaeser in this volume.

and problems of the modern research university. Here the argument proceeds by analysis but also with historical reference. The final level of reflection, and, necessarily, the most abstract, will be to propose, in outline form, a response to the problems of the idea of the research university while, hopefully, retaining its possibilities. On this plane of reflection, the task is the critical reconstruction of the idea of the university and its relation to the formation of human character. This final level of reflection likewise mixes theological and humanistic thinking as necessary for the reconstruction of the idea of the university. Why those modes of thinking are necessary for the task of reconstruction will become obvious in the course of these reflections.

Now this strategy of reflection, I should note, rests on a basic assumption that I will not defend, other than trying to redeem it through the course of the essay itself. Human beings are participants in the lived dynamics of reality, and especially so through natural languages and the history of peoples. Stated otherwise, the meaning of our humanity is refracted through those processes in which we participate, natural and social. Accordingly, we must interpret those processes —and their institutional forms—in order to understand our lives as well the possibilities and limitations encountered in lived reality.

The assumption about the interpretation of things human itself poses a problem that undergirds the modern research university and is central to the argument of this essay, namely, what is the relation, if any, between knowledge of the world of facts and knowledge entailed in the conduct of life. Some thinkers, including some authors in this book, draw a sharp distinction between these domains of knowledge, such that the findings of the research university—the world of facts—has little if anything to do with the conduct of life. Without eliding the distinction, I will argue the contrary point, as ancient thinkers like Aristotle did and also some contemporary ones.[3] Why? Insofar as researchers—scientists in the largest sense of the word—are human beings, their labors have at least a practical aim, and the researchers will, come what may, be shaped by their specific scientific practice. Likewise, as acting and thinking beings, people hold beliefs that they ought to examine to determine their truth and rightness. The ancient Socratic idea that the unexamined life is not worth living did not deny the need for knowledge of the world, even if Socrates's favored focus was human conduct. On my understanding, the Socratic idea merely meant that the most basic task facing human beings is how to live, and that every resource should be used to answer that in some way, including the search knowledge or the arts for their own sakes. They, too, enrich life. Besides, the twentieth century and much current life testify to the profound dangers when the search for knowledge is unmoored from actual life.

---

[3] For one contemporary example, see Stephen Toulmin, *Return to Reason* (Cambridge, MA: Harvard University Press, 2001).

As practical acting beings, we are participants and interpreters in the dynamics of lived reality, and given this fact, inquiry is necessarily hermeneutical and practical in character. In order to explore that fact and its import for the idea of the university, we begin with some simple and well-known historical observations.

The Bologna Idea and Its Demise

While the challenges facing major modern research universities around the world are known, it is important to have them in mind. It is not clear what, if anything, unifies the work of research universities and thereby what warrants calling them "universities" in any precise sense of the term. The Latin *universitas* (a whole) does not designate simply an institution of higher teaching and research that awards advanced degrees in various fields. It was meant to designate that the universe of knowledge has some coherence and so is an ordered cosmos rather than a chaotic collection of faculties. The oldest university in the West is the University of Bologna, founded in 1088. Its motto is "Nourishing Mother of the Studies" (*studiorum*), and the term "university" was coined at its founding.[4] It has been argued that the "unity" of the medieval universities, Paris to Oxford and Bologna to Salamanca, was grounded in Christian convictions.[5] Recall that Saint Augustine's treatise *De Doctrina Christiana* set the agenda for education well into the late Middle Ages. To be sure, theology was, as often noted, the "queen of the sciences," but that did not mean there was no discord and disagreement about the task and structure of education. For instance, there were conflicts between Dominicans and Franciscans at Paris and elsewhere.[6] Nevertheless, the conception of the university was that of an ordered whole needed to fund the work of studies set within a religious cosmology.

---

[4] See https://www.unibo.it/it.

[5] Recall that the great universities were usually founded by religious orders and often held to Saint Paul's advice to his follower Timothy to guard the deposit of faith (1 Tim. 6:20–21). The university taught the seven liberal arts, of course, but they had a religious end and purpose. By the time of Thomas Aquinas (1225–74) as a Dominican at the University of Paris, theology itself was conceived as both a wisdom (*sapientia*) and a science (*scientia*) and thereby interrelated moral formation and the attaining of knowledge rooted in the being of God.

[6] On the different orders in the medieval universities, see Pope Benedict XVI, "Franciscan and Dominican Orders in the Middle Ages," https://www.ewtn.com/catholicism/library/franciscan-and-dominican-orders-in-the-middle-ages-6257). The purpose of this essay is not historical, but it will be important to note historical developments in order to grasp the situation of the contemporary university.

The religious grounds and horizon of the university, no matter how conceived or disputed, meant that the university is to represent the presupposed unity of reason. Whether or not human reason was keyed into, participated in, the divine *logos* was hotly debated. Yet the power of human reason to interpret and understand the natural and social orders and to guide conduct was generally accepted. And so, too, was the idea that education was not only about the gaining and creating of knowledge, but also a form of *paideia*, the formation of character, whether clerical or not. Thus, at its origins, that university entailed claims about (1) the coherence of study in a religious context, (2) the nature and scope of human reason, and (3) the university's purpose, which was, in good measure, the religious, moral, and intellectual formation of students and scholars. While each of these claims was disputed, the necessity of their interrelation, variously conceived, remained at the core of any idea of the university. In a word, religious conviction and even divine revelation were not somehow seen at odds with the claims and limits of reason.

A quick glance at contemporary universities, including their curricula, shows the utter lack of the three features of classical universities just noted: a religious or moral backing and horizon to study, an idea of the unity of human reason, and a belief in the possibility of human character formation within the context of inquiry. Contemporary universities are a collection of discrete disciplines with their own methods, purposes, and scholarly norms that lead, inevitably, to intellectual silos lacking communication with other silos. The disciplines have been incredible engines in the creation of knowledge in virtually every field of scholarly endeavor, but there is also no real shared conception of reason or intellectual norms. The topic of the unity of the university itself is rarely debated, and its loss seemingly unlamented. Undergraduate education rarely enables students the means to integrate their different studies into a coherent intellectual whole. The result is intellectual disorientation or early professionalization. Graduate students too often are merely educated to be the next generation of occupants of the silos. Further, the idea of the moral formation of students is foreign to most universities, except the most conservative religious ones and many Catholic universities.

Added to these institutional and curricular matters are a host of other challenges that impact virtually every research university. Increasingly, research and learning are driven primarily, if not solely, by economic concerns. Students seek a university degree in order to enter an occupation. The idea of a profession or calling (*Berufung*) has been lost, especially a religious vocation, and it has been replaced with the idea and rhetoric of occupations. Research is funded by medical, technological, military, sports, and political sources in order to further their interests. In the case of sports, at least in the United States, athletics not only bring in millions of dollars of revenue to major universities but are also the seedbed for global professional sports. The connections between universities and the military as well as technological and medical interests are well known. Not surprisingly, fundraising—especially among so-called private, as opposed to public, universities in the United States—is a constant feature of university administration often employing many development officers and, in some places, multiple units throughout universities dedicated to fund raising.[7] The point is that each of the social systems explored in this series of books is related to the modern university, and the coin of the realm for those relations is just that—coin. If there is a coherence to the university, it is an economic one.

How did this odd situation come to be within research universities? That question is, of course, in one sense a topic for the social history of the transition of Western societies into modernity. The social history of the university in the West is beyond the scope of this essay. However, there are obviously important intellectual shifts between the founding of the great medieval universities and the contemporary research university. The next step in this argument is briefly to note these shifts, each of which is well known, and which together, I contend, elided the idea of the university as traditionally conceived. These three forces are not individually the cause of our current situation. It is only when each aligns and interacts with the others that conditions are set for the emergence of the modern university and the end of the Bologna ideal. The purpose of this essay is not, as for some scholars, to somehow retrieve and restore the classical medieval university![8] The purpose is to reconceive the idea of the university under present conditions that nevertheless advance the three concerns noted above: an account to reason, the formation of character, and a coherence backed by postsecular rather than strictly religious (Christian), secular, or economic convictions.

Shifts within Western Modernity

To designate "Western modernity" as the intellectual environment that helps to explain the current state of the research university is no doubt correct. Yet it is also vague and misleading, since, as scholars have noted, there are in fact, globally speaking, many modernities. Further, the singular designation of modernity fails to grasp that within the various social systems, what counts as modern differs from system to system—say, in media, politics, or economics. Accounting for

---

[7] Increasingly, the distinction between private and public universities in the United States is being elided, as state-run schools (that is, public universities) face cuts in public funding. Additionally, many European and British schools face the grim prospects of having to begin fund raising in order to finance their work.

[8] The most renowned advocate of some version of retrieval is the philosopher Alasdair MacIntyre in his works *After Virtue: A Study in Moral Theory* (Notre Dame, IN: University of Notre Dame Press, 1980) and *Three Rival Versions of Moral Enquiry: Encyclopaedia, Genealogy, and Tradition* (London: Duckworth, 1990).

these differences is one task of this series of books. And while it is true, as thinkers like Max Weber, Talcott Parsons, and Niklas Luhmann in different ways argue, that "modern" societies are characterized by systemic pluralism and therefore do not find coherence in any one system, that observation merely demands attention to specific systems. It is also the case, as noted above, that these systems—say, the educational system—while marked by their own values and norms, are reflexively interrelated and interdependent and therefore cannot be construed as isolated processes or social action. That being said, I want to note shifts that, I believe, are seminal for understanding the state of the contemporary research university.

Reason and Knowledge

Mid-twentieth-century theologians, like Paul Tillich, and philosophers, such as Martin Heidegger, made an important point when they drew a distinction between ontic and ontological reason.[9] The point was, as noted above, that in the ancient and medieval worlds, reason was conceived to have ontological depth and connection. There was, as it is sometimes put, a rationality continuum, such that human reason was connected to the *logos* structuring and animating reality.[10] Of course, this point, again, was debated, with nominalists rejecting the claims about reason and focusing instead on will. But the philosophical point being made by the likes of Tillich and others was that the mark of modernity is a restriction of reason to ontic realities cut off from claims about the meaning of Being, questions of value, and matters of ultimate human concern.

The backdrop to the stunting of reason solely to ontic concerns, and thus the inability to give a rational account for the ends of human action, was partly the rise of "scientific," meaning experimental, rationality. From Francis Bacon onward, the task of "reason" was the development of the most efficient means to human desired ends. This made curiosity, not awe, the primary virtue, and inquiry, not wisdom, the task of science, which defined truth as the experimental verification of a theory by means of empirical results. The scientific attitude was one of observation and distance with respect to what was under examination. One sought, as it was put, value-neutral inquiry rightly free from personal prejudice but also, oddly, supposedly free of personal participation by the researcher as well. Not only did this mark a radical shift in conceptions of reason and knowledge, but it also ensconced what we may call two principles important for the research university.

---

[9] Paul Tillich, *Systematic Theology*, vol. 1 (Chicago: University of Chicago Press, 2012) and Martin Heidegger, *Being and Time* (New York: Harper, 1962).

[10] I want to thank Michael Welker for this useful concept.

The first principle is the priority of method over content.[11] In order for any ostensive discipline of thought to validate the truth status of its claims, it had to follow the rationality of the experimental, or scientific, method. This focus on method expelled not only appeals to revealed truth but also, importantly, intuitive or a priori knowledge.[12] Knowledge claims are experimentally and empirically verified, including those that appeal to a tradition of rationality. This redefined the rationality continuum not in terms of the depth and scope of reason but, rather, with respect to a rational procedure. In order to don the mantel of reason, a discipline had, then, to establish that its subject matter—say, anthropology—was not subsumable under some other subject matter—for example, history—and thus represented a sui generis arena of inquiry. Further, the discipline had to show that its "rational procedure" was the same as, or at least analogous to, that of every other legitimate discipline in order to claim its place in the university.

The force of this claim about reason and validity within the priority of method is most clearly seen, interestingly, with the rise of the modern study of religion.[13] The task, started by Friedrich Schleiermacher in the nineteenth century, was to isolate a sui generis object of study, the human feeling (*Gefühl*) of absolute dependence on a "whence" other than itself, not reductive to rational metaphysics or ethics.[14] This feeling can then be traced through time within a single religion or explored within various religions. As he put it, "within the religions you are to discover religion."[15] The study of religion had a distinct subject matter, but it was to proceed through historical and cultural analysis to verify its claims. Despite the wild difference among the modern theories of religion—for example, Emile Durkheim on collective effervescence, William James and the varieties of religious experience, or Karl Marx's theory of ideology (to name a few)—the demand to isolate a unique subject matter within shared procedural method was the price religious studies had to pay in order to enter the university. The same was true of other disciplines as well.

The second principle developed within the modern shift to experimental method was the consequence of (1) the dethroning of theology as queen of the

---

[11] On this, see Hans-Georg Gadamer, *Truth and Method* (New York: Continuum, 1975).

[12] The crucial counterpoint to modern empirical method was first asserted by Kant in his arguments about synthetic a priori claims, an issue I cannot explore in this essay.

[13] For a very different approach to the study of religion, see William Schweiker and David A. Clairmont, *Religious Ethics: Meaning and Method* (Chichester, UK: Wiley Blackwell, 2020).

[14] It is important to remember that Schleiermacher was one of the founding fathers of the University of Berlin (Humboldt University), the first modern research university. Its motto is *Universitas litterarum*.

[15] Friedrich Schleiermacher, *On Religion: Speeches to Its Cultured Despisers* [1799], trans. R. Crouter (Cambridge: Cambridge University Press, 1988), 190.

sciences, and thus the loss of a religious and moral purpose to study, and (2) instigating the conflict of the faculties (*Der Streit der Fakultäten*), as Immanuel Kant put it in 1798, around the idea of the freedom of inquiry. Kant's point was that at least with philosophy, one must be able to think for oneself without fear of political censorship and thus have the truth status of claims determined by open and free argument.[16] That procedure, we might say, was the humanistic analogue to the experimental method in the natural sciences. It also meant that the university became a context for determining which so-called sciences, especially theology, were in fact sciences. In other words, the second principle had to do with the disciplinary identity wherein any ostensive discipline had to guard its intellectual place within the university from being subsumed into some other discipline amid free inquiry. In this sense, the conflict of faculties, or disciplines, means the unending contest for membership in the university. As noted above, this has led to intellectual silos, on one hand, and on the other, in the current university, the seeming triumph of economic, procedural rationality. The silos replicate Max Weber's account of modern differentiated and rationalized societies as a war among value spheres and as nothing less than a war among gods.[17]

Yet matters are more complex than just described, and complex in ways important for the constructive argument of this essay. A variety of thinkers from a variety of fields (physics, philosophy, theology, philosophy of science, etc.) have challenged the modern Baconian ideas of method, reason, and knowledge noted above. Often lumped together under the banner of postmodernism, an admittedly vague term in my judgment, the idea, in part, is that aside from perception and conception, human beings seek understanding through interpretation.[18] What is more, the practice of interpretation can never exile the interpreter and claim to assume the role of omniscient scientific observer through perceptible or a priori claims. The interpreter, additionally, exists within complex networks of signification (for example, natural languages), differentiated social systems that must, come what may, reflexively interact and adjust to each other, and, further, within complex natural processes and ecologies. This means that knowledge is a synthetic practice: it must integrate an array of claims, and the validity of claims to knowledge is defined by their scope and illuminative power to orient further research.

Interrelatedness, networks, reflexive, autopoietic systems, participation, and action spheres are some of the watchwords of the day aiming to signal new ac-

---

[16] J. S. Mill, *On Liberty and the Subjection of Women* (New York: Penguin Classics, 2007).

[17] See H. Richard Niebuhr, *Radical Monotheism and Western Culture: With Supplementary Essays* (Louisville, KY: Westminster/John Knox Press, 1993).

[18] The literature here is mountainous and led by thinkers in the late twentieth century like Stephen Toulmin, Thomas Kuhn, John Polkinghorne, A. N. Whitehead, Paul Feyerabend, Imre Lakatos, Michael Polanyi, and on and on.

counts of knowledge and reason beyond "modern" paradigms. However, what is not at all clear is whether this shift from observation to participation, from silos of inquiry to collaborative research (like the work of this book!), is, in fact, informing the structure and purpose of the contemporary research university. I return to this question later. For now, we turn to social shifts in the conception of humanity.

The Crooked Timber of Humanity

In 1784, several years after his great *Critique of Pure Reason* (1781), and long before worrying about the conflict of faculties, Immanuel Kant published his *Idea of a Universal History from a Cosmopolitan Purpose.* In that text, Kant sought to chart the development of history toward an unrealized cosmopolitan and moral federation of states. He made this optimistic proposal while admitting that "Out of the crooked timber of humanity, no straight thing was ever made."[19] With that admission about humanity, Kant captured a shift to modern thought away from the Bologna idea of education, a shift that was also partly Protestant in nature. This modern shift predates Kant, of course, not only in the thought of Martin Luther and his conception of fallen humanity but also, and most powerfully articulated, in the political philosophy of Thomas Hobbes that shaped subsequent social-contract theory. At issue, for the sake of the present inquiry, is the extent to which the character of human beings is fundamentally open to improvement so that education is a kind of *paideia*.

Hobbes's point was that political and social thought must take human beings as they are, not as one thinks they ought to be. Ancient and medieval virtue theory, and its supporting educational ideal, assumed the perfectibility of human beings aimed at well-being (*eudaimonia*). With Hobbes (and before him a line of Pauline thinkers from Augustine to Luther), the idea was that human beings in a state of nature (Hobbes) or as fallen, sinful creatures (Augustine, Luther), are driven by fear, by the will to dominate others, and have little, if any, capacity to reform their own lives. Given this, it is important to develop political and social systems that constrain the human will-to-power, calm peoples' fears about the security of their lives, and attain some measure of social tranquility. Luther, for instance, thought that the civil order existed to seek peace and restrain wickedness. But the peace of the earthly kingdom was insured by force, by the sword, which held people in awe. The magistrate was the mask of God's vengeance and justice.[20]

---

[19] Immanuel Kant, *Idea for a Universal History with a Cosmopolitan Aim*, ed. Amelie Oksenberg Rorty and James Schmidt (Cambridge: Cambridge University Press, 2007).

[20] Luther's writings on this topic, such as "On Christian Freedom," "Temporal Authority: The Extent to Which It Should Be Obeyed," and "Against the Robbing and Murdering Hoards," are all well known.

Debates arose, of course, about the extent of citizens' liberty with respect to a sovereign state. Hobbes left little space for dissent; so did Luther.[21] What is just and right, according to Hobbes, is what the sovereign, the Leviathan, declares. There is no cosmic or theological grounding or horizon of the right, just, and good in reason. Accordingly, if a citizen dissents from the sovereign's decree, having already consented to assign one's natural right to power to that sovereign, the only option is to flee the state. In doing so, one returns to the terrifying state of nature, the war of each against each, from which only the Leviathan offers escape.[22] Later social contract theorists sought to extend the domain of liberty (J. S. Mill), the possibility of working towards a moral Kingdom of Ends (Kant), and the protecting of property (J. Locke). The American founders asserted the inalienable natural rights to include life, liberty, and the pursuit of happiness. And the debate about liberty and the social contract continues to our day among thinkers as diverse as John Rawls, Jürgen Habermas, and Charles Taylor, to name a few.

The crux of the matter in terms of this essay was the intent of social contract theory and, importantly, early capitalist economic theorists like Adam Smith as well as moral philosophers (David Hume). Their intent was to develop social systems (politics; economics) wherein individual self-interest aimed at maximizing its power and utility could be harnessed to further the social, common good without reforming human nature. In that way, the crooked timber of humanity can make a straight thing, that is, social tranquility. Hobbesian "man" seeks to maximize his power, but in order to be saved from the state of nature, he is driven by reason to consign that right to the state, an artificial man as Hobbes called it, that affords citizens a degree of civil tranquility. *Homo economicus* likewise seeks to maximize wealth with little interest in the customer, employer, or employees, but the market through its invisible hand increases wealth with a minimum of moral demands on economic agents. Max Weber even traced the rise of capitalism out of Protestant demands for inner-worldly asceticism motivated by a desire for salvation. Working out one's salvation with diligence and frugality situated one within the structure of capitalism, a structure, Weber thought, that had become, in the modern world, an iron cage.[23]

These developments are of course part of the rise of modern differentiated societies where different social systems (politics, economics, media, education, etc.) reflexively interact and thus constrain and support each other. And, of

---

[21] On this, John Calvin differed somewhat. Not only does he affirm a version of natural law, restored and healed by revelation, but he also notes the right of lower magistrates to revolt if, and only if, the sovereign forgoes sacred duties. See John Calvin, *Institutes of the Christian Religion*, bk. 4, 20.

[22] See Thomas Hobbes, *Leviathan* (New York: Penguin Classics, 2017).

[23] Max Weber, *The Protestant Ethic and the Spirit of Capitalism*, trans. with intro. T. Parsons, foreword R. H. Tawney (New York: Charles Scribner's Sons, 1958).

course, there were other developments in social thought and theory, especially among conservatives, Catholics, and various Protestant groups and sects (see, for example, Anglicanism and Methodism), that focused on the moral development and even perfection of persons. In fact, contemporary theories of education (essentialism, perennialism, progressivism, behaviorism, etc.) are divided along these lines, that is, the extent to which education can and should seek to form students' character morally and socially.

The liberal insight of social thought is that the crooked timber of humanity will not be transformed, and therefore social systems, rather than individual actors, are the means for human advancement. Social systems can constrain, construct, and further the lives of individuals and, further, are therefore not explainable with reference to individual human actors. When that insight is applied to education, the conditions are ripe for the research university to come into existence. There is no need to worry about the moral betterment of students or society, and research is carried out within individual disciplines that interact, as we have seen already, around *sui generis* subject matters within shared rational procedures.

However, just as with contemporary shifts about reason and knowledge, there are counter forces to social theories that atomize the university and dismiss that task of *paideia* as important for the research university. Interestingly, these developments are often related to but also reach beyond the borders of the contemporary university. Research projects are the next step, we might say, in the differentiation of societies applied to research and education, but with a postmodern and global twist. Major research universities, as well as some free-standing philanthropic foundations, have established research units around the world precisely to further collaborative research on basic, global problems. So, too, have some scholars sought and found funding for this kind of collaborative research that intentionally breaks down silos by focusing attention on basic problems.[24] The idea is to conceive of the various academic disciplines not as individual arenas of expertise and knowledge production but, rather, as resources for exploring questions and projects at the intersections of disciplines. As James M. Gustafson noted decades ago, "Intellectual, academic, and practical problems and interests

---

[24] For example, Michael Welker and I have run a number of these projects. I was also the principal investigator (PI), with Günter Thomas of Bochum University as the associate investigator, for the Enhancing Life Project, which brought together thirty-five scholars from around the world and from disciplines as diverse as medicine, communication studies, law, theology, history, etc., to explore the meaning and criteria for enhancing life, especially human life. For materials and information on this project, see enhancinglife.uchicago.edu.

in our time fit less and less the traditional divisions of the [modern] academy."[25] In terms of the coherence of research, the queen is most certainly dead. Yet so, too, is the modernist presumption that any one discipline can, from with its own resources, answer challenges that fall within and at the margins of its expertise.

However, these developments in research face a profound challenge and have yet to address their import for the structure and purpose of the contemporary university. The challenge is that in order to escape the disciplinary silos, it is necessary for researchers either (1) to learn the concepts, theories, and methods of other disciplines in order to explore the intersections productive of knowledge or (2) to develop new conceptual frameworks and methods that articulate the intersections among disciplines. Projects use both strategies of reflection, but without doing so, collaborative research will be *ad hoc* or actually dominated by one disciplinary framework. With respect to these new globalized research projects, too little has been done at the level of advanced teaching to enable a new generation of scholars to advance this agenda. Sadly, the demands of the academic market and the pressure on students to secure jobs force most, if not all, students back into the silos, since these disciplinary structures often determine job placement and the academy itself. In that way, up-and-coming scholars remain spectators and not participants in these emergent research projects and their possible contribution to advancing the university system.

The Horizons of Understanding

One of the conclusions from the above all-too-brief history and analysis is that contemporary modes of research, call them postmodern or not, have denounced the attitude of the scientific "observer" in favor of reinserting the human in the dynamics of nature and society as agents. This rejection has not meant a lessening of demands for truth or validation, despite what some critics believe. It has, rather, meant a shift to collaborative and intersubjective or communicative validation and truth. It has also brought with it a shift in understanding the dynamics of lived reality. "So, we must develop," as Stephen Toulmin notes, "a more coordinated view of the world, embracing both the world of nature and the world of humanity—a view capable of integrating, not merely aggregating, our scientific understanding and capable of doing so *with practice in view*."[26] In other words, once we understand the researcher as an active participant in collaborative work, any field of research will have, come what may, relevance and import for the con-

---

[25] James M. Gustafson, *Intersections: Science, Theology, and Ethics* (Cleveland, OH: Pilgrim Press, 1996), 146, addition mine.

[26] Stephen Toulmin, *The Return to Cosmology: Postmodern Science and the Theology of Nature* (Berkeley: University of California Press, 1982), 255–56, italics in original.

duct of human life, for practice. In the age of possible chemical and nuclear warfare, gross economic inequality, and, at present, the race to address the spread of a deadly pandemic, the practical import of each form of research ought to be appraised. I return to this point below, since it is obviously central to this essay and this book.

Understanding that we, as persons and researchers, are agents and not spectators within the dynamics of lived reality denotes a fact and poses a question that remains debated within the current academy. That fact is that agents are, come what may, shaped by and also shape those practices and processes of which they are a part. In this sense, the topic of this book and this essay is a settled one. Every social system, every institution, and every practice shapes human character, even as those systems, institutions, and practices manifest the lives of agents. The question posed once we adopt an agential perspective is a philosophically and theologically difficult one. Is the horizon of human understanding exhausted by natural and social processes in a way that, religiously speaking, sanctifies those processes? In other words, and to recall the Bologna idea, are reason's depth and scope defined by natural and social processes alone? Call that position reductive naturalism, ardent secularism, the immanent frame (Charles Taylor), or dreadful immanence (Robert Bellah).[27] Insofar as we are participants in the dynamics of lived reality, is that "secularistic" picture of reality adequate to thought and experience, or does it leave us inarticulate about the scope of our lives?

The Russian religious philosopher Nikolai Berdyaev noted, about the twentieth century, that the "processes of sanctifying the natural-historical, processes really social in their origin, have gained final predominance over those forces working for the transfiguration of life, over the prophetic element in religion."[28] Modern capitalism, communism, colonialism, and now neoliberal global capitalism and technology have sought to enfold human life within themselves. Paradoxically, there is an *overhumanization* of the world, as David Klemm and I have called it. Human-made systems enfold natural as well as social and communicative processes and yet constrict and endanger our humanity.[29] Overhumanization also denies the belief, Christian or otherwise (say, human rights discourse), that human beings take precedence over abstract systems. Importantly, that is an axiological and not methodological critique of systems. Obviously, some research projects must focus on systems and not persons. The question is whether or not

---

[27] Charles Taylor, *A Secular Age* (Cambridge, MA: Harvard University Press, 2007), and Robert Bellah, *Religion in Human Evolution: From the Paleolithic to the Axial Age* (Cambridge, MA: Harvard/Belknap, 2011).

[28] Nicolas Berdyaev, *The Fate of Man in the Modern World*, trans. D. A. Lowrie (San Rafael, CA: Semantron Press, 2009), 119.

[29] David E. Klemm and William Schweiker, *Religion and the Human Future* (Chichester, UK: Wiley-Blackwell, 2010).

human beings and other living realities have a moral dignity and status that cannot be elided by social systems, but which those systems can and ought to serve.

Put otherwise, are life and living things a horizon of human understanding and truth claims as well as the linguistic, social, and natural systems in which we participate? Again, if we take seriously the postmodern idea that we are agents and participants in the dynamics of reality, and that research must have practice in view, then life (and not just being-towards-death), natural ecologies (and not just social systems), and language in use among speakers (and not just semiotic systems) are conditions of understanding. Thus, much like the shifts traced above in knowledge and reason as well as in persons and social systems, here, too, is one that marks our postsecular age: human life and probably all living things are open to multiple horizons of meaning and truth and thus not understandable within any one horizon. If that is not the case, then the argument of this essay and maybe this whole book is moot. In order to answer that challenge, I necessarily shift from history and analysis to the attempt to reconstruct the idea of the research university.

The Research University in View of Practice

Thus far the argument of this essay has been to trace developments around knowledge, persons, social systems, and, finally, the horizons of understanding in order to grasp the losses and also possibilities found in the demise of the Bologna idea and the rise of the modern university. At each step of the argument, we have seen the emergence of postmodern configurations that deeply impact the conduct of research, insofar as researchers are seen as participants in view of practice. Each step also contributed concepts needed to advance a reconfiguration of the university: from observer to participant and agent; from discrete disciplines to intersections among research agendas; and from a unitary horizon of understanding to a diversity of horizons. These concepts provide ways for us to construe and interpret the dynamics of lived reality not as a unitary whole but as productive antinomies among the horizons of understanding. For agents and participants, the horizon of human understanding includes life *and* being-towards-death, natural ecologies *and* social systems, language in use among speakers *and* semiotic systems. The challenge, I submit, is how to render these antinomies productive and not destructive. That would enable us to advance, as Toulmin put it, "a view capable of integrating, not merely aggregating, our scientific understanding and capable of doing so *with practice in view.*"[30]

The possibility of the contemporary research university that has emerged from this inquiry is to enact the reflexive intersection of the work of disciplines

---

[30] Toulmin, *The Return to Cosmology*, 255–56, italics in original.

that aim to interpret and understand the complexities of the world from diverse perspectives. To participate in such research, to be an agent within the university, is to grasp the integration of knowledge not reducible to any one perspective or to a strict logical unity. As such, two related but different practical aims are in view.

One aim of this conception of the university is to humanize research by highlighting the agency of researchers and therefore the responsibility they have for the production of knowledge. This does not deny, but in fact accentuates, the specific methods, theories, and purposes of disciplines or research projects. It also, however, relativizes them in relation to the aim of understanding the researcher as a responsible agent in knowledge creation. One should not gain the whole world of knowledge and lose one's soul (cf. Matthew 16:26)! What is more, teaching in this context means that students are enabled and required to see how their various studies are integrated with respect to their own interests—this is the mark of intellectual freedom—and therefore how they, too, are participants and agents in education. This is the intellectual responsibility that researchers and teachers should enable students to assume. The specific details of the integrating and humanizing tasks of research and teaching are beyond the scope of this essay. But it must be noted that so conceived, the university reconstructs the Bologna concern for reason, now defined in terms of grasping and interpreting intersections and also the agency and character of students and research in terms of assuming responsibility for knowledge creation.

The second practical aim is distinctly moral in character, and, like the first aim, it reconstructs part of the Bologna idea. Researchers and students are not simply responsible for their creation and integration of knowledge. They are also, given the nature of participation in the university, responsible to and for each other and, in varying degrees, the wider public as well. The moral aim here is to make the university a *just* institution that respects and enhances the integrity of life.[31] On this account, any proposed research or pedagogical agenda must pass the test that it respects the integrity of the dynamics of learning and discovery, even as it must also show how it will enhance both of these constitutive dynamics of the lived reality of the university. This of course poses profound questions that the university itself must address within free inquiry aimed at finding and sustaining the better argument: what does it mean to respect others; what is the enhancement of life, and how can it be measured, if at all; what are the dynamics of living realities such that they command respect and elicit the desire for their enhancement? These questions, and especially the third, open the university as an institution of research and instruction to examine from all of its disciplinary perspectives the meaning and worth of the dynamics of lived reality. In this way, the

---

[31] On the conception of justice institutions, especially the university, see *Paul Ricoeur and the Hope of Higher Education: The Just University*, ed. Daniel Boscaljon and Jeffrey F. Keuss (Lanham, MD: Lexington Press, 2020).

contemporary research university does not assume a religious or metaphysical backing for its work. By the same token, it does not and cannot deny those questions as themselves integral to its practice. We might go so far as to say that the practical and moral aim of the practice of the university is the warrant for exploring the theological and metaphysical horizons of human worth and understanding. The research university is then something like a living hermeneutics of morals that warrants respecting and enhancing the integrity of life, especially human life and our responsibility for living realities.[32]

In less grand terms, we conclude that the two practical aims of the research university reconstruct elements in the Bologna model in ways fit for our age, whatever the age is called. And, perhaps in ways that can and must be contested, it prescribes a specific moral code and ethical idea of the good from within the dynamics of rational inquiry and teaching. That is, inquiry and teaching ought to respect and enhance the integrity of life from the perspective of the distinctive task of the university in the creation and communication of knowledge. In this way, the wholeness, if not the unity, of the university is enacted, so that once again there is order and purpose to its work that warrants its name.

---

[32] See William Schweiker, "Groundwork for the Hermeneutics of Morals: Paul Ricoeur and the Future of Ethics," in *The Journal of Religion* (forthcoming).

Analyzing Actually Existing Ethics
A Hermeneutic-Institutionalist Approach

Andreas Glaeser

In this chapter, I explore how actually existing ethics can be fruitfully analyzed as assemblages of institutions.[1] To nonsociologists this move may appear odd at first, because the term "institution" is associated in everyday language with formal entities governed by specific sets of written rules, housed in designated buildings, and staffed with officers—the institutions of government, for example. These are species of institutions, all right, but very particular ones endowed with staff to look after their own survival. It is better to call such institutions organizations. Clearly, ethics mostly do not fall into this category.[2] Organized ethics usually become law. For sociologists, the term "institution" refers to any stable social arrangement that is formed and maintained by human beings. Greeting formulas, sets of roles, or ordinary language itself are institutions in this sense, just as much as the papacy or a central bank, even though the former are not organized, whereas the latter are. My exploration of ethics as institutions will rely on a neo-Weberian hermeneutic theory of institutions that emphasizes the constitutive dependence of all institutions on other institutions.[3] For ethics, this means that, on

---

[1] In this essay I use the words "ethics" and "morality" interchangeably. I am, of course, familiar with the efforts to distinguish them not only in philosophy (see Bernard Williams, *Ethics and the Limits of Philosophy* [Cambridge, MA: Harvard University Press, 1985], 6) but also in parts of the social sciences (see Webb Keane, *Ethical Life: Its Natural and Social Histories* [Princeton: Princeton University Press, 2016]). Yet I think there are good sociological reasons not to separate them, because both the distinctions suggested merely emphasize different moments in processes of institutionalization. More on this below.

[2] Ethics boards of professions are, of course, organized in this sense. They constitute a phenomenon that is halfway between everyday ethics and the law.

[3] Given this centrality of ethics and the prominence given to it by Durkheim and by Weber, it is remarkable the degree to which the social sciences have dropped the topic for a while. See Émile Durkheim, *De la division du travail social* (Paris: Presses Universitaires de France, 1893); id., *Formes élémentaires de la vie religieuse* [1912] (Paris: Presses Univeri-

one hand, much like languages and methods of time keeping, they often play an infrastructural role in the formation of many other institutions. On the other hand, it means that ethics depend on prima facie extraethical institutions, such as language and the organization of social relations. My argument is simply that to understand the diversity, fragmentation, and transformation of actually existing ethics, including dramatic episodes of apparent ethical breakdown or, conversely, of ethical flourishing, it is key to understand ethics in relation to a wider range of other institutional formations and their development.[4]

Let me begin this undertaking with a working definition of ethics. Sociologically speaking, ethics can be conceived of as encompassing all *instituted* and thus collective *efforts* to direct human behavior in *socially desirable* directions with the expectation of *voluntary* habituated or reasoned compliance. Such efforts typically make use of stories, character images, idioms, precepts, norms, values, induce-

---

taires de France, 1960); and id., *Leçons de sociologie: Physique des mœrs et du droit* [1915] (Paris: Presses Universitaires de France, 1950). See Max Weber, "Entwicklungstendenzen in der Lage der ostelbischen Landarbeiter," in *Gesammelte Aufsätze zur Sozial- und Wirtschaftsgeschichte* [1894] (Tübingen: J. C. B. Mohr [Paul Siebeck], 1988); id., "Die Protestantische Ethik und der Geist des Kapitalismus" [1904/05], in Weber, *Gesammelte Aufsätze zur Religionssoziologie*, vol. 1 (Tübingen: J. C. B. Mohr [Paul Siebeck], 1920), 1–206; and id., "Zwischenbetrachtung: Theorie der Stufen und Richtungen religiöser Weltablehnung," in ibid., 536–73.

For an analysis of why the social sciences dropped ethics as a central concern, see Steven Hitlin and Stephen Vaisey, "The New Sociology of Morality," *Annual Review of Sociology* 39 (2013): 51–68. Since the 1990 s, however, there has been a remarkable revival in both sociology and anthropology. For an overview of sociology, see Steven Hitlin and Stephen Vaisey, eds., *Handbook of the Sociology of Morality* (New York: Springer, 2010); for an overview of anthropology, see Michael Lambek, ed., *Ordinary Ethics: Anthropology, Language and Action* (New York: Fordham University Press, 2010). Influential texts include Luc Boltanski and Laurent Thévenot, *On Justification: Economies of Worth*, trans. Catherine Porter (Princeton: Princeton University Press, 1991); Michèle Lamont, *Money, Morals, Manners* (Princeton: Princeton University Press, 1992); Joel Robbins, *Becoming Sinners: Christianity and Moral Torment in a Papua New Guinea Society* (Berkeley: University of California Press, 2004); James D. Faubion, *An Anthropology of Ethics* (Cambridge: Cambridge University Press, 2011); James Laidlaw, *The Subject of Virtue: An Anthropology of Ethics and Freedom* (Cambridge: Cambridge University Press, 2014); and Gabriel Abend, *The Moral Background: An Inquiry into the History of Business Ethics* (Princeton: Princeton University Press, 2014).

4   The frequently cited examples of ethical breakdown pertain to situations in which "good" ordinary human beings become mass murderers or cruel torturers. Archetypical examples about the sudden flourishing of ethical behavior stem from strangers selflessly helping each other in crisis situations, such as natural catastrophes.

ments, and theories which are, for this reason, part of ethics.[5] Ethics can also be used as the name for the instituted results of such efforts, the patterned track record of socially evaluated performances. In this sense, one can speak of the ethics of a particular sociation, a family, a laboratory, a trading floor, or even a profession or nation. What is or is not deemed socially desirable can and often is subject to intense contestation. Depending on the political capabilities of the contestants, this may lead to various kinds of outcomes about whose vision of the social good is to be instituted in what way. Politics is, as I will show below, in a very specific sense central to ethics, as ethics are central to politics (if not in the way in which politics and ethics are usually discussed together).

The Ethics-Sociality Link

Ethics have emerged throughout all known history and across all cultures, subcultures, and local milieus that social scientists have studied. Given the historical and ethnographic record, it is safe to generalize that ethics emerge in any big or small, more durable *self-conscious* association of human beings, and that ethics are in some fundamental sense a constitutive component of such self-conscious sociations. A second prominent feature of the empirical record is the immense diversity in the actual content of ethics across contexts, time, and sociations. Even where some prohibitions or recommendations appear as features of a very wide range of ethics—take, for example, killing others, or incest—the boundaries drawn between condoned and condemned killing and sexual contact vary significantly. What is prescribed in one social configuration is proscribed in another. Accordingly, ethical universals can be stated only at a very high level of abstraction.[6] That humans everywhere are in some way subject to ethics is a universal. How precisely their lives are shaped by ethics is not.

In the same way that historical and ethnographic research has shown ethics to vary across time and space, it has demonstrated that the sociality of human beings likewise exhibits extraordinary plasticity in quantitative and qualitative relatedness. To see this, one does not even have to go to the extremes of comparing kind and number and structure of relations of a typical hunter-gatherer to that of a typical contemporary human being. It is quite enough to remember how much the relationship between men and women, parents and children, employers and em-

---

[5] Durkheim saw such inducements in the form of "sanctions" as the definitive characteristic of ethics.

[6] For efforts in this direction, see D. E. Brown, "Human Universals and Their Implications," in *Being Humans: Anthropological Universality and Particularity in Transdisciplinary Perspectives*, ed. N. Roughley (New York: Walter de Gruyter, 2000). For a discussion, see Keane, *Ethical Life*, passim.

ployees has changed only in recent memory. That human beings exist only socially is a universal. How precisely they exist socially is not.

The link between sociality and ethics becomes all the more complex if one considers that by no means all forms of sociality entail the development of corresponding ethics. This point can be illustrated by the fact that, for example, the entanglement of modern consumers in extraordinarily complex supply chains with myriad producers around the world has by no means led to a widely shared ethics of consumptive practices, isolated efforts (such as fair-trade coffee) notwithstanding. To understand better why humans develop substantively distinct ethics in some forms of sociation but not in others, and why ethics vary so much in time and space, it appears fruitful to come first to a better understanding of what precisely is at stake in human sociality. Such an inquiry is all the more important since, in modern times, religious and philosophical forms of thought have come to dominate, and these strongly favor varieties of ontological individualism that deny or give short shrift to human beings' constitutive sociality. These forms of thought are rooted in such figures as the individual soul conceived as a substance with a distinct origin and a distinct ultimate fate, and its modern utilitarian cognates in the autonomous rational decision maker of utilitarianism, Nietzsche's Zarathustra, or Sartre's human being condemned to be free. From such perspectives, individuality is prior to sociality. And community is ultimately conceived as a voluntary association. Given the results of research across a wide variety of fields of study, however, ontological individualism has become highly implausible as a basis for all but a set of narrowly circumscribed normatively articulated interests.[7]

Metatheoretically Reconceptualizing Sociality and Its Link to Ethics

There are at least four classical themes in thinking about the sociality of human beings. The first argues genealogically, emphasizing the necessary embeddedness of every human in sociations which care for raising offspring into adults. The second stresses the horizontal interdependence generated by the division of labor. The third focuses on asymmetrical power relations and hierarchical forms of interdependence. And the fourth, finally, stresses that humans have their language from those who raise them, and thus always make sense of the world in terms borrowed from them. These four traditions of thinking about human sociality have more often than not been discussed in isolation from each other. To see how the relatedness foregrounded by each is better thought of as interconnected

---

[7] Neoclassical economics is, of course, very useful if, for example, particular kinds of quantifiable optimization problems are at stake.

with the others, it is useful to bring these classical themes under the auspices of a unifying theory. Doing so will foreground a set of hermeneutic principles, with the help of which a very wide variety of historically specific socialities can be analyzed in fine gradations. A fruitful candidate for such an undertaking is the neo-Weberian hermeneutic theory of institutions, which I have developed over the past decade and a half. This move appears useful because ethics are, sociologically speaking, instituted themselves, no matter whether they are conceived as rules anchored in norms, as virtues defining the aims of character formation, or as consequentialist reasoning that grounds decision making. The hermeneutic institutionalism I present here is based on a specific consequently processual social ontology, which implies hermeneutic institutionalism as a method for designing and conducting research. Programmatically, I call both together consequently processual hermeneutic institutionalism, or CPHI for short.[8] I will introduce CPHI step by step while probing its implications for understanding ethics as both an assemblage of institutions in its own right and as a supporting, infrastructural institution for the formation of other institutions.

Social Life as Process

The basic idea of CPHI is very simple and should be rather uncontroversial. Social life exists in actions which are, in many ways, responses to prior actions of both self and others while giving rise to further actions in self and others. Put differently, social life proceeds in complex flows of action-reaction effects. Hence, the reference to *processes* in the name for the theory. Basic sociality is established through such flows. Everybody whose actions have an effect on others is thus connected to that person. Within the flow of actions and reactions, ethics are manifest in the *manner* in which a particular actor responds to previous actions by giving pride of place to prior communications about socially desirable acts. Ethics are

---

[8] As will become apparent from what follows, this model takes important cues from the social hermeneutics of Giambattista Vico (*The New Science*, 1744) and Johann Gottfried Herder (*On the Origin of Language*, 1772), the hermeneutic sociology of Weber, the phenomenology of Alfred Schütz (*The Phenomenology of the Social World*, 1932) and his students Peter Berger and Thomas Luckmann (*The Social Construction of Reality*, 1966), the pragmatism of George Herbert Mead (*Mind, Self, and* Society, 1934) and the philosophy of the later Wittgenstein (*Philosophical Investigations*, 1953). I have motivated and defended this model extensively in other writings and can here only point the reader to these texts. See Andreas Glaeser, *Political Epistemics: The Secret Police, the Opposition, and the End of East German Socialism* (Chicago: University of Chicago Press, 2011), and id., "Hermeneutic Institutionalism: Towards a New Synthesis," *Qualitative Sociology* 37 (2014): 207–47.

also manifest in the manner in which actors anticipate the social desirability of the consequences of their actions. In short, ethics are a particular modality of generating effects from being affected, namely, a modality answerable to what is upheld as socially desirable.

Institutions—Self-Similar Processes

All of the more stable aspects of social life—that is to say, institutions—exist in the repetition of identifiably self-similar action-reaction flows. Looked at under the magnifying glass of CPHI, structures are processes. Here, then, lies the reason to designate the model as *consequently* processualist. Much of human sociality is instituted or mediated through institutions. Family relations, friendships, and alliances are made and remade in activity flows. Even the more fleeting forms of relatedness—the transaction between particular buyers and sellers, the one-off encounter with a professional—usually take place within institutionalized frameworks, such as markets or firms. The relationship between ethics and institutions is twofold. For one, ethics consist in assemblages of a range of different institutions. A person is just insofar as she continues to act in just ways. An individual act is just insofar as it replicates models of just actions. Stories as repositories of character ideals, and idioms exhorting people to act in specific ways, need to be instituted in ongoing discourse. But then ethics also play a helping role in the formation of other institutions, and this has everything to do with the need for regularization and predictability. Promises, oaths, and contracts—as well as the ways in which such commitments are stabilized as habits with the help of cultural models such as "the reliable partner," "the good parent," "the law-abiding citizen"—are of obvious importance for the formation and maintenance of institutions. In fact, wherever there are institutions, it is useful to probe for the existence of associated ethics.[9]

---

[9] Institutionalists in economics and political science may object that one can achieve such regularization with incentives alone. Yet, as research has shown time and again, there is no general natural human response to so-called incentives, since they have to be understood as such and reacted to as such. In other words, one first has to become a particular sort of person to be responsive to incentives, a becoming that typically involves some form of ethics. And that is exactly what has happened historically (classical studies: Weber; Aleksander Luria, *Cognitive Development: Its Cultural and Social Foundations*, 1934). Benjamin Franklin's aphorisms in *Poor Richard's Almanack* (1733–58), and *Advice to a Young Tradesman* (1748), and, needless to say, Jeremy Bentham's own effort to propagate utilitarian principles are cases in point.

Understandings—Directing and Orienting Action

The account I have given so far has a yawning gap in its middle. On one hand, I have depicted social life as a continuous process of activity-flows; on the other, I have argued that institutions ought to be considered as self-similarly replicated flows. Yet I have not explained how self-similar replication and, thus, patterns and order become possible in the first place. To begin with this task, it helps to recall that the very idea of action implies that it is ordered, oriented, and directed behavior. What guides actions are processes of understanding that consciously or unconsciously differentiate the world into constitutive components while integrating them again into a whole. To do so requires the good offices of some medium that exists above and beyond the immediate context of acting as something already pretty stable and preordered. In other words, the ordering of actions into activity patterns—the process of institutionalization—hinges on the prior existence of media that are in fact institutions themselves.[10]

Different media give rise to different forms of understanding, because each medium offers distinct possibilities and limitations for making sense of the world in analyzing and synthesizing it. Indo-European languages find acting subjects and acted upon objects everywhere, simply because the grammar of these languages is fundamentally organized in that way; algebra remakes the world into variables and coefficients that are integrated through operators forming equations, thus turning the world into a play of balanced, quantitative variation—simply because algebra is structured that way.[11] In a first cut, it makes sense to distinguish broadly between discursive, emotive, and different kinds of sensuous understandings precisely because they are enabled by distinct culturally configurable symbolic and biosemiotics media.[12] With this attention to the role that var-

---

[10] Languages have often even served as the paradigm case of institutions par excellence.

[11] For classical discussions of such structuring, see Benjamin Lee Whorf, "The Relation of Habitual Thought and Behavior to Language" [1944], in *Language, Thought and Reality: Selected Writings of Benjamin Lee Whorf*, ed. John B. Caroll (Cambridge, MA: MIT Press, 1966) 134–59, for ordinary languages, and George Lakoff and Raffael Nuñez, *Where Mathematics Comes From: How the Embodied Mind Brings Mathematics About* (New York: Basic Books, 2001).

[12] Although not as readily objectifiable as thought in language, the biosemiosis of feelings and perception can nevertheless also be configured culturally. To the degree that they can, these biosemiotics media are institutions very much like the symbolic media. After all, feelings and the senses can be cultivated and refined. One learns to see, hear, feel, taste in particular ways. On the importance of facial muscles in the biosemiotics of feeling, see Paul Ekman and Erika Rosenberg, eds., *What the Face Reveals: Basic and Applied Studies of Spontaneous Expression Using the Facial Action Coding System (FACS)* (Oxford: Oxford University Press, 1997).

ious understandings generated in already instituted media play in forming institutions, it becomes clear why the institutionalism proposed here is in fact hermeneutic, even if it is an expanded hermeneuticism that takes emotions and the senses seriously.

What, then, do ethics have to do with understanding in this sense? My thesis is simply that one way in which ethics emerge (the first of three) is a very simple type of experience: In the retrospective reflection upon particular action-reaction effect chains involving at least two but potentially many more people, the enchainment is either comparatively liked or disliked by the participants. Ethics emerge from here as an effort to repeat favorably and avoid unfavorably evaluated interactions.

Imagine a deer-hunting expedition in a hunter-gatherer society. Noise-making drivers coming from several directions have to scare the deer into fleeing toward a few strategically placed killers armed with stone knives. At the beginning of the expedition, the drivers are still relatively far apart, and it takes some skill in maneuvering through the forest in such a way that the deer does not break through the acoustic dragnet and flee in the other direction. Think how the members of the party may make sense of a good expedition, in which barely any deer escaped, compared to an *average* or *bad* one, or how they would compare the relative performance of the drivers or killers with each other.

If these sorts of experiences can count as paradigmatic for at least one way in which actually existing ethics emerge—and I think they can—then ethics build on particular types of judgments (a subclass of understandings). In Indo-European languages, these judgments differentiate distinctive basic elements: a subject, two objects (or object classes), and an evaluative category. They integrate these elements as a statement of comparison between the two objects by the subject in light of the evaluative category. The evaluative categories are available discursively through particular locutions. In English, these are grounded in notions of *better/worse* and, metaphorically related to it, higher/lower, more/less, etc. In emotive understandings, the comparative evaluation manifests as relative degrees of *desire* and aversion and sensuously as more or less *pleasing* to eye, ear, tongue, nose, and touch. To continue with the example above, one might obtain a report such as this: "In A's opinion, B's noise-making movements have been much more effective than C's." Depending on cultural conventions, the evaluating subject can be a human being or some transcendent entity, such as a god or an objective law. For one member of the party might say—instead of "in my opinion"—"the goddess of the hunt loves B and frowns upon C," or, sagaciously anticipating Kant, "C's noisemaking movement falls short of being exemplary to all the hunting parties from one edge of the water to the other." In these kinds of judgments, the objects of the evaluative comparison can also be objects in the more narrow sense that they are things. For example: "This knife is better made than that one [that is, because its blade cuts better, does not break off as easily, etc.]." Finally, it is important to remember that many judgments are rendered in elliptical form by dropping the subject and or the comparative object. One can say simply "B is a good driver" or "this is a bad knife." It is important to note how these judgments are contingent on the prior availability of instituted media, on languages, cultivated manners of feeling and sensing.

Judgments are ethical—or one could also say properly moralizing—only under three conditions. First, that the objects of comparative evaluation must be ultimately either actions, actors themselves, or otherwise attributable in a relevant way to actions or actors. In the knife example, this could be because the better one is better made or specially blessed by a shaman, made by a legendary stone cutter, or cut from stone from the mountain under special protection of the goddess of the hunt. Second, the evaluative category must be de facto treated by the sociation as particularly *relevant* to its interactions in a particular situation. And third, the person passing the judgment is authorized by the community to pass such judgment.

Validations—Objectifying Understanding

How do situationally specific ethical judgments become moral precepts that are available as institutionalized templates before the action even begins? For institutionalization to happen, processes of understanding must congeal into more objectified forms. The agents of this transformation are *validating* action-reaction sequences which lift, as it were, specific performances of analysis and synthesis inherent in the flow of actions and reaction out of the stream of happenings into a more memorable, situationally transposable form. One could also say that validating events transform processes of understand*ing* (present participle, continuous) into schematized understanding*s* (gerund) which enable learning. Analytically, it makes sense to distinguish at least three types of processes through which validational effects come about.[13] They are generated, first, through the *recognition* of actors' understandings by others reckoned to be authorities on the particular kind of understanding.[14] In the example from the last section, the hunters would *praise* the good driver and *scold* the bad one, for example, thus affirming a particular kind of judgment. Second, validational effects can come about through corroboration by the experience of successes and failures in acting, where an explicit or implicit evaluation of the action success reflects back on the action-guiding un-

---

[13] For purposes beyond the scope of this chapter, they can be further subdivided; see Glaeser, *Political Epistemics*.

[14] The more differentiated societies become, the more differentiated people's networks of authority tend to be. Parents are authorities on some matters (a steadily smaller number as children age), friends on others. Physicians are considered authorities in their field but not usually on matters of ethics, etc.

derstandings. Both the good and the bad driver may learn from assessing what they have done. And, third, validational effects manifest in resonance, that is, in the fit of the understanding validated with the actor's already extant understandings. If both good and bad drivers have a self-image as alert and vigilant, then positive resonances follow from good and negative ones from bad performances.

Understandings, the objectified form of orienting and direction action, exist in continuous use and validation. But that is to say that they are institutions. Recognition immediately links actors' understandings directly to those of other actors; corroboration does so indirectly, through the mostly institutional character of the environment in which actions typically unfold;[15] and resonance also ties actors indirectly to others by virtue of the fact that what any particular understanding resonates with is per force another understanding that is maintained in recognition and/or corroboration. All of this is to say that understandings are social not only because humans mimetically acquire them from others, but also because they are actualized and maintained in processes of validation in which others always play a role. This has immediate consequences for actors. Positive validations actualize understandings and thus make them more suitable for action guidance. Negative validations achieve the opposite effect. Agency—the ability of actors to perform certain actions—is possible precisely because acting is contingent on extant understandings that are in turn, crucially dependent on sufficient positive validation. The agency that human beings have is therefore an institution formed through all three validational effects.[16] The ability to act morally is an agency in this sense.

But this is not all. The stable understandings through which human beings interface with the world make up their personality. Thus, their character, including its virtues, is an institution. So is their body, which is reproduced in the consumption of food as well as in physical activity. What is eaten, and what muscular and mental capacities get exercised, are yet again based on understandings. The conclusion is dramatic: human beings are *thoroughly* instituted beings, not only because they must live in an institutional environment created in collaboration with others through whom they can satisfy their material needs, but also, more fundamentally, because the ways they sense, feel, and think themselves in the world, their inner lives, their agency and identity, are the result of processes of institutionalization. If that were not the case, they would neither be able to col-

---

[15] The boundary case here is purely natural features of the environment. The kinesthetic understandings underpinning fundamental skills—such as sitting up, walking, swimming, or biking—are formed through the unfailing corroborative forces of gravity, resistance, lift, and so on.

[16] It is easy to see how circular effects may come about: success breeds praise, breeds more success, more positive self-feelings, etc.

laborate with others to form the outside world in which they live nor be able to live in it with any semblance of success.[17]

The implications of these thoughts for a theory of how particular ethics may or may not take hold in everyday interaction are profound. Qua force of recognition, all members of a person's network of authority play a significant role in making and remaking her character, as well as in shaping her agency and her identity. Such networks include not only friends and relatives but also experts, news sources, authors, stars, pundits, influencers, literally any authority within whose reach actors place themselves. In a less visible manner, people also support the two forms of validation, since they, too, hinge on institutional arrangements. Qua corroboration, the distribution of opportunities for practicing certain kinds of activities is similarly influential on the sense a person has of her agency, her personality, and her identity. Since this distribution is often governed by institutions, it is again concrete people, each with a name and an address, who share in making and remaking people.[18] Qua resonance, the external mnemonic environments proffer and thus foreground certain understandings at the expense of others, thus validating some understandings of actors positively and others negatively. This external mnemonic environment, which aids in constructing personal memories, includes mass-mediated discourses and images, religious and national holidays with their recurring rituals, professional categories of newsworthiness, narrative

---

[17] Even where people do not discursively understand how they are dependent on others, they can emotively know it. Phenomenally, this emotive knowledge becomes available, for example, in attachments to others, and especially those others who play a central role as authorities in recognition and those who may enable access to corroborating experiences. For people living in what Irving Goffman calls total institutions, such attachment can be to people who, looked at from the outside, appear as extreme violators of the person's dignity, thus explaining the so-called Stockholm syndrome. See Irving Goffman, *Asylums: Essays on the Social Situation of Mental Patients and Other Inmates* (Garden City, NY: Anchor Books, 1961).

[18] Take the ability to swim, for example. First an understanding is needed that human beings can swim at all. Furthermore, one needs knowledge about how to swim. So far, what matters is the distribution for the mimetic acquisition of such understandings and the recognition of these understandings by others. Both are, of course, instituted. But nobody knows how to swim without practicing it. Thus, one needs a suitable body of water, which may be natural, such as oceans, lakes, and rivers in whose proximity some people are lucky enough to live while others do not. Yet even access to these natural bodies of water can be institutionally managed by regulating access to beaches and shores, etc. Finally, one could build artificial bodies of water, the access to which could be so generously regulated that most people come within reach of the possibility of learning to swim.

and linguistic conventions, monuments, street names, and so on.[19] It, too, is institutionalized.

Equipped with the concept of validation, we can now understand how judgments of performances in particular situations can turn into precepts and norms. If judgments like the ones in the above example are repeated, the actors so censured may wish to avoid negative and try to incur positive judgments from their coactors. The motivation for this move lies simply in the fact that they need others not only for maintaining a positive reputation within the sociation, but also for generating and maintaining a positive self-image and a sense of agency. Under these circumstances, "you are a good driver" or "you make great knives" can be converted by self or well-meaning others into "*be* a good driver/knife maker." Or generalized: "be excellent in whatever you do." In anticipation, the retrospective judgment becomes an exhortation, a piece of advice, a command. The consequentialism underpinning the judgment is, looking forward, turned into deontology. And, as I have argued above, both are ultimately valuable to the community and self only if judgment and command become habituated into personality or character. And it is as character—integrated disposition—that judgment and exhortation become virtue.

The concept of validation can also shed an interesting light on the social, spatial, and temporal limits of ethics. Based on the kinds of understandings discussed further above, ethics need to be maintained institutionally by a continuous stream of recognitions, corroborations, and resonances. Thus, the boundaries for the validation of ethics are coextensive with the limits of sufficient validation. Not surprisingly, then, the distribution of validating events for particular ethical understandings ends often at the boundaries of a particular sociation and the reach of the people vocally carrying it. Every family will develop a family ethics maintained by the judgments and exhortations, memory practices, and distribution of experiences of its members. So will every office, every club, and every translocal sociation, such as a nation. Once a domain is established, there is prima facie nothing that guarantees the absence of ethical factionalism created by different people validating different judgments—just that each faction be large enough to maintain its separate ethics, while maintaining just enough overlap between the factions to ensure the continuation of the overarching sociation itself. Thus, split ethics lead to subsociations.

The more differentiated and, thus, structured by a multitude of overlapping distinct sociations a social environment is, the more people live concurrently in a plurality of specific ethics. Nothing guarantees that these ethics cohere in any sense—neither in the point of crystallization formed by one person nor in any par-

---

[19] Think of the organization of cities in Europe as an example. Baroque cities in Europe converge on the palace; self-governed cities converge on town hall and market. Monuments foreground particular people as exemplars.

ticular sociation. They can be based on starkly different understandings of what is good and relevant, because precisely those understandings vary with contexts and across sociations. As long as these worlds are organized into institutionally distinct environments—that is, as long as the activities informed by these ethics take place at different times, at different locations, with different interlocutors— people remain mostly unfazed by these differences. Cutthroat hedge-fund managers or traders at work can also be doting parents, loving partners, and pious members of a religious congregation—that is, as long as they spend enough time in each of these sociations to have its specific ethics reproduced as part of their situationally activated character. It is a plot recipe for both comedy and tragedy to let distinct spheres intersect and either laughingly shrug off the schizophrenia of life, or break a character with life's inherent contradictions. Cognitive dissonance is not a natural phenomenon but the result of some instituted environment proclaiming the desirability of the unity of character across all contexts.[20] That is what all fundamentalisms of a philosophical, religious, or political nature will demand, and that is precisely why they can be attractive to people who are worn out by the contradictions in their lives.

Institutiosis—the Meshing of Institutions

I have proposed to study institutions as existing in regularized action-reaction effect flows. Regularization, however, depends on stably objectified understandings serving as guides orienting and directing action. For these to form and remain actualized, my argument goes, regular validation is necessary. That, however, can issue forth with sufficient regularity only if the validating authorities themselves operate with a stable set of understandings of the world (the good=-steadfast parent, friend, teacher, mentor, partner) or if the action environments and mnemonic environments are maintained in a form that produces constancy in corroboration and resonance. But that is to say that one kind of institution depends on others: actions on understandings, understandings on validations, validations on issuing institutions. The institutions farther down this chain operate as affordances for those preceding them. One could also appeal to the down-the-chain institutions as infrastructures for everything further up. I call this chain of

---

[20] The fundamental problem of the social psychological research tradition built on Leon Festinger's work is its blatant disregard of culture. See Festinger, *Cognitive Dissonance* (Evanston, IL: Row, Peterson, 1957). Weber had already pointed in 1916 ("Zwischenbetrachtung") in a much more fruitful direction.

forever-deferred moorings institutiosis.[21] The regularization of action flows can take place only in reference to something that is already more stable. And in that sense, already established institutions play a constitutive role in the processes of forming new institutions.

I have already pointed to the fact that ethics have a key role to play in grounding institutions. Certain parts of ethics are more specifically geared toward the maintenance of specific institutions. A simple example is the Ten Commandments injunction, "Honor thy father and thy mother," which directly supports parental authority. The infrastructural role that such specific injunctions play is limited to these institutions. Nevertheless, there is always the possibility of a metaphorical transposition across institutional domains that share certain structural features. "Honor thy father" can thus shade into "honor thy God" and "honor thy king," or vice versa. Qua resonance, the very fact that the first precept is already well-established increases the chance that it can be mobilized for the latter two, notably if metaphorical bridges in understanding are built: "thy God is like thy father"; "thy king represents God on earth."

Other ethics are, in the very structure of their underlying understandings, more general in emphasizing modalities of acting: "be punctual," "exercise care," "keep promises." These can serve as infrastructures for a very large variety of institutions. And precisely because this is so, they are also most likely maintained in very diverse interaction contexts and across many different sociations and thus are more stable. They play a role akin to languages or calendars as the most frequently enrolled infrastructural institutions around.[22]

A second dimension of institutiosis emerges if we consider that most actions partake in the reproduction of several institutions at the same time. Marriage vows not only legally found the institution of a particular marriage but also partake in the institutionalization of ritual in which they are spoken, the moral notion of commitment, the linguistic form of an oath, etc. Fully institutionalized ethics offer an excellent example for the interweaving of institutiosis. Ethical judgments support precepts, precepts support virtuous characters, and these are ultimately the source for the consistent use of judgments. The various components of ethics buttress each other like the various straws in a nest. Thus, we can see that rather than presenting three distinct and competing approaches, virtue ethics, deontology, and consequentialism figure as three different moments in a process of institutionalization that is complete only in regard to all three. As I have argued

---

[21] I am adopting here Charles Sanders Peirce's notion of semiosis, in which signs refer to each other in infinite chains for my purposes. Note that there is no absolute order in institutiosis. The infrastructural relation is always relative to context.

[22] It is not surprising, therefore, that in spite of major social transformation, keeping promises or speaking the truth is as fresh as ever as an ethical precept, while honoring god, king, and father is not—in spite of the fact that all of these precepts are ancient.

further above, consequentialist reasoning gives rise to judgments; their repetition and anticipation lead to deontology, which can take a firm hold only in the virtues of character.

Projective Articulation—Expanding the Reach of Activities

One last word about institutions in general. Actions not only produce effects in others through direct face-to face encounters. The basic human faculties of memory and imagination put actors from the beginning into a horizon of past and expected activities. Moreover, history shows how ingenious human beings are in coming up with constantly new techniques to help them projectively articulate their actions across time and space. This can be done by transporting and storing objectifications of actions which can, even without the presence of the actor, trigger reactions in others all on their own. All artifacts, including goods, pieces of art, texts, written calculations, graphs, pictures, films, and so on, fall into this category. Projective articulation is thus dependent on technologies of objectification, transportation, exchange, and storage as well as on institutions and organizations further developing, teaching, and, especially, applying these technologies.[23] Writing can objectify thought (and, albeit to a lesser extent, feeling and perception), which can then be assembled into scrolls or books to be duplicated in scribal or print workshops, from where they can circulate in various ways to produce effects in faraway places and times. Note that technology alone is not sufficient, but that organizations with dedicated staff are needed to make it happen. Other spatiotemporally projected effects come about by forming enduring features of the natural and built environments or simply by producing goods that are traded across space.

Each technique of objectifying and projectively articulating activities significantly expands their potential reach. For ethics as institutions, this means that they, too, can now be formed over much wider time spans and across much wider territory. Also, small groups can maintain their ethics more easily against an immediate social environment governed by different mores if these groups are sustained from the outside. Particular kinds of ethics can thus become defining

---

[23] Historically, the development of political institutions aimed at establishing control over ever expanding territories—that is, states as well as distant trade—as well as territorially expanding cults and missionary religions have been particularly influential if not in directly stimulating the invention of such techniques, then certainly in instituting and developing them further. See, for example, Michael Mann, *The Sources of Social Power*, vol. 1-A, *History of Power from the Beginning to AD 1760* (Cambridge: Cambridge University Press, 1986).

across territory and the ages. History is replete with examples of the uses of projective articulations to form and maintain ethics across space and time.

Knowledge, Care, and Agency in the Emergence and Transformation of Ethics

The profound effects that humans have on shaping each other can influence actually existing ethics only to the degree that these effects are known. Thus, changes in the knowledge how human activities impinge on others directly or indirectly may have considerable repercussions for ethics. Psychoanalysis and developmental psychology, for example, have created knowledge that makes it much more apparent through what innocuous-seeming exchanges parents, siblings, and friends shape children. At the same time, changing family sizes, changing institutional care arrangements, as well as changing economic conditions have altered the understandings of children's relevance for the reproduction of a broad range of institutions. Through the combined effect of both changes in knowledge and relevance, the ethics of childrearing have undergone profound changes.

The work of Marx showed already in the midnineteenth century how markets and modern production techniques systematically destroy people's knowledge about their social relations.[24] With the increasing spatial and social distance across which goods are traded, neither consumers nor producers know anything about each other, in spite of the fact that they wield influence on each other. With an ever-increasing division of labor within and across production sites, workers cease to know how they affect and are affected by their anonymous coworkers. These Marxian findings of "abstraction" can be generalized to all techniques of projective articulation, which by necessity make it much more difficult, if not impossible, for actors to know what the consequences of their actions will be. Innovations in projective articulations literally create an ethical vortex because they prevent the spontaneous emergence of a community of judgment which is coextensive with the reach of effects. It takes countervailing innovations in the knowledge of action effects—such as Marx's—to make a revival of ethics possible. One historical example for such an effort to revive the ethical after its destruction is the cultivation of solidarity in the workers' movement. Consumer activism is another. Fair trade, animal welfare, and green labels aim to create the conditions for the possibility to consume ethically, that is, mindfully with regard to the effects that consumption has on others around the world as well as on the natural environment.

---

[24] The key concepts here are alienation (*Die deutsche Ideologie*, 1846) and commodity fetishism (*Das Kapital*, 1867).

Knowledge impinges on ethics in still other ways. Sometimes distal manifestations of action effects begin to generate feedback effects that may force a rethinking of the consequences of actions for others and the environment. This is the case when distal effects finally become visible either through a large increase in magnitude or with the help of more effective techniques of projective articulation. The new visibility of human impact can then, in turn, trigger the proposal and possible adoption of new ethics. The many ways in which rising human populations and fossil-fuel-powered economic growth have impacted the natural environment, ranging from ecosystems destruction to global warming, offer many examples for such feedback-loop-engendered developments of new ethics caused by magnitude-in-effect changes.[25] And, indeed, there are now not only environmental ethics—with many components stretching the gamut, from carbon-footprint accounting and biodiversity and climate-conscious shopping to recycling—but also efforts to rethink the ways in which humans exist in and with the world. Certain forms of terrorism and global refugee movements are an example of how newly available forms of travel and communication establish feedback loops for foreign and economic policy decisions that previously did not exist. Alas, new ethics have developed along these lines.

Knowledge is not the only constraint on the possibility for ethics to emerge. Even if there is knowledge, it matters a great deal whether the action effects manifesting elsewhere are perceived as in some sense relevant or not. People may simply not care what effects they produce in faraway places and distant times. "Out of sight, out of mind"; "Après mois le déluge!" Indeed, as Marx's analysis suggested, some institutional arrangements—global capitalist economies included—can hold only precisely because they systematically obscure action effects.

Imaginaries delimiting the sociation to which one affectively belongs influence the evaluation of relevance of potential action effects, because they delimit an inside and an outside, a moral cartography of care and carelessness. Changing social imaginaries thus have the prospect of altering the limits of care. This is particularly effective not only where a central organization is charged with cultivating the imaginary, but where the problems created across space or time become the problems of this organization. In such cases, the organization feels compelled to let everyone know how they affect each other. These organizations may act, then, as catalyzers for the development of new ethics of care. Increasing the size

---

[25] As vastly expanding markets have disabled knowledge about human connections, the environmental crisis, too, has been hastened along by a knowledge problem. Insight into these dynamics was blocked by notably Europenoid knowledge systems that have seen culture and nature as distinct spheres requiring distinct modalities of knowing. Culture was defined as humanly molded, nature as being independent of human interference. Ethics belonged to the first, not the second. In fact, however, the planetary ecosystems at all levels have become institutions that must be addressed as such.

of political units has historically had this effect, which becomes palpable through the promotion of new forms of solidarity. The emergence of new nation-states in the nineteenth and the twentieth centuries is an excellent case in point.[26] Religious organizations, too, have provided imaginaries which have increased the domain of care—in extremis to encompass all of humankind.

For ethical judgments to take hold, they not only need to be enabled by knowledge elucidating action/actor-effect links and imaginaries that underwrite some form of care for these effects. What matters in the last instance is that people who know and care also know concretely how precisely to make a difference in their action. The scholarly writings of Freud, Piaget, and their successors required translation into self-help action plans to take hold. Accordingly, people need not only information and exhortation but also concrete action alternatives.

Even with the best of knowledge and the sincerest of cares, many action effects—and most definitively those materializing only in the future—will remain unknown. In this context, ethics have developed something of a rule-of-thumb character, connecting the hope for minimal detrimental effect with relatively simple rules. The hope motivating these rules is often underwritten by metaphysical systems that provide comprehensive accounts about the connective fabric of all happenings. Various religions, philosophies, and the animating ideas behind the modern sciences provide such metaphysical systems. Practitioners of the Abrahamic religions have, for example, cultivated attitudes that favor obeisance to divine will in the assumption that the divine ordering of all happenings is ultimately to the best. Kant's categorical imperative is an artfully derived rule of thumb that counts on a rationally ordered universe. Bentham's exuberant hope to provide a system of total action accounting was already countered by the best of his philosophical successors,[27] such as Mill, who emphasized the importance of rules of thumb that have proven themselves historically.

Ideas of accountability and responsibility (and its cultural cognates) become challengingly complicated when people become aware of exploding action effect chains which, at least at the margins, will remain untraceable. As the investigation has shown so far, any meaningful notion of accountability is contingent on knowledge, care, and effective agency. Beyond even the best currently available knowledge of action effects, care, and alternatives, there will remain a portion that can be addressed only by forgiveness.

---

[26] Max Weber, *Wirtschaft und Gesellschaft: Grundriss der verstehenden Soziologie* [1922] (Tübingen: J. C. B. Mohr [Paul Siebeck], 1972), 528, speaks about nationhood as a value that imposes a feeling of solidarity. For the role of imaginaries in nation building see Benedict Anderson, *Imagined Communities* (London: Verso, 1983).

[27] The economists took a more naive turn, at least until Pigou introduced the notion of externalities in the 1920 s.

Freedom

It might appear now that CPHI offers just another version of the perfectly socialized, that is, completely socially determined human being. That, however, is not the case, as I hope to show in this section. This is an important step, because ethics exist in the knowledge that human beings are quite capable to resist the collective effort to direct their actions toward socially desirable ends and in accord with socially endorsed norms. Conforming to these efforts rather than counteracting them, and doing so voluntarily either by reasoned choice or freely acquired habit, is precisely what gives an act or continuous pattern of acting its specific ethical value in the eyes of the sociation sponsoring the ethics. But whence this freedom to resist the ire of judgment, the force of precept, and whence the idea how to do otherwise in a substantively different way? Answers to this question have two distinct parts. The first wonders about the source of the power to say no to attempts at influencing. This is freedom *from*, or *negative* freedom. The second inquires about the source of the capability to imagine an alternative direction for action that is noncongruent with what is demanded and that nevertheless shows all the properties of ordered action. This is freedom *to*, or *positive* freedom.[28]

Consistent with the commitment to hermeneutics, the starting point for my considerations is the historical record of people's own concern with freedom. These concerns have shifted considerably over time and have taken on quite a range of hues in various contexts.[29] Is there a way to make sociological sense of such varied experiences across time? Is there a way to theorize freedom in a manner that is loadable with the specific concerns and the specific language of times past and across cultures? Clues to a sociological theory of freedom go all the way back to the analyses of modern life through which early sociologists left their mark. Especially early German-speaking sociologists insisted that life in modern societies is life in a plurality of incongruous sociations producing diverse de-

---

[28] The distinction has been made popular by Isaiah Berlin, "Two Concepts of Liberty," in *The Proper Study of Mankind: An Anthology of Essays* (New York: Farrar, Strauss, Geroux, 1958).

[29] Historical overviews over the idea of freedom across time and concepts are provided by Christian Meier Christian et al., "Freiheit," in *Geschichtliche Grundbegriffe: Historisches Lexikon zur politisch-sozialen Sprache in Deutschland*, vol. 2, ed. Otto Brunner, Werner Conze, and Reinhart Koselleck (Stuttgart: Klett-Cotta, 1975), 425–542; Kurt Raaflaub, *The Discovery of Freedom in Ancient Greece* (Chicago: University of Chicago Press, 1985); Orlando Patterson, *Freedom in the Making of the Modern World*, vol. 1 (New York: Basic Books, 1991); Jerome B. Schneewind, *The Invention of Autonomy: A History of Modern Moral Philosophy* (Cambridge: Cambridge University Press, 1998); and Quentin Skinner and Martin van Gelderen, *Freedom and the Construction of Europe*, 2 vols. (Cambridge: Cambridge University Press, 2020).

mands on their members.[30] Weber emphasized that this plurality can, under certain circumstances, generate enormous tensions for modern human beings because each "sphere of social life" is characterized by its own supreme value. And these are, he argued, often enough not only in conflict with each other but in direct competition. Weber's concern remains with tension-reducing institutional creations and the motivations they induce as motors of historical change.

Simmel went further for the purposes at hand. He emphasized that people's movement in and out of a plurality of "social circles" creates the very possibility for freedom and links freedom to the emergence of individuality. According to him, plurality and the pervasive awareness of plurality imply that no particular circle can operate as a total institution.[31] The time spent in any sociation is always limited. No person is dependent for her or his self-maintenance on any particular one institution. For Simmel, human beings in differentiated societies are neither dependent nor independent, but plurally dependent across various contexts. That makes a difference because it opens a venue for resisting particular local pressures simply by leaving and/or by pointing to the demands of others as, under certain circumstances, an acceptable excuse for refusing them. Thus, a certain wiggle room emerges, a freedom from demands to conform. Take, for example, the modern child oscillating between home, school, club, and friendship network activities. In school, the child can resist the demands of, say, a gym teacher, with prohibitions from home; at home, the same child can counter parents' demand to do chores "right now" by pointing to excessive homework on this very day. Similarly, the demands of the club can be played off against the peer pressures in friendship networks, notably in cases where using the family as an excuse would sound "lame," etc.

Just as important, however, life in each sociation offers a different glimpse of what it means to be a particular person, and what actions have to be performed to reproduce it as it is. Women marrying into other families, even other social locations, know that life can be organized differently. People may experience themselves as dominant in some circles and as subordinate in another. Here they are eloquent, there they are mostly quiet. And so they become equipped with alternative understandings of what they could be and what they could do and, more important, how they could be within a particular social environment. And what would hinder them, under these circumstances, from trying out in one context a stance they have developed in another?[32] Their interactants may be surprised,

---

[30] Particularly important are Georg Simmel, *Soziologie* (Frankfurt a. M.: Suhrkamp, 1908) and Weber, "Zwischenbetrachtung."

[31] Goffman, *Asylums*.

[32] I am leaning here on Hannah Arendt's Augustine-inspired notion of freedom as the capacity to begin something new. See, for instance, Arendt, "What is Freedom," in *Between Past and Future: Eight Exercises in Political Thought* (New York: Penguin, 2006), 142–69.

they may react in unpredicted ways, the field of understandings currently actualized within the sociation may begin to shift, if ever so slightly. What emerges from this playful transposition is, in all likelihood, neither what the outside model smuggled into a different context was, nor the regnant local model, but something different, perhaps even something "new."

Freedom in this sense emerges from an interplay of three moves: first, a social jiujitsu, in which a plurality of expectations is skillfully leveraged against each other; second, the playful and somewhat adventurous use of metaphorical transpositions of understandings and practices from one social context to another; and, third, the sheepish or cunning performance of unexpected action to see what happens. Freedom is, sociologically speaking, a craft and, therefore, a skill that grows with practice.[33] It can be further supported and heightened by creating the space for reflexively anticipating some of these moves in the imagination to form a horizon of possibility that replaces single-track behavior which, owing to the absence of clear alternatives, would not even be conceived as conformity, but as simple factuality, as "that's how it is."

CPHI helps to expand the Simmelian model to even smaller-scale microdynamics of interacting. When I speak of action-reaction effect flows, I do not mean to suggest that prior actions in any simple way cause (in the sense of "determine") the reaction. For given the model, the question would have to be, which one of the many? Those that come closest to being proximate? Those that have underwritten the actualizations of the diverse understandings brought to bear on the situation? All? Quantitative metaphors of vectors and resultants would be utterly misleading, not only because there is nothing that could automatically be commensurate between such qualitatively diverse influences, but because, in the interweaving of institutiosis, later influences are highly dependent on earlier ones. Instead of a resultant, the response is an *answer* produced not so much by maneuvering through, but maneuvering with and against, the many influences of relevant prior actions.

After all, reactions are mediated by understandings across all three modes and possible alternatives within each. Discourses working with a plurality of mod-

---

Although Arendt is clearly expressing something very important here, she has left it standing in her work as a bit of a mystery—and I think quite deliberately so. What I try to do here is to give the concept processual richness and, with it, sociological heft. For this is precisely what would be needed to make it politically relevant.

[33] I have benefited greatly from Peter Bieri's work in thinking about freedom as a craft. See his *Das Handwerk der Freiheit: Über die Entdeckung des eigenen Willens* (Munich: Carl Hanser, 2001). Of course, the idea that freedom is a learnable craft can be traced back in the Europeanoid world at least to the Stoa. Hindu, Buddhist, and Taoist notions of freedom were similarly conceived. All of these traditions work with a notion of individual inner freedom which is problematic in light of CPHI.

els can lead to a plurality of possible orientations and directions; emotions can be deeply ambivalent, suggesting both desires and aversions concurrently; and of the senses, we have at least five to give us different takes of the world. Reactions are thus plurally mediated, not necessarily determined at all, but they can be the result of a crafty way of responding that need not even be conscious. In common English parlance, such craft is recognized and indeed admired generally as ingenuity and, more specifically, as wit in discourse, as savvy in tactics, as maturity in feeling. A person who has managed to habituate such ingenuity in a particular domain of acting is described as sovereign within it. Within the microdynamics of interacting, too, the craft of freedom can be enhanced by generating some inner distance from the expected speed in linking actions and reactions. Freedom grows by allowing for the skilled introduction of delay fuses that create a space for reflection.

Like every other skill, the craft of freedom is built on particular understandings that orient and direct it. Knowledge about how to play off demands against each other, how to delay a response, how to imagine alternatives falls into this category. Moreover, to say that freedom is a craft means that it can bloom only where these understandings are in fact instituted with the help of continuous validations. Nobody is free on their own, but depends on the help of others who recognize freedom-supporting understandings, and who help to maintain experiential and mnemonic environments that enhance these understandings. Freedom is therefore not an individual property at all, but a social one. This is also to say that freedom is available in different measures to different people in different contexts. It is contingent and can be cultivated or not. And that, of course, has consequences for ethics. If freedom is the precondition for responsibility, then people have rather variant capacities for responsibility in different contexts and across time. The law acknowledges this, even though its tools for assessing this variation of freedom are rather primitive.

Ethics and Politics

Ethics can emerge or change in a completely decentralized, distributed manner, much in the same way that most of language does. The interplay of understandings and validations provides tools to analyze institutionalization and deinstitutionalization in such uncentrally coordinated processes. Most people occasionally act as impromptu ethical entrepreneurs by venturing ethical judgments that they may not have heard in this way in this particular sociation. Of course, one swallow does not a summer make, and whether or not such ventures will lead to the emergence of an additional or altered thread in the fabric of a sociation's ethics depends entirely on how others react to the moralizing incident. Successful entrepreneurship resonates with others who then begin to mimic the judgment because it fits with their own understandings of this and similar situations, with what they believe and feel to be true about them. It might also fit with their own ideas about where things should be going. With sufficient circulation and repetition, judgments then turn into precepts that likewise need to make the rounds within the sociation to ensure a successful integration of the new strand of understandings into a sufficient number of characters within a sociation such that judgments, precepts, and characters are sustainably instituted.

Ethics can come about also in a completely different way. The entrepreneurship can be self-conscious and deliberate rather than impromptu; the response of others can become the object of organized attempts to influence them rather than letting them decide spontaneously what to do. From the perspective of CPHI, politics is the deliberate effort to form, alter, or abolish institutions. Politics thus conceived is contingent on three kinds of knowledge: on imaginaries that the world could be otherwise; on sociological insight into how to bring that otherwise into being; and on mobilizational knowledge that successfully informs activities to bring all those on board who are needed to effect the desired institutional consequences. But that is to say that ethics can be an object of politics, and it very often is. All organized religions form and maintain their ethics deliberately. They typically have ethical imaginaries, and they know how to institute it. Missionizing religions aim at finding not only acolytes in worship but also carriers of the associated ethics. Nation-states have deliberately used the expanding school systems that have underwritten their own existence to promulgate some sort of national ethics, which they preach at the expense of competing genealogical or more encompassing religious ethics. In the same vein, activists promote fair trade, biodiversity, animal rights, and environmental ethics. States and trade associations set up committees to draft ethical guidelines and substate enforcement procedures for professions such as medicine, law, or research in the life sciences.

As I have mentioned before, ethics also can be an important supporting institution for political efforts to form other kinds of institutions. Ethics are appealed to in political mobilization, and the experience of membership in and ethically guided effort is often a reward for partaking in politics. No wonder, then, that the powerful have always aimed to shape ethics to their liking. But that does not mean, of course, that ethics are nothing but the right of the stronger, because it is by no means a given that the stronger will succeed in their political efforts. For the same reason that ethics can provide powerful tools, ethics can also be an impediment for particular political efforts. Genealogical ethics undercut the formation of larger political units; insider privileges of sociation members, such as internal codes of honor protected by an outward wall of silence, are an impediment to crime-fighting endeavors everywhere.

Conclusions: Toward a Sociological Metaethics

The Hebrew Bible formulates a core part of its ethics in the form of second-person imperatives addressing individual persons. So, for example, in the first of the Ten Commandments: "Thou shalt have no other Gods before me."[34] The same form of address is used later in the Christian New Testament, for example: "And as ye would that men should do to you, do ye also to them likewise."[35] Kant, in his pre-critical period, related the branches of philosophy as he saw them as answers to a set of four questions. Ethics were presented as an answer to "What should I do?" He answers himself in his practical philosophy with the categorical imperative that reads, for example, its second formulation in the *Groundwork of the Metaphysics of Morals*, "Act as if the maxim of your action should, through your will, become a general law of nature."[36]

I offer these three prominent examples as a way of directing attention to the fact that ethics are generally thought of as relating to individuals and their behavior. If what I have argued in this essay deserves to be taken seriously, then this focus on individuals is seriously deficient. Since human beings are instituted beings living in institutional environments, to whose reproduction they wittingly and unwittingly contribute, the more foundational question for an ethics would have to be, "What sort of institutions should *we* generate, to make it possible for *us* to live the lives we deem worth living?" In short, "What are good institutions?"

For most of history, this question was seen as always already answered by reference to some transcendence, of which divinities, cosmic laws, and nature are archetypical examples. Today, many larger institution forming projects in the Europeanoid world involve people who do not agree on such transcendences, even where the participants may hold on to some transcendence within the networks of authority in which they maneuver. Even the concept of nature as set forth by their eponymous sciences has lost the position as a universally acknowledged transcendent. So the question of the good life in the good society has become one that needs to be addressed anew and in a different form. In the absence of transcendences that are persuasive to most participants, answers to the question need to involve a broad, inclusive, and equal public debate to see whether there could not be points of convergence. It is on the basis of such a shared vision that we should decide what the institutions would have to look like to support it, including associated ethics. All of this does not mean that some sort of core consensus is prima facie out of reach. Do we want people to be free? Do we want them to be able to act responsibly? Do we want them to care for others, possibly even all others? Do we want them to be able to be politically active to shape the environment in which

---

[34] Exodus 20:2.
[35] Luke 6:31.
[36] Immanuel Kant, *Gesammelte Schriften*, Akademie-Ausgabe 4:421.

they live? Well, if so, then this has consequences for the kinds of institutions we should want and those that we should begin to dismantle.

Absolute Truth—A Toxic Chimera?

Bernold Fiedler

Prologue

The universal prerogative of religion over ethical education is much contested today as old-fashioned, outdated and obsolete, private and subjective, unscientific, sectarian, or outright abusive. Natural science, in contrast, is considered beyond dispute, even though its ethical record is equally dubious, at best. In education, science is mostly taught, and misunderstood, as a fixed canon of known facts. Science is presented as established laws of nature, carved in stone in the unfortunately inscrutable symbolism of mathematics.

Both equally beyond the doubt of mortals, religion and mathematics come gilded with the value of truth—for seemingly diametrically opposite reasons. Whether their concepts are based on pure logic or pure faith, both appear as last bastions of Absolute Truth in an otherwise pluralistic mind set. Both appear enshrouded with the mystique of the unfathomable. And neither is thought to be subject to majority vote—quite contrary to the pacifying relativism and arbitrariness of the assertion that "everyone has their own truth." How can we still dare to teach the undemocratic absolutes of mathematics and religion?

The provocative apologetics in this chapter mostly explores the mathematical side. Katz[1] provides a relatively accessible historical background on many of the mathematical topics below.

Definition and Toxic Chimeras

Truth, the Greek goddess Ἀλήθεια (Aletheia), known as Veritas to the Romans, daughter of Time-Chronos or sometimes Zeus, lives forgotten and enigmatically

---

[1] V. J. Katz, *A History of Mathematics* (New York: Harper Collins, 1993).

hidden in the obscurity of a deep well.² In Greek, so Martin Heidegger lets us know,³ her name hints at an unconcealment, an unforgetting, an unhiding. Truth is detected, uncovered, emerging, and exposed to broad daylight as naked truth. When truth is thus revealed or unveiled, her impartial innocence is in stark contrast to seductive Salome, who dances and unveils to a lecherous audience, herself an instrument of sinister intrigue. The range from investigative journalism to paparazzi tabloids, for example, covers that spectrum of nakedness. Veritas, the Roman version of truth, leans toward rectitude, rightness, or correctness. The virtue of correctness is probably invoked when mathematicians formally check logical tautologies, via truth tables, or verify their tedious calculations and algorithms. Sworn testimony, in various formulations, languages, and legal systems, refers to both ἀλήθεια and *veritas* in the absolute obligation to tell "the truth, the whole truth, and nothing but the truth." An example of religious truth, finally, as indisputable revelation, is incarnate in the fourteenth century "Ave verum corpus," as enshrined by Wolfgang Amadeus Mozart.⁴ For brevity and simplicity, I will limit comments on religious aspects to an Abrahamic perspective and context. The intriguing complexities and refinements of the idea of Truth in Asian culture remain beyond the reach of this chapter.

Pluralism offers many chimerical shapes and shades of truth. Lopsided fundamentalism—Bible thumping, and, say, science thumping—unilaterally announce themselves to be in possession of the one and only absolute truth, respectively and exclusively. The equally dogmatic relativism of "everyone has their own truths" is less pacifying than it may sound. Just as absolutist in character, it rejects the very possibility of any absolute truth—besides itself. The travesties of contradictory conspiracy theories and the popularity of fake news in the echo chambers of social media vociferously claim the virtues of democratic diversity and free speech, exclusively in their own respective favor. Professional spin doctors mock truth for a living, with murky concoctions of *Deutungshoheit*, Orwellian "Newspeak," language control—and a remarkable affinity toward defining and bending political correctness. The boastfully declared objective of these pundits is the profitable manipulation of public opinion. Success is measured in terms of changed legal perceptions, the selling of candidates, and victory in democratic elections.

The supreme value of truth, in contrast, receives unanimous praise in countless university mottos, and in near unison ranging from Soviet ПРАВДА (*Pravda*) to the unofficial motto of the U.S. Central Intelligence Agency (CIA), "The truth shall set you free" (John 8:32). Noam Chomsky declares, "It is the responsibility of

---

[2] In view of this mythological identification of Truth as a goddess, I refer to Truth throughout this chapter as a feminine entity rather than "it."
[3] M. Heidegger, *Sein und Zeit* (Tübingen: Niemeyer, 1927).
[4] W. A. Mozart, "Ave verum corpus," KV618, 1791.

intellectuals to speak the truth and to expose lies."[5] And Heidegger, in his "Rektorratsrede," remarks,

> "Die deutsche Studentenschaft ist auf dem Marsch. Und wen sie sucht, das sind jene Führer, durch die sie ihre eigene Bestimmung zur gegründeten, wissenden Wahrheit erheben und in die Klarheit des deutend-wirkenden Wortes und Werkes stellen will."
> (The German student body is on the march. And *whom* it seeks are those leaders through whom it is determined to elevate its own destiny toward founded, knowing truth, and to place it into the clarity of the interpreting-effective word and work.)[6]

As politically wizened pluralist skeptics, of course, we then have to ask with seasoned Pontius Pilate, "What is truth?" (John 18:38).

In the beginning, we follow Thomas Aquinas,[7] Q16 *De veritate*, verbatim. He refers to, and reinterprets, Isaac Israeli ben Solomon and Aristotle before him, when he defines Truth as *adaequatio rei et intellectus*, an adequateness or correspondence between the thing or object, *res*, and its representations in our intellect. Meanwhile, the sibylline *adaequatio* has become central to natural science in the guise of mathematical models and laws of nature. See the section on "Laws of Nature" below.

Truth comes with a most significant necessary condition attached. Immediately, we have to require consistency, that is, Truth is free from self-contradiction. A lie, that is, a conflict between what is and what is said, contradicts Truth. A lie is a lie, and neither an "alternative fact" nor Truth. In particular, Truth cannot contradict Truth herself. Deconstructionist Averroes points out,

> "If in reality there ... existed ... the possibility of two opposites, even for the twinkling of an eye, there would no longer be any permanent knowledge of anything."[8] He goes on to say: "When the theologians admit that the opposite of everything existing is equally possible, ... [then] there is no fixed standard for His will ... according to which things must happen. For this reason the theologians are open to all the scandalous implications with which they are charged. For true knowledge is the knowledge of a thing as it is in reality."[9]

---

[5] N. Chomsky, "The Responsibility of Intellectuals," *The New York Review of Books* 8 (1967).

[6] M. Heidegger, "Rektoratsrede," University of Freiburg, May 1933.

[7] Thomas Aquinas, *Summa Theologica* (1265–74).

[8] Averroes (Ibn Rushd), *The Incoherence of the Incoherence*, Gibb Memorial Series, new series 19, trans. S. van den Bergh, 2 vols. (Oxford: Oxford University Press, 1954), 1:374.

[9] Ibid., 2:219.

Consistency is the principal *Law of Truth*, from which many other properties—and complications—derive. Although consistency is a necessary condition, we do not consider that mere property as a sufficient condition for Truth. For example, we are not particularly interested in true but meaningless statements, like the entries of a telephone book. As a necessary property of Truth, however, consistency can be used quite effectively to weed out self-contradictory statements. See sections on paradoxes, antinomies, and consistency, below.

The Thomist definition conveniently separates things, or objects, from the intellect of the subject contemplating them. Much criticized, at least this separation elegantly avoids self-referential circles involving the thinking subject, as an object. Immutable things also make truth independent of any specific realization, instantiation, or intellectual representation. In that sense, Truth reaches beyond the particular individual who knows, and intellectually represents, this or that aspect of truth.

Two related properties follow. Truth becomes *universal:* Truth does not depend on who encounters and discovers her, or when and where, or in which form and language. This is implicit in the absence of self-contradiction: Truth here and there, or now and then, should mutually agree and coincide. For example, Truth becomes translatable. Truth herself is immutable, *mutatis mutandis*, and becomes *absolute:* detached and independent from ephemerals like location, history, cultural background, social status, language, and even the particular material or neural representation in the particular mind of a particular intellect. *Absolute Truth* is singular, not plural. Today, religious revelation and mathematical proof form just about the last bastions of such a concept.

Sectarianism, religious and political strife, pogroms, terrorism, and war are among the more toxic companions of the chimera of purported absolute truth. The quest for Truth herself is never the driving intention behind such divisive confrontations, of course. The purported absolute is instrumentalized, exploited, mocked, and abused. Truth becomes enslaved for pseudocultural warfare, fed by pseudologic and narcissistic infantilism, driven by ulterior motives like greed, power, domination, and conquest. It is not Truth herself which is discredited by such machinations. Obscurantism, with hidden ulterior motives, takes her hostage in her well and replaces her purity with alluringly glittering, but diabolically poisoning, chimeras.

With Truth as an established value, perhaps even a passion, or an obsession, the question remains how to truly and honestly catch a glimpse of her, how to pursue her, reach, and perhaps embrace her. Far from Augustine's image of Truth as a lioness who defends herself, once exposed, Ἀλήθεια mostly leads a most reclusive existence.

Although Truth, once revealed, seems to induce consensus, such consensus could be manufactured.[10] In any event, invariable Truth herself is not subject to majority vote. Uncovering Truth, even mere scientific truth, seems a highly mysterious and strenuous process. Intuition may help, or imagination, or genius. Honest, diligent, and tenacious intellectual work certainly does. Or conducive circumstances, fortunate errors, and plain good luck. Checking Truth however, once found and converted to intelligible form, seems a more manageable task, shared by many. In mathematics, this may amount to the verification of a given calculation or derivation. In natural sciences, more cautiously and potentially open-ended, it may involve the falsification of ever temporary, ever refined working hypotheses.[11]

Mathematical *Adaequatio*

Let us get a little more precise, mathematically. Here mathematics stands only for a particularly simple, limited, and therefore well-defined mode of thought. Law, philosophy, language, religion, and even the natural sciences are much more complex by comparison.

If the *res* side of the Thomist *adaequatio* seems relatively clear, scientifically speaking, the *intellectus* part requires some actual "incarnation," some mindful representation, some word, some language, preferably some λόγος (logos). Mathematics steps in here, the designated "universal language of science." Evidently, the mathematical formulas of Isaac Newton, James Maxwell, Albert Einstein, Erwin Schrödinger, Werner Heisenberg, and many others define the language in which the laws of nature appear to be carved in stone.

The lamentable and, to outsiders, inscrutably hermetic logographic symbolism of mathematics reflects that universality: the meaning conveyed becomes independent of any phonetic or language particulars and carries independent graphical significance for the initiate.

However, does our Thomist definition of Truth apply to mathematics at all? This requires an *adaequatio* between mathematics, viewed as *intellectus*, and some "things." In natural science, those things are essentially material and distinct from the mathematical descriptions of their phenomenology. But what are the things, then, the objects, of mathematics? When speaking of mathematical truth—detached, universal, and absolute—do we refer to anything outside pure mathematics at all?

---

[10] E. S. Herman and N. Chomsky, *Manufacturing Consent: The Political Economy of the Mass Media* (New York: Pantheon Books, 1988).

[11] K. Popper, *Logik der Forschung. Zur Erkenntnistheorie der modernen Naturwissenschaft* (Vienna: Springer, 1935).

Consider, for simplicity, the positive integers 1, 2, 3, etc. When we count things—say apples—we use such numbers. (Some animals count, too—quite adequately, somehow.) When we count a bunch of apples—mathematically speaking: a set a—we have an *adaequatio* between those apples and our count, provided we count correctly. But we might count a set b of bananas, instead. In fact, we might end up with a count of $b = 3$ bananas, and the same count $a = 3$ of apples, or the same count of just any other things. So far, numbers are just counts of stuff.

Next, we may abstract from a apples and b bananas, and just consider that number $a = b = 3$ as a new object. To have the same count of things in two different sets a and b then means that we can label the things in a by the things in b, and vice versa, by an artificial one-to-one correspondence between them. Next, we may consider the total count $a+b = 6$ of our apples and bananas, even after we have already eaten them all. Or we may arrange a rectangle of two rows, one of $a = 3$ (imagined) apples and a second one of $b = a = 3$ (imagined) bananas, and conclude that we have $2 \cdot 3 = 2\,a = a+a = a+b = 6$ things—without any thing in sight anywhere.

The numbers 1, 2, 3, etc., originated from such counts, by abstraction from the counted objects. But we can now consider those numbers themselves as things, on a higher level. Any *abstraction* is of that type: we consider mental representations, on the *intellectus* side, as new objects of reflective thought, as new things, on a next-higher transcending metalevel. We may consider, for example, numbers that exceed any actual number of real objects in the (finite) universe. We can explore rules concerning addition, multiplication, primality, distribution of prime numbers, and so on.

When we speak of "truth" in the more encompassing sense, we may ask about the truth of mathematical abstractions or, again more generally, about the Truth of mathematics. More ambitiously, we may ascend to the question: "Is Truth true"? The risk of self-referential cycles looms large, in such ascent.

We present a few paradoxes and an antinomy in the next two sections, and some humbling caveats of incompleteness and determinism in subsequent section. The section on Laws of Nature, as *applications* of mathematics, returns to the *adaequatio* with the real thing—mostly with a focus on some physics.

Paradoxes

The principal Law of Truth requires Truth to be consistent, that is, free from self-contradiction. *Paradoxes* look self-contradictory but are not. On a higher level, the contradictions can, and will, be resolved. In that sense, paradoxes fall short of constituting *antinomies:* unresolvable contradictions, toxic to Truth and logic. Let us consider three examples to illustrate the point.

Can a circle be a rectangle? Of course not, one might think, because a rectangle possesses four corners, while a circle does not possess any. In three dimensions, however, it is easy to resolve the seeming paradox. Let us grab a can of coke or beer. Depending on how we hold the can, out in the sunshine, the shadow may assume different shapes. Circular and rectangular shapes are extreme cases, for the same can. In other words, one and the same three-dimensional object may possess incongruous two-dimensional projections. Similarly, the same four-dimensional object may possess incongruous three-dimensional projections, and so on. In physics, the resolutions of the quantum wave-particle paradox by Schrödinger's wave equation or Heisenberg's equivalent matrix mechanics come to mind.

Our second paradox involves linked rings. For linking, think of two rings manufactured so that they become inseparable, like two successive links in a chain. They cannot be unlinked, except by destruction, elimination, or opening of one of the rings. Now consider three rings. *Is it possible to link three rings, inseparably, such that elimination of any one ring unlinks the other two rings, too?*

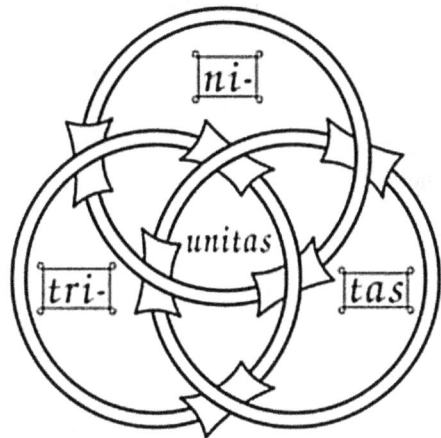

Figure 1: The three Borromean Rings in a thirteenth-century allegory of the Christian Trinity. Eliminating any one ring makes the remaining rings fall apart. The challenge is to discover similar designs involving 4, 5, 6, etc., rings. Do not feel discouraged if you fail at first. Imagination is more important than knowledge.

The question is worth some contemplation before looking up the answer. The challenge appears to be a clear impossibility, at first, as linking and separation contradict each other. The Borromean Rings,[12] however, provide a positive an-

---

[12] A. N. Didron, *Christian Iconography; or, the History of Christian Art in the Middle Ages*, transl. M. Stokes (London: George Bell, 1907; public domain), vol. 2, fig. 139.

swer; see figure 1. They appear on the coat of arms of the Borromeo family in north Italy, in the fifteenth century. The figure has been used much earlier to symbolize the paradoxical mystery of the Trinity. The relevant area of topological knot theory, and its relation to physics, is an exciting classical and current field of active research.

The *Hausdorff paradox*,[13] or *Banach-Tarski paradox*,[14] our third example, defies common sense completely—but not mathematical logic. Consider a solid three-dimensional ball B, say, of gold to trigger greed and public interest. Felix Hausdorff decomposes B into *three* equal parts (except for a single added center point), such that any *two* of them can be recombined to form an exact copy of the whole original ball B. The third of the equal parts is left over. Here two parts or balls are considered equal if they are identical copies after a three-dimensional rotation and translation. In particular, the ball does not get any smaller, in the process.

The proof exceeds the mathematical techniques developed in this little primer. The paradox is based on the mathematical concept of the continuum, rather than atomistic physics. Moreover, the proof uses the *axiom of choice*, a set theoretic device accepted by the overwhelming majority of mathematicians.

On the practical side, we caution greedy readers that it is not possible to attribute physical weight to any of the three equal parts. (In mathematical jargon, the volume of the parts is not measurable, in the sense of Henri Lebesgue). Otherwise, we could add the volumes of three or two identical parts, respectively, to obtain a veritable contradiction of arithmetic: 3 = 2.

Antinomies

The increasingly bewildering paradoxes of the previous section did not constitute mathematical contradictions. Antinomies, in contrast, launch a frontal attack against the principal Law of Truth itself: they actively seek self-contradiction.

Precursors commonly arose in self-referential structures. A classical (but not quite convincing) paradigm is the Cretan Epimenides, who tells us that all Cretans lie. Sancho Panza is confronted with a legal antinomy involving capital punishment for lying.[15] In theology, self-referential complications of thinking the absolute have been amply discussed, for example, in connection with omnipo-

---

[13] F. Hausdorff, *Grundzüge der Mengenlehre* (Leipzig: Veit, 1914), 469–72.

[14] S. Banach and A. Tarski, "Sur la décomposition des ensembles de points en parties respectivement congruentes," *Fund. Math* 6 (1924): 244–77.

[15] M. de Cervantes Saavedra, *Segunda Parte del Ingenioso Cavallero Don Quixote de La Mancha* (Madrid, 1615).

tence: can God contradict himself, and the like. See, for example, Averroes,[16] Maimonides,[17] and the geometry argument of Thomas Aquinas,[18] which we will recall in the section on religion, below. It is easy to recognize such statements as self-contradictory and discard them.

Mathematicians, as seekers of Absolute Truth,[19] have to take antinomies particularly seriously. Indeed, *ex falso quodlibet* warns that anything, true or false, can be derived from a self-contradictory statement. Moreover, *proof by contradiction* or *indirect proof* is a common mathematical device, typically when contemplating infinitely many objects—for example, the positive integers 1, 2, 3, etc. Such indirect proofs just assume the original claim to be false. They then use that falseness, as an additional assumption, to derive a contradiction.

Because mathematics, like Truth, supposedly does not contradict itself, the original claim cannot have been false. Therefore, the claim must be true: *tertium non datur*. In classical perspective, that strategy of indirect proof is a special case of *reductio ad absurdum*. For illustration, let us prove the following claim: among the positive integers 1, 2, 3, etc., there does not exist any largest one. An indirect proof assumes this original claim to be false: let n denote the largest integer, then. But the integer $n + 1$ is larger than n. This contradicts the defining property of n. And this contradiction proves the original claim.

An *antinomy*, as defined by Kant,[20] requires a construction where *both a claim and its opposite lead to contradictions*. Unfortunately, his specific examples fail to meet current standards of mathematical logic.

The *Russell antinomy*, however, delivered. The contradiction arises by self-reference, much as in the introductory examples, but in an entirely mathematical framework. The construction is based on sets, that is, lists of objects called elements. In his first letter to Gottlob Frege[21] (written in excellent German), Bertrand Russell defines a set B which collects all those sets A which do not contain themselves as elements. Russell then asks whether the set B contains itself as an element or not. He remarks that the set B must contain itself as an element, if it is assumed that it does not. Similarly, however, B cannot contain itself as an element, if it is assumed that it does. Either assumption leads to a contradiction. And

---

[16] Averroes (Ibn Rushd), *The Incoherence of the Incoherence*.
[17] M. Maimonides, *The Guide for the Perplexed* (Cairo, ca. 1176–90).
[18] Thomas Aquinas, *Summa Theologica*.
[19] A. and B. Strugatzky, Понедельник начинается в субботу (Monday Begins on Saturday) (Moscow, 1965).
[20] I. Kant, *Critik der reinen Vernunft* (Riga: Hartknoch, 1781), I.2.2.2.2.
[21] B. Russell, "Russell an Frege, 16.06.1902," in *Wissenschaftlicher Briefwechsel* (Hamburg: Felix Meiner Verlag, 1976).

tertium non datur! Frege's reply[22] to this frontal attack on his system of formal logics was a mix of personal shock and honest acclaim.

Fuzzy logic, by the way, which associates a continuum of truth values ranging from 0 = false to 1 = true to a statement, is not a way out. All it does is to replace the truth tables of classical logic with a calculus equivalent to conditional probabilities.

The horror of Russell's antinomy was, and remains, such that mathematical set theory today carefully forbids constructions like Russell's set B, to avoid self-referential contradictions. And proof by contradiction remained a principal mathematical device, happily forever after—until the next antinomy arises from her hideout.

Consistency and Incompleteness

The absence of self-contradictions in the axioms of arithmetic is the second in David Hilbert's legendary set of twenty-three mathematical problems presented at the Paris International Congress of Mathematics in 1900.[23] In other words, would it be possible to prove that a mathematical statement and its negation cannot be simultaneously true, at least for statements concerning the positive integers 1, 2, 3, etc.? With reference to our principal Law of Truth, this desideratum is called *consistency* of (integer) arithmetic.

Entscheidbarkeit (completeness; literally, decidability; that term is used in a more narrow, computational sense today) is closer to the *tertium non datur.* Although there are several variants of this notion, our presentation will mercifully forsake the full splendor of academic complications, for simplicity. Suppose we have some mathematical statement A: can we decide whether or not A is true, given our axiomatic context, for example, of arithmetic? To show that A is true, we require a proof in finitely many steps, based on the underlying axioms. To refute the truth of A, we have to prove, in finitely many steps, that claim A is false. In short, are we capable of proving either A or the negation of A? If this is always the case, we call the underlying axiomatic system *complete* or *decidable.*

Hilbert's program, formally presented in the 1920 s, aimed to formulate all mathematics in axiomatic form, and to prove both consistency and completeness within that framework. In 1930, Kurt Gödel sensationally deconstructed Hilbert's

---

[22] G. Frege, "Letter to Russell, 22.6.1902," in *The Frege Reader,* ed. Michael Beaney (Oxford: Wiley, 1997).

[23] D. Hilbert, "Mathematische Probleme," *Archiv der Mathematik und Physik* 3 (1901): 44–63 and 213–37.

program with his famous *incompleteness theorems*.[24] (The originally announced sequel of Gödel's paper never appeared.) Assuming consistency, Gödel constructed a statement A of arithmetic which was neither provable nor refutable. Even more specifically, he showed that *consistency of arithmetic is not provable*, from within that same set of axioms.

This turns out to be a rather general, if deplorable, fact. Euclidean geometry, fundamental to mathematical education for millennia, is also affected. The axiomatization of geometry by David Hilbert since 1899,[25] for example, contains the notion of the infinitely long real line, and hence of arithmetic. Therefore, a purely geometric proof of consistency of Euclidean geometry must remain elusive, unless the axiomatics of the real numbers is *assumed* to be consistent, a priori. Tarski and others have presented reduced sets of axioms for geometry, where consistency can be proved to hold true, from within.[26] However, that advantage comes at a steep price: such "geometries" have to sacrifice the intuitive geometric notions of the infinite line and of the continuum.

But Gödel proved even more. In fact, there always exist extra statements A', extraneous to any given system of axioms A containing arithmetic, such that the following property holds true. If the system of A is consistent—that is, without contradiction—then the system remains consistent if we adjoin the truth of A' as a new axiom. However, the system remains equally consistent if we adjoin the negation of A' as a new axiom.[27] A longstanding question in the realm of real numbers was known as the continuum hypothesis, the first Hilbert problem.[28] Already in 1878, Georg Cantor had asked whether there could exist any subset C of the continuum of all real numbers, that is, of the real line, such that C contains more points than the integers do, but fewer points than the real line itself. The nonexistence of such an "in-between" set is called the *continuum hypothesis* (CH). Here "fewer" and "more" are defined by counting: two sets are considered equally large if all elements of the one set can be labeled by the elements of the other, and vice versa. Note how this extends our finite counts of apples and bananas, above, to comparative counts of infinities, that is, of mere mathematical thing" without any further reference to actual objects in the real world. In the Hausdorff paradox, we already encountered remarkable properties of the ball, a three-dimensional continuum.

---

[24] K. Gödel, "Über formal unentscheidbare Sätze der Principia Mathematica und verwandter Systeme I," *Monatshefte für Mathematik und Physik* 38 (1931): 173-98.

[25] D. Hilbert, *Grundlagen der Geometrie* (Stuttgart: Teubner, 1903).

[26] A. Tarski and S. Givant, "Tarski's system of geometry," *Bulletin of Symbolic Logic* 5 (1999): 175-214.

[27] Gödel, "Über formal unentscheidbare Sätze der Principia Mathematica und verwandter Systeme I."

[28] Hilbert, "Mathematische Probleme."

Until 1938, nobody had been able to reach a decision on the continuum hypothesis. It was Gödel,[29] again, who showed the following. If the axiomatics of the reals (for experts: in the precise meaning of Zermelo and Fraenkel) is consistent, then consistency persists under the additional assumption that (CH) is true. Everybody was quite happy and took that result as the next best thing to a proof of (CH) itself. In 1963, however, Paul Cohen[30] showed that consistency remains equally valid under the additional assumption that (CH) is false. Conclusion: the validity of (CH) turned out to be undecidable, under the assumption of consistency, and became a matter of taste. Had Absolute Truth thus become a matter of taste, a choice of predilection among various axiomatics in the abstract glass bead game of mathematics?

The term "incompleteness," more generally, suggests an extension process for axiomatic systems containing integer arithmetic. When we encounter any undecidable statement A of interest, we may well add the assumption that A is true to our set of axioms. Or we may add the negation of A as our latest pet axiom. The extension process preserves the property of consistency, in case consistency held true before extension. But the extended system, still containing arithmetic, will again contain undecidable statements, and so on, ad infinitum. Such processes are perhaps reminiscent of Karl Jaspers's ascent *zum Umgreifenden des Umgreifenden*[31] (toward transcendence of transcendence), or an iteration of Hegel's dialectic *Aufhebung* (sublation), ad infinitum.

Laws of Nature

So far, we have explored the mathematical side, the *intellectus* aspect, of the Thomist *adaequatio*. Concerning the *res* aspect, we have pointed at natural science. But how about the *adaequatio* in all those mathematically formulated laws of nature?

In 1894, Heinrich Hertz explained the *adaequatio* between a real-world object and its mathematical model as follows:

---

[29] K. Gödel, "The Consistency of the Axiom of Choice and of the generalized Continuum-Hypothesis with the Axioms of Set Theory," *Annals of Mathematics Studies* 17 (1952): 207–08.

[30] P. J. Cohen, "The Independence of the Continuum Hypothesis I and II," in *Proceedings of the National Academy of Sciences* (1963 and 1964), 105–10 and 1143–48.

[31] K. Jaspers, *Der philosophische Glaube angesichts der Offenbarung* (Munich: Piper, 1962).

Absolute Truth—A Toxic Chimera? 77

"Wir machen uns innere Scheinbilder oder Symbole der äußeren Gegenstände, und zwar machen wir sie von solcher Art, daß die denknotwendigen Folgen der Bilder stets wieder die Bilder seien von den naturnotwendigen Folgen der abgebildeten Gegenstände."

(We produce inner mirages/images/models or symbols of the external objects, such that the consequences of the images, by abstract thought, always shall be the images of the consequences, in nature, of the objects which the images describe.)[32]

In other words, we project the real world into the realm of mathematical structures, and require the projection (alias mathematical modeling) to commute with the causal and dynamic consequences. The projection is the Thomist *adaequatio*, from *rei* to *intellectus*. Whether we first watch what actually happens in nature's sequences of cause and effect, and then project the result into mathematical symbolism, or whether we first project to that realm of mathematical ideas and then derive the mathematical consequences remains intellectually equivalent. At least this is the objective of the mathematical formalisms offered by Newton, Maxwell, Einstein, Schrödinger, Heisenberg, and so many others. Well, is that actually so?

The Hertz definition involves at least three subtleties. First, the *adaequatio* projection might fail to be surjective—that is, it might fail to cover the full range of the mathematical modeling space: there may be variants of a formula in the mathematical model which do not arise from any real object. The popular chimera of tachyons[33] is an example. The starting point is Einstein's formulas of special relativity, which frequently include Lorentz or Minkowski terms like the square root of $1-v^2/c^2$. Here c is the velocity of light, and v is the velocity of some object, for example, a particle. To make sense of the Lorentzian square root, it is assumed that no particle moves faster than light. Conveniently, the term $1-v^2/c^2$ then remains nonnegative, and its square root is a real number. Mathematicians, of course, have long developed the concept of square roots of negative numbers as well, calling them imaginary. (Complex numbers—that is, sums of real and imaginary numbers—are essential to quantum mechanics.) So it is very easy to define the Lorentz root for velocities v larger than light speed c itself. We obtain mathematical descriptions of hypothetical particles, alluringly called *tachyons*, with, depending on preference, imaginary mass and real energy, or imaginary energy and real mass, and so on. This does not mathematically prove, or even just hint at, the actual existence of any tachyon at all on the *res* side of the real world. The use of the Lorentz root is just symbolic, like a magical incantation of imaginary spirits. The validity of such mathematical voodoo in the real world is nil. Less well-

---

[32] H. Hertz, *Die Principien der Mechanik in neuem Zusammenhange dargestellt* (Leipzig: J. A. Barth, 1894).

[33] O. M. P. Bilaniuk, V. K. Deshpande, and E. C. G. Sudarshan, "'Meta' Relativity," *American Journal of Physics* 30 (1962): 718–23.

known, in imaginary time the mathematical pendulum, and even the Kepler motions of the planets themselves, possess additional invisible periods of their associated elliptic integrals.[34] This beautiful mathematical theory has been developed by Abel, Jacobi, Weierstrass, and many others. Pure mathematics, however, neither predicts nor precludes any associated imaginary physics: only observation does.

Second, the *adaequatio* projections of Hertz typically fail to be injective—that is, they fail to describe a one-to-one correspondence: several quite different real objects can be represented by one and the same mathematical model. This is actually good news when it happens. Wind tunnels are an engineering example, based on a scaling invariance of the equations for aerodynamics. Small model planes can faithfully reproduce the aerodynamics of large airplanes via a mathematical *adaequatio*. Alfred Lotka provides another example.[35] In 1920, he suggested a theoretical mathematical model for oscillating chemical reactions. In 1928, the same model was developed by Vito Volterra,[36] independently, to describe ecological interactions in a predator-prey system. Any analog computer, still popular in the 1970 s, is an example where a variety of physical processes are used to project onto given mathematical equations of interest. FitzHugh and Nagumo,[37] for example, simulated a simplified Hodgkin-Huxley model for the electric conduction of nerve impulses by a purely electronic, nonbiological device involving a few tunnel diodes. Quantum computing, when successful, may boil down to a similar idea someday. As a caveat, we add that intriguing similarities between the Maxwell equations for light waves and the equations of fluid dynamics suggested some "ether," which remained elusive.

Third, *adaequatio* projections may even fail to be properly defined maps: different mathematical models may well describe one and the same physical reality. The Ptolemaic approach, for example, via cycles, epicycles, and epi-epicycles, had achieved a quite accurate description of the perceived planetary motions in the sky—numerically superior, by then, to the conceptual inaccuracies of the inadequately circular Copernican revolutions. Admittedly, the Kepler ellipses[38] are much more elegant than the Ptolemaic system in their perfect simplicity. But, of course, they contain all the cumbersome Ptolemaic complications, to perfection, as a corollary on apparent motions. In modern mathematical language, this can be

---

[34] E. Freitag and R. Busam, *Complex Analysis* (Heidelberg: Springer, 2005).
[35] A. J. Lotka, "Analytical Note on Certain Rhythmic Relations in Organic Systems," *Proceedings of the National Academy of Sciences* 6 (1920): 410–15.
[36] V. Volterra, *Leçons sur la Théorie Mathématique de la Lutte pour la Vie* (Paris: Gauthier-Villars, 1931).
[37] E. M. Izhikevich and R. FitzHugh, "FitzHugh-Nagumo Model," *Scholarpedia* 1, no. 9 (2006): 1349, doi:10.4249/scholarpedia.1349.
[38] J. Kepler, *Harmonices Mundi* (Linz: J. Plank, G. Tampach, 1619).

subsumed under the name of a Fourier series,[39] also known as harmonics in music theory.[40]

Current hype around artificial intelligence and machine learning abandons wholesale any diligent attempts of modeling and causal understanding by simple mathematical laws. This is due to the frustrating difficulties of precise mathematical descriptions in a less-than-ideal real world fraught with untraceable errors, unknown influences, and frustrating complexities. At the core of that perceived shortcut through the Gordian knot of a proper *adaequatio*, however, are still certain mathematical approximation theorems for general functions, as inspired and developed by the neural network community.

With all those caveats at hand, we still have to conclude that the Thomist *adaequatio* just works, at least on the very restricted levels of mere scientific or mathematical thought. Abstract constructs and structures from the mathematical storehouses just apply in too many, and too varied, scientific contexts to be attributed to blind chance and coincidence alone. They just "fit"[41] reality way too often. Except, nobody knows why. For example, Max Planck remarks:

> My original decision to devote myself to science was a direct result of the discovery (which has never ceased to fill me with enthusiasm since my early youth) of the far from obvious fact that the laws of human reasoning coincide with the laws governing the sequences of the impressions we receive from the world around us; and that, therefore, pure reasoning can enable man to gain an insight into their mechanisms. In this connection, it is of paramount importance that the outside world is something independent from man, something absolute, and the quest for the laws which apply to this absolute appeared to me as the most sublime scientific life-task.[42]

Concerning "pure reasoning" then, how about consistency, that necessary condition and principal Law of Truth, in all those laws of nature? Above, we have explored consistency as a mathematical prerequisite and a problem of pure logic, unrelated to the real world. This has led to the vexing problem why mathematics fits reality so well. But suppose we consider mathematics and logic as just derived, distilled, and abstracted from real world observation. Then, where does consistency of mathematics derive from, that principal article of faith of all mathematicians? Either way, the tacit assumption of a noncontradictory, self-

---

[39] W. E. Boyce and R. C. DiPrima, *Elementary Differential Equations and Boundary Value Problems* (New York: Wiley, 2001).

[40] P. Hindemith, *Unterweisung im Tonsatz I. Theoretischer Teil* (Mainz: B. Schott's Söhne, 1937).

[41] J. Hüfner, "Wie konnte es gelingen, die Quantenwelt mathematisch zu verstehen?" (Neversdorf: Manuscript), 201.

[42] M. Planck, *Wissenschaftliche Selbstbiographie* (Leipzig: Barth, 1948).

consistent "Nature"—that is, of *consistency of nature*, runs deep in the scientific community.

The distance from the sun to the Earth, for example, and hence the vast scale of the solar system, had been measured by the Venus transits in 1761 and 1769 with reasonable reliability. Due to the enormous distances, any adequate energy source of the sun to heat Earth conceivable at the time, like coal burning or contractive heating, would have expired after a few millennia. This was quite consistent with biblical chronologies, then. In the nineteenth century, however, combined progress in geochronology and the fossil record produced a veritable contradiction between the estimated millions or billions of years actually required, and the limited millennia of available solar power. Note that the contradiction arose within natural science, with Darwinian evolution just a collaterally religious aspect. Not until 1939 did Hans Bethe[43] resolve the paradox, theoretically, by the fusion answer. Confirmation by measurements of the solar neutrino flux, including corrections for neutrino oscillation, took until 2002. With centuries of patience, theory and observation finally did fit. In between, of course, no one had lost faith in the consistency of nature.

Or consider James Maxwell.[44] He completed his ingenious description of all classical phenomena involving electricity and magnetism based on consistency. In fact, he famously added a "displacement current" term in one of his equations, just to avoid a mathematical contradiction. And nature herself actually complies with his purely theoretical argument!

The equivalent mathematical reconciliations of the paradoxical wave-particle dualism in quantum mechanics, by Schrödinger's wave equation and Heisenberg's matrix mechanics, are another historical example.

Today, measurements of Doppler data indicate that spiral galaxies seem to rotate approximately rigidly. Newtonian gravity, based on the observable mass distribution, predicts a significantly slower rotation of the outer parts. The substantial discrepancy is attributed to the invisible presence of dark matter. Unfortunately, nobody knows what that is supposed to be. The concept, however, is vivid testimony to the unshaken faith of physicists in the tacit dogma of consistency of nature.

Religion

Singlehandedly, Goethe equates legal, mathematical, scientific, and religious Truth: "Ein durchgreifender Advokat in einer gerechten Sache, ein durchdringen-

---

[43] H. A. Bethe, "Energy Production in Stars," *Physical Review* 55 (1939): 434–56.
[44] J. C. Maxwell, "On Physical Lines of Force III: The Theory of Molecular Vortices Applied to Statical Electricity," *Philosophical Magazine* 23 (1861): 12–24.

der Mathematiker vor dem Sternenhimmel erscheinen beide gleich gottähnlich." (An effective advocate in a just cause, a penetrating mathematician facing the celestial sky appear both equally god-like.)[45]

Let us approach the religious aspect from the mathematical and scientific side, which we have followed above. Somewhat timidly, perhaps also with the howling Boeotians of Gauss[46] in mind, Eugene Wigner ponders "The unreasonable effectiveness of mathematics in the natural sciences." "On a more cheerful note," he concludes: "The miracle of the appropriateness of the language of mathematics for the formulation of the laws of physics is a wonderful gift which we neither understand nor deserve. We should be grateful for it and hope that it will remain valid in future research and that it will extend, for better or for worse, to our pleasure even though perhaps also to our bafflement, to wide branches of learning."[47]

A "baffling" *adaequatio* is "gratefully" welcomed as a "wonderful gift," even a "miracle." Or only a transitory and ephemeral coincidence, perhaps?

We encountered, above, consistency, the absence of self-contradiction, as a principal Law of Truth. After Russell's sobering antinomy and struggles with incompleteness, we transferred the thorny issue to the natural sciences. Do laws of nature contradict themselves? We do not even ask, yet, who or what is speaking in the name of Nature here. But inconsistencies of those universally observed laws, independent of social, cultural, political, or religious background of the observer, should certainly be conceivable. Why, for example, should there be any reproducible experimental results at all? Why should observed data fit into any logical schemes which actually work? Just because this is all our mind can grasp? Certainly, the minds of dreamers, poets, readers of fantasy and science fiction, and particularly of children do not suffer such limitations. In fact, our question concerning consistency of nature is much more radical, much more fundamental, than a mere "anthropic principle," which rather unimaginatively postulates and mystifies an anthropocentric fine tuning of various universal constants—taking all known laws of nature for granted, a priori.

No scientist will accept an inconsistent law of nature. It is understood, as a matter of course, that nature is consistent indeed. So mercilessly consistent, in fact, that her blind Darwinian brutality sends Nietzsche into a delirious quest for "truth" beyond any conventional standards of love, charity, mercy, or morals. He answers Pontius Pilate as follows:

---

[45] J. W. von Goethe, *Wilhelm Meisters Wanderjahre. II. Betrachtungen im Sinne der Wanderer* (Weimar: Böhlau, 1825).

[46] C. F. Gauss, "Gauss an Bessel, 27. Januar 1829," in *Briefwechsel zwischen Gauss und Bessel* (Leipzig: W. Engelmann, 1880).

[47] E. P. Wigner, "The Unreasonable Effectiveness of Mathematics in the Natural Sciences," *Communications on Pure and Applied Mathematics* 13 (1960): 1–14.

Was ist also Wahrheit? Ein bewegliches Heer von Metaphern, Metonymien, Anthropomorphismen, kurz eine Summe von menschlichen Relationen, die, poetisch und rhetorisch gesteigert, übertragen, geschmückt wurden, und die nach langem Gebrauch einem Volke fest, kanonisch und verbindlich dünken: die Wahrheiten sind Illusionen, von denen man vergessen hat, daß sie welche sind, Metaphern, die abgenutzt und sinnlich kraftlos geworden sind, Münzen, die ihr Bild verloren haben und nun als Metall, nicht mehr als Münzen, in Betracht kommen. Wir wissen immer noch nicht, woher der Trieb zur Wahrheit stammt: denn bis jetzt haben wir nur von der Verpflichtung gehört, die die Gesellschaft, um zu existieren, stellt: wahrhaft zu sein, das heißt die usuellen Metaphern zu brauchen, also moralisch ausgedrückt: von der Verpflichtung, nach einer festen Konvention zu lügen, herdenweise in einem für alle verbindlichen Stile zu lügen."

(What then is truth? A mobile army of metaphors, metonyms, anthropomorphisms, in short, a sum of human relations, which, poetically and rhetorically enhanced, transposed, embellished, seem firm, canonical, and obligatory to a people, after long use: truths are illusions, about which one has forgotten that this is what they are, metaphors which are worn out and without sensuous power, coins which have lost their image and now matter as metal [only], no longer as coins. We still do not know where the urge for truth originates from: for as yet we have only heard about the obligation imposed by society, in order to exist: to be truthful means compliance with the customary metaphors, i.e. in moral terms: the obligation to lie according to fixed convention, to lie herd-like in a style mandatory for all.)[48]

Nietzsche lashes out against religious and social convention. Above, however, we tracked some aspects of pure mathematics as a solitary intellectual development, purely by and in itself, solipsistically detached from the fetters of the real world, social or otherwise, but with "baffling" applicability. The real continuum and the complex plane, for example, provably mathematical constructs of the nineteenth century, are favored pervasively throughout physics, including the most recent and esoteric variants of string theory. Those purely intellectual constructs were no longer derived from any physics. So why should they apply to anything?

But let us suppose, following Nietzsche, that all our mathematical developments are just social conventions, too: herd-like rituals, somewhat boring perhaps, much too nonsensical and academic for his taste. As a further concession, let us consider mathematics, even purest mathematics in all wounded pride, as a mere secondary phenomenon of the mind, as essentially applied from the start, subconsciously perhaps, as merely derived from the real world, by some vague process of abstraction.

Now, Truth is singular, not plural—even for Nietzsche. And neither nature nor *adaequatio* is mere social convention: just do away with the "convention" of gravi-

---

[48] F. W. Nietzsche, "Über Wahrheit und Lüge im außermoralischen Sinne," in *Nietzsches Werke: Schriften und Entwürfe 1872 bis 1876* (Leipzig: Koegel, 1896).

tation and levitate for a while, in case of lingering doubt. In comparison to mathematics, then—which fails to prove its own consistency due to self-referential troubles—might natural science be any better off? If consistency comes for free in science, mathematics should follow suit, gladly released from its self-referential burden.

No scientist, and Nietzsche even less, knows how it comes to be that nature does not contradict itself. Any scientific proof of that most tacit, most hidden assumption of natural science should run into self-referential troubles, just as mathematics did.

Religious faith, then, closes more than a mere gap when declaring nature the *creation* of the One God—any law of nature included. Theology, after all, and not philosophy or science or mathematics, her handmaidens, is the foremost attempt to think the Absolute. This, finally, shifts consistency, our principal Law of Truth, to the domain of religion—all grandeur and toxicity included.

But how about miracles? Miracles are popular. So popular, indeed, that they run rampant in the genres of fairy tales, fantasy, and science fiction. But, wouldn't miracle stories, universally popular in all religions as well, contradict the true laws of nature, almost by definition? And didn't we just banish the mathematically exact, but uncomfortably alchemistic, duplication of a golden ball (not to speak of bread and fish) from the real world as a mere mathematical Hausdorff paradox based on the undecidable axiom of choice?

Thomas Aquinas teaches how miracles, and hence omnipotence, are constrained by geometry: "Further, a thing cannot be done miraculously ... contrary to the conclusions of geometry, which are infallible deductions from common principles—for instance, that the three angles of a triangle should not be equal to two right angles."[49]

Not entirely convincing after non-Euclidean geometry[50] by the non-Boeotians Gauss,[51] J. Bolyai, Lobachevsky, and Poincaré, of course, performs just that impossible geometric "miracle": on the sphere with angle sums strictly exceeding 180 degrees, and on the hyperbolic disk with sums strictly less than 180 degrees.

Concerning the conversion of water to wine (John 2:1–11), for example, Augustine imparts some light of reason on the miracle tale. He points at the much greater, quite real miracle: how the vine converts rain to grapes, and ultimately to wine, quite naturally, repeatably, reliably, and accessible to natural science. "But we do not wonder at the latter, because it happens every year: it has lost its miraculousness by its constant recurrence. And yet it suggests a greater consideration than that which was done in the water pots. For who is there that considers

---

[49] Thomas Aquinas, *Summa Theologica*, III Suppl. 83.3.2.
[50] Katz, *A History of Mathematics*.
[51] Gauss, "Gauss an Bessel, 27. Januar 1829."

the works of God, whereby this whole world is governed and regulated, who is not amazed and overwhelmed with miracles?"[52]

On such level of understanding, it is the laws of creation, commonly called laws of nature, which become the true miracle—and not a tale which contradicts chemistry and conservation of mass. The false dichotomy between science and faith, a vengeful construction of the nineteenth century, is overcome here in the two books of one and the same revelation: *liber scripturae and liber naturae.*

The Faustian quest of the scientist for universal, and hence absolute, Truth is essentially religious indeed. We encountered above the dogmatic faith of scientists in the consistency of nature. When particle physicists today strive for a Grand Unified Theory (GUT), a Theory of Everything (TOE), or a SUperSYmmetry (SUSY) extension of the standard model of particle physics, their quest comes with the same quasi-religious impulse and appeal—particularly to the young and brilliant. The popular TV character Sheldon Cooper of *The Big Bang Theory* is an example. In the episode "The Benefactor Factor," the archetype of a graduate student nerd proclaims that his purpose is "to tear the mask off nature and stare at the face of God."[53]

True scientists are yearning for discrepancies in their knowledge, and they should, if only for ambition: firm faith in the consistency of nature welcomes such discrepancies as the safest indicator of future discoveries. Such faith reveals itself when much-hoped-for discrepancies between theory and measurements at the Large Hadron Collider are preemptively called New Physics. Without such faith in Truth, in the unifying and universal light of reason, equally transcending both naive creationism and naive atheism, research would remain futile: why accumulate ever more inconsistencies? The research process itself would deteriorate to a convention, indeed, a mere tradition, scientifically "and rhetorically enhanced, transposed, embellished, ... canonical ... after long use."[54]

Why, indeed, should there exist any unifying Truth at all, veiled and hidden behind all discrepancies? At that very core, the question for the existence of Absolute Truth reappears. Even Nietzsche, in rare modesty, declares his ignorance as to the origin of our "urge for truth." For whatever reason, ambition, dedication, and spending run high to detect, to uncover, unveil, and unravel the beyond, the invisible and transcending.

The deep parallel between the scientific and the religious quest for the Absolute is as obvious as it is suspect for Nietzsche:

---

[52] Augustine of Hippo, "Tractatus in Iohannis Evangelium" (416).
[53] R. E. Lowe, "The Cooper Conundrum: Good Lord, Who's Tolerating Whom?," in *The Big Bang Theory and Philosophy: Rock, Paper, Scissors, Aristotle, Locke,* ed. D. A. Kowalski (Hoboken, NJ: Wiley, 2012).
[54] Nietzsche, "Über Wahrheit und Lüge im außermoralischen Sinne."

Doch man wird es begriffen haben, worauf ich hinaus will, nämlich daß es immer noch ein metaphysischer Glaube ist, auf dem unser Glaube an die Wissenschaft ruht,—daß auch wir Erkennenden von heute, wir Gottlosen und Antimetaphysiker, auch unser Feuer noch von dem Brande nehmen, den ein Jahrtausende alter Glaube entzündet hat, jener Christen-Glaube, der auch der Glaube Platos war, daß Gott die Wahrheit ist, daß die Wahrheit göttlich ist.... Aber wie, wenn dies gerade immer mehr unglaubwürdig wird, wenn Nichts sich mehr als göttlich erweist, es sei denn der Irrtum, die Blindheit, die Lüge,—wenn Gott selbst sich als unsre längste Lüge erweist?

(But it will now have been understood, what I have in mind, namely, how it is still a metaphysical faith, on which our faith in Science is based—that we also, the knowing, the godless, and antimetaphysical, still take our fire from the conflagration which a millennia-old faith has kindled, that Christian faith, which was the faith of Plato as well, that God is truth, that all truth is divine. But what if just that keeps losing credibility, what if nothing turns out divine anymore, except error, blindness, and falsehood—what if God himself is revealed to be our most persistent lie?)[55]

It is safe to conjecture that Nietzsche was even less informed about the basics of natural science than the present author is about the basics of philosophy. His "Fröhliche Wissenschaft" was more inclined, anyway, toward a Provençal chimera of singer, knight, and free spirit than toward diligent scientific nerdity. With striking lucidity, however, Nietzsche exposes the deep parallelism of that metaphysical faith in the Absolute which underlies both religion and science. This agrees much with our compilation of parallels between the mathematical, the scientific, and the religious idea of Absolute Truth.

Nietzsche argues with an end in mind: the abolition of God. We, in contrast, start from progress in science. We just have to recall the independence of scientific fact from the interpreting intellect to arrive at a fundamental objection: scientific fact does not underly papal verdict anymore—but it does not bend to serve Nietzsche's purpose, either.

The scope of Truth, in the true sense of the suspiciously popular motto "The truth shall set you free" (John 8:32), extends much beyond mere science, of course. Such Truth is revealed in the λόγος of creation, and becomes God incarnate—much transcending mere syllogism, logic, and even laws of nature.

Progress toward Truth is a narrow and thorny path: a path for humankind, but also for each individual. A path of life, maybe, but never complete in the here and now. It is such a path that Benedict XVI refers to when he denounces "possession of truth": "Only if we allow ourselves to be guided and moved by the truth, do we remain in it. Only if we are, with it and in it, pilgrims of truth, then it is in us and for us."[56]

---

[55] F. W. Nietzsche, *Die fröhliche Wissenschaft* (Chemnitz: Schmeitzner, 1882).
[56] J. Ratzinger, Benedict XVI, "Homily," September 12, 2013.

Pope Francis points at the same path aspect of "via, veritas, vita" (John 14:6), when he comments on "absolute truth."[57] And Karl Popper joins in, from the more limited scientific perspective: "Der Ehrgeiz, Recht zu behalten, verrät ein Missverständnis: nicht der Besitz von Wissen, von unumstößlichen Wahrheiten macht den Wissenschaftler, sondern das rücksichtslose, unablässige Suchen nach Wahrheit." (The obsession to be right betrays a misunderstanding: it is not his possession of knowledge, of irrefutable truths, which forms the man of science, but his irreverently critical, untiring quest for Truth.)[58]

Conclusions

Starting from the definition of Truth by Thomas Aquinas as *adaequatio rei et intellectus*, we have attempted to completely revert his original approach. For him, the divine principle of the Absolute was the primary cause of all truth and consistency in creation, and any human observation could, at best, incompletely reflect such eternal perfection.

Our secular journey toward Truth started at the opposite end: at pure mathematical logic, its paradoxes, antinomies, and incompleteness. We have encountered Gödel's undecidability results,[59] including an ascent in logical consistency reminiscent of the *Umgreifenden des Um greifenden*[60] or perhaps Hegel's dialectic *Aufhebung*. Further reflection on the Thomist *adaequatio* led to the question of *consistency of nature*. This turned out to be the ultimate article of faith underlying all of natural science—a faith based on most diligent observation and, by now, the accumulated insight of centuries of agnostic scientific endeavor. As far as nature is concerned—that is, starting from physics rather than the metaphysical—that extremely fruitful scientific dogma posits the ultimate resolvability of the paradoxical and inconsistent in the light of reason.

On a more secular, postparadise note, what did Mephistopheles jot down as a motto for that reverential first-year student who arrived for mentoring? "Eritis sicut Deus, scientes bonum et malum" ("You will be like God, knowing good and evil": Genesis 3:5).[61] We also recall King Solomon, who asked for a heart "to discern between good and evil," with the best intention to govern and judge (1 Kings 3:9).

---

[57] J. M. Bergoglio, Francis, "Dialogo aperto con i non credenti," *La Repubblica*, September 2013.

[58] Popper, *Logik der Forschung. Zur Erkenntnistheorie der modernen Naturwissenschaft.*

[59] Gödel, "Über formal unentscheidbare Sätze der Principia Mathematica und verwandter Systeme I."

[60] Jaspers, *Der philosophische Glaube angesichts der Offenbarung.*

[61] J. W. von Goethe, *Faust. Eine Tragödie* (Tübingen: Cotta, 1808), Studierzimmer 2.

How about turning that toxic motto of the Luciferian light-bearer into a challenge, then? A Promethean impulse to jointly face an infinite challenge which we are too weak, too limited to meet as solipsistic individuals. A challenge to trust reason and Truth, wherever they may lead. A challenge which includes the ethical as a prerequisite. A challenge not conceited by chimeras of diabolic allure and promise. A challenge to pursue reason, in the Augustinian sense of divine enlightenment, always wary of chimeras and delusions: not in toxic pride, but in humility.

We cannot ever meet that challenge and face the unfiltered light of Absolute Truth. She will remain an absolute goal, always partially hidden, always beyond. Hidden, but not entirely inaccessible to our searching mind, hopefully, at least in principle. Comprehension of the infinite may require infinite time[62]—but calculating an actual limit or at least proving its existence does not. There is progress. There is hope. Truth, after all, might be meant to become comprehensible, to become known, eventually, almost. Perhaps the Mephistophelian temptation does qualify as a university motto, after all?

Absolute Truth is not a possession. She remains a goal of our search and our research, ongoing, beyond the individual or the generation, over and over again. Our quest for the universal value of Truth has been, is, and will remain a quest for the Absolute. Progress may be slow: it may measure in millennia, forever incomplete. But such progress is worth living for, everywhere, and at all times.

Acknowledgment. This is an abridged and revised version of notes for the consultation at FIIT / Wissenschaftsforum Heidelberg, April 2019. Far beyond wonderful hospitality, I am indebted to our host, Michael Welker: his guiding inspiration and gentle prodding helped orient my postmodern confusions toward seeking Truth beyond mere mathematics. Jia-Yuan Dai and Yuya Tokuta opened a door to East Asian thought on Truth, much beyond the scope of my little essay. Jörg Hüfner clarified my uncertainties on what the object side of Truth might be, in mathematics, and he patiently tried to coach my rudimentary grasp of physics. Rüdiger Bittner contributed penetrating friendly criticism, based on actual benevolent reading. Nicola Vassena, my former student in mathematics and continuing mentor in music, guided me toward Nietzsche, Ivano Vassena toward Husserl, and Vittorio Hösle toward intersubjectivity in general. Hannes Stuke supplied me with Kant, and Sebastian Fiedler shared his expertise on the Big Bang Theory. They all helped significantly to focus my meandering thoughts. Patricia Hăbăşescu assisted much with the literature. And all my group at Berlin, past and present, as well as all participants of the consultation, generously shared their philosophical challenges of my numerous inconsistencies.

---

[62] Strugatzky, Понедельник начинается в субботу (Monday Begins on Saturday).

Can Academic Research Be a Moral Guide?

Rüdiger Bittner

Let us understand broadly the terms of the question before us. Let us take research not in contrast to teaching but comprising it, in line with an important tradition of thought on higher learning which sees academic research and teaching as endeavors that need to be joined for either to be as fruitful as it can be. Let us take "academic" to refer to what is done not only in universities and public research institutions but also in the research departments of private companies and by individual investigators without institutional affiliation. And let us use the word "science" in what follows not in the narrow English sense of "natural science" but as an equivalent of German *Wissenschaft*, which includes social science, jurisprudence, and the humanities as well. Thus broadly understood, academic research is the entire body of work devoted to producing and transmitting advanced knowledge. Talk of advanced or higher knowledge in turn needs to be understood in social, not material terms. Some bit of knowledge is "advanced" not in itself but by not being accessible to the bulk of the relevant population.

Academic research so understood is organized differently in different countries, but at least the developed countries all devote a large part of their workforce to this sector. Thus, Germany in 2018 spent a bit more than 3 percent of its gross national product on what in the statistics is called research and development, and this figure has risen considerably in the past fifteen years. It has risen enormously over the past four hundred years. Modern science, inaugurated by authors like Galileo, not only changed the ways in which advanced knowledge is gained, and changed them definitively for all we know. Thanks to its great success in all sorts of fields—not just in physics, where it started—it became an important productive force, to borrow Karl Marx's term.[1] This is why it grew so massively: modern economies do not prosper without a vigorous and innovative research sector. Thus, contrary to the popular talk of postmodernism, we still live and move under

---

[1] Karl Marx, "Zur Kritik der politischen Ökonomie" [1859], in Karl Marx and Friedrich Engels, *Werke*, vol. 13 (Berlin: Dietz, 1961), 8f. See also G. A. Cohen, *Karl Marx's Theory of History* (Princeton, NJ: Princeton University Press, 1978), 45–47.

the auspices of modern science. We do science the way our seventeenth-century forebears taught us to do it, and, under the arrangement reached subsequently, science earns its keep, a generous keep to be sure, by the service it provides to the economy.

The question before us, however, does not concern the service that science provides by expanding our knowledge of the material world and thus opening the road to technical innovations, or by expanding our knowledge of the social world and thus allowing us to organize our cooperation more profitably. It inquires whether science, always in the broad understanding given above, can by itself provide moral guidance. It inquires whether academic research, not by *what* it finds out, but by *how* it does, indeed by the very presence of such an undertaking in current societies, has an educational value, or could have it if it were used properly. Could academic research function as the place where we can learn how to live right and how to live together in a fruitful way, and where also what we thus learn can be preserved for adoption or rejection or, as seems most likely, for further development by the next generation, as they will see fit?

No, academic research does not, in its practice or in its very existence, hold moral resources of this sort. In countless ways, it has contributed by its findings to many of us living more comfortably now than people did before. It has contributed and will contribute to discovering good ways to deal with particular problems arising. It cannot contribute to our learning to live right, individually or collectively. It helps with practical, but not particularly with moral, problems.

To support this skeptical answer, I shall offer two arguments—one, philosophical, examining the credentials of the traditional idea that knowledge is a necessary foundation for living right; the other, drawing on experience, on what I have learned about academic research from living in the present and living in academia. After skepticism, good news: the moral guidance that we do not get from academic research we also do not need. Left to our own devices, we may be doing fine.

1

A formative strand in our tradition sees in higher learning both the best way to live and the condition for ordering lives toward the good—the lives of individuals as well as those of whole communities. Plato put forward this dual conception with characteristic force. Thus, he has Socrates, in his apology before the court of Athens, memorably state:

> It is the greatest good for human beings every day to be speaking to one another about virtue and about the other things you heard me talk about with others, examining both myself and them.²

And the famous doctrine of the philosopher-kings is a consequence of the thought that advanced knowledge is what those need who are to govern people's lives:

> As long as philosophers do not rule as kings in cities, or what are now called kings and rulers do not genuinely and sufficiently do philosophy, political capacity and philosophy coming to the same thing, and as long as the various natures of those who now pursue either of these separately are not by force excluded, there is no end of the misery in cities, my dear Glaucon, I even believe no end of the misery of humankind.³

So on this view, to acquire true knowledge is a good, indeed the best, thing for humans to do; and nobody should undertake to direct people's steps unarmed with knowledge, for knowledge is in the last resort knowledge of the good, the highest knowable.⁴

This is not the place to pursue the reception and further developments of these thoughts in Aristotle, in Stoic philosophy, and in Christian writings. Suffice it to say that the classical, that is, premodern tradition was to a large extent committed to this Platonic heritage and so to seeing knowledge and the good internally connected, internally in contrast to being merely linked via the good effects that knowledge sometimes brings to the knower and to others who use that knowledge.

However, the relevance of the Platonic line of thought for our present topic may be contested. It was philosophy that Plato wanted the future rulers of his city to study from the ground up, but philosophy is a marginal field in today's academic research. So the Platonic link of knowledge and the good does not seem to have any bearing on the question of the moral resources held by this research. In reply, it must be admitted that *what* the Platonic rulers know after years of studying in the Academy differs from the knowledge provided by current academic research from which we might hope to receive moral guidance in present societies. Still, this material difference does not affect the basic point of the Platonic thought, which is that knowing the world, and hence our place in it, is in the end the only proper foundation for directing our own and others' steps. "Know thyself," the god in Delphi is reported to have told those who entered his temple. That did not mean, as we now tend to take it, know your inner self. Such a thing was not yet invented. It meant, know your place. As it is a modest place, knowing it will teach you mod-

---

² Plato, *Apology of Socrates*, 38a.
³ Plato, *Republic*, 473c–d.
⁴ Plato, *Republic*, 518c–d.

esty and so will keep you from overstepping your bounds.[5] More sophisticated, but still growing from the same conception, is the Stoic doctrine of living in accordance with nature,[6] a doctrine which has found adherents right to the present: to know the whole, of which we form merely a part, can lead us to act in a way befitting us.

This idea of knowledge capable of guiding us has lost its power. Not because knowledge is so hard to come by. Sometimes it is, sometimes it is not; that is not the point. The point is that the knowables have lost their ethical significance. They have become mere facts, certainly to be reckoned with in practical matters, but without a directive force of their own. A remarkable passage in David Hume's *Treatise of Human Nature* illustrates the change. In every system of morality, he tells us, he always remarked

> that the author proceeds for some time in the ordinary way of reasoning, and establishes the being of a God, or makes observations concerning human affairs; when of a sudden I am surpriz'd to find, that instead of the usual copulations of propositions, *is*, and *is not*, I meet with no proposition that is not connected with an *ought*, or an *ought not*. This change is imperceptible; but is, however, of the last consequence.[7]

Many took Hume to make a logical point here, namely, that you cannot derive an *ought* from an *is*, an inference which came to be called the naturalistic fallacy. In fact, there is no rule of logic prohibiting it,[8] and Hume's point is instead the material one that things like god's existence and the way human affairs go do not, as the Platonic tradition thought, carry a message as to how we should live; the knowables are mute regarding morals. Kant's separation of theoretical and practical reason is rooted in the same conviction. Yes, for Kant it must be reason which tells us how to go, but that can only be for him a reason apart, a practical one, since what we used to call reason, theoretical reason, which establishes such things as the being of a god or makes observations concerning human affairs, is unable to

---

[5] Pierre Aubenque, *La prudence chez Aristote* (Paris: Presses Universitaires de France, 1963).

[6] Hans von Arnim, ed., *Stoicorum veterum fragmenta* (Leipzig: Teubner, 1903), 3:4-9, 12-17. See also Gisela Striker, "Following Nature: A Study in Stoic Ethics," in *Essays on Hellenistic Epistemology and Ethics*, ed. Gisela Striker (Cambridge: Cambridge University Press, 1996), 221-80.

[7] David Hume, *A Treatise of Human Nature*, ed. P. H. Nidditch (Oxford: Oxford University Press, 1978), 469.

[8] As Karl Popper held. See "What Can Logic Do for Philosophy?," *Logical Positivism and Ethics, Proceedings of the Aristotelian Society*, Suppl. vol. 22 (1948): 154.

tell us how to go.⁹ The shedding of the Platonic conception can then be seen completed in Max Weber's rough comment that it is "just incontestable" that science does not answer the question of how to live.¹⁰

You may ask what, in the end, recommends leaving the Platonic line of thought. Isn't it natural to expect guidance regarding what to do from understanding our place in the world? Surely it is natural, in the sense that it has become a habit to think this way. And why abandon this habit? For skeptical reasons. We do not have grounds to believe that the world of which we form a part makes any comprehensive sense, and neither do we, therefore, have grounds to believe that how things are contains any message as to how to go on from where we happen to be. The knowables turned mute in matters of how to live, because we do not have any reason to listen to them in these matters.

2

Turning to academic research as we know it from current experience, we find that it cannot provide ethical guidance, first of all because it is not one thing and thus does not speak with one voice. It is a mere collection of activities of a large number of people. While the activities resemble each other sufficiently to be subsumed under the common term "academic research," they cannot be usefully understood as making up one comprehensive activity. We researchers do not form a team or indeed an army united by a common purpose. Just as misleading, therefore, is talk of academic research as a social system. The expression suggests systematicity: elements joined under an intelligible plan that covers the field in question completely. In this sense, academic research is far from forming a system. It is a bunch of diverse intellectual activities running hither and thither, like children on a schoolyard.

It may be objected that academic research does have a common purpose, which is truth, and that this shared direction assembles researchers into a community, the community of truth-seekers. To reason in this way, however, is to be misled by the specious singular "truth." There is not this one thing truth which, from different directions, we all try to approach, like a tower. There are only truths, that is, true statements or true thoughts, and truth is just the common quality of these statements or thoughts. We researchers, then, do not pursue the

---

⁹   Immanuel Kant, *Grundlegung zur Metaphysik der Sitten*, in *Kant's gesammelte Schriften, Werke*, vol. 4, ed. Kgl. Preußische Akademie der Wissenschaften (Berlin: Reimer, 1903), 404.

¹⁰ Max Weber, "Wissenschaft als Beruf," in *Gesammelte Aufsätze zur Wissenschaftslehre*, 5th ed., ed. J. Winckelmann (Tübingen: Mohr Siebeck, 1982), 598. The German words are *schlechthin unbestreitbar*.

truth. At best we pursue truths, but different people different ones, so there is no common enterprise here.

In fact, we do not even pursue simply truths.[11] Saying something merely true is too easy. Any phone book gives you a large (and the series of natural numbers gives you an inexhaustible) supply of truths. Academic research aims for interesting truths. With that criterion in place, however, we researchers become competitors. While one truth cannot be truer than another, it can be more interesting, whatever the standard by which this is measured, and so we come under pressure to show the truth we found to be more interesting than the one somebody else found. Here is where fraud enters, different methods of fraud offering themselves in different fields, from rigging the data, as in medicine and social science, to enunciating bold- or profound-seeming nonsense, which is more common in the humanities. That there is such a thing as academic fraud is precisely due to researchers' selling their products on a market as other producers do—markets are fraud's natural habitat. The research market admittedly has its peculiarities. One of these is the fact that the value of products is often assessed not by consumers but by competing suppliers, that is, in a peer-review procedure. Another is the fact that the state, everywhere providing a large part of the funds for academic research, has a powerful, if often indirect, influence on the decisions about truths being more or less interesting. In any case, the important point is that the success researchers are striving for needs to be understood as success within competitive research institutions. What we researchers are after, one could say, is not truth, but truth that brings tenure, for example.

Not that anything is wrong with seeking tenure or more generally with fighting one's way through competitive institutions. With respect to the present argument, though, the thing to note is that we academic researchers do not hold a position above the fray from where we could offer ethical guidance to others. We are fray ourselves, like anybody else, and our practice can thus not be presumed to hold special sources of ethical orientation.

Nor do we hold ourselves as researchers to a particular ethos. True, you should properly indicate how you collected your data and should quote the sources you used in your writing, but these are technical rules, the first ensuring that a bias in your data selection can more easily be detected, the second preventing your adorning yourself with borrowed plumes, this however being something you should not do anyway, whether you are doing research or other things. Admittedly, on this line of argument there may not remain any professional ethos anywhere, as one has been held to exist, for instance, in the medical profession. All the alleged rules of a professional ethos may turn out to have only technical significance. However, this is a consequence that may actually be welcomed.

---

[11] Nelson Goodman, "Art and Inquiry," in *Problems and Projects* (Indianapolis, IN: Bobbs-Merrill, 1972), 117.

Academic research is not in a position to offer ethical guidance, secondly, because it does not enjoy authority with the public at large. The learned are respected for what they know in their fields. They are not trusted to lead people right with regard to broader questions. We follow the doctor's advice when sick and let our attorney fix the legal problem into which we got entangled. Beyond such special issues, we are not likely to give them credit. It is telling that the report on the state of the German economy that is every year submitted by five leading economists to the German government is always received with gratitude and highest respect, but its recommendations are never followed. They are not even adduced in subsequent political discussions in support of pursuing this rather than that political course; they disappear right away in the drawers. Small wonder, in the end: the expertise of economists is seen as limited to purely economic matters, hence, as lacking authority when it comes to political problems. Even less, then, will researchers be trusted should they presume to tell us how to live. Rather the opposite: there is a hidden but widespread suspicion that advanced learning, however admirable it may be in its particular field, makes people less competent to find good ways in real life. This prejudice may in part explain as well why politics does not care about the advice coming from economists. Such advice is looked down upon precisely as being "academic," in a derogatory sense of the word. So even if, contrary to the previous argument, higher learning were to have moral resources in store, it would not find people's ears open for it.

There was a time when at least some people of higher learning did enjoy an authority which no longer comes with higher learning nowadays. The ministers of the Christian church, supposedly knowing about the path to salvation, used to hold unrivalled authority with respect to how people should live. Yet that authority they owed not to their learning specifically, but to being considered guardians of, and dispensers from, a treasure of grace the power of which was supposed precisely to lie beyond the grasp of human learning. So their case in fact confirms the rule that higher learning does not bring the authority to guide people's lives.

As for academic research devoted especially to laying open what is right to do —that is, ethical research as undertaken in theology and philosophy—it cannot teach people an ethics which was alien to them before, the way one would teach them a foreign language, nor does this research anywhere pretend to do so. Rather, it can help people to understand better the ethical convictions they already come equipped with. It can help to put these to the test and thereby to diminish or strengthen people's confidence in them, but it cannot give its hearers an ethical orientation which before being taught they simply lacked. Thus, it can usefully be understood as resembling teaching people their own language—after all, many of my readers, like myself, will have studied in school for years the language which they already knew best.

3

The point can be generalized. If ethical research in particular does not provide recipients with an ethical outlook but enlightens them on the basis of one they already hold, the same will be true of higher learning in general. Sure enough, different academic disciplines will bring different kinds of enlightenment, with pure mathematics, as opposed to applied mathematics, perhaps marking the thin end of ethical relevance. Still, once we talk about knowledge of the world in which we live, any piece of advanced knowledge may at times contribute to improving, which is to say, to refining, extending, restricting, sharpening our view of what it is right to do in a given situation. As mentioned at the beginning, modern societies to a large extent live by the advanced knowledge they assemble. Small wonder, then, that such knowledge sometimes needs to be brought in to find out what it is right to do. Think of the broad array of knowledge that you need if you want to avoid contributing to the destruction of the planet. Of course, you cannot acquire all this knowledge by yourself, you have to ask the experts. Still, without in some way taking recourse to advanced knowledge, you cannot figure out what it is right to do. Indeed, any knowledge, be it advanced or humble, may at times contribute to one's finding that out. However, the knowledge that helps you find out does not, as in the Platonic tradition, itself tell you how to go. It is not knowledge of the good in itself, whatever that may be, it is knowledge of how the world goes. Yet by using such knowledge, you may come to see what is good for you to do.

Therefore, the moral orientation which, according to the argument of the previous two sections, higher learning will not provide is also a thing we do not need. We are not lost in the woods as regards how to live, we are right in the middle of trying to find our way. That the moral understanding we have reached so far, individually or on average, could still be improved is a trivial thing to say: any bit of understanding we have gained, unless it be purely formal, can be further improved. We do not need, however, moral orientation in the literal sense of setting up people's moral compass from scratch, since they already have one and use and improve it. To contribute to that improvement is all that learning, higher or not, should be expected to do.

Why, then, is there so much complaint about the lack of moral orientation in contemporary societies? Probably because our moral convictions are more diverse, or just more visibly diverse, than they used to be, and what one person does in following hers may, in the eyes of another who holds different views, betray a lack of orientation. (Orientation is nearly always found lacking in others.) So the reason for the complaint is, in short, pluralism: we do not form a moral community, and that produces the appearance of moral disorientation. Pluralism, though, should not be news; it has been our condition at least since the Reformation, and therefore should give no grounds for complaining. Contrary to what is commonly assumed, we can well live together while disagreeing on how one should live. It is true, the idea seems hard to give up that somewhere deep down we are at one as to how one should live, or at any rate that the good people among us are. John Rawls, for instance, having insisted on pluralism being a permanent feature of modern democratic societies, nonetheless hopes for a social unity founded on an overlapping consensus among the opposing doctrines held in them.[12] In effect, this is just to maintain, against the evidence, that pluralism is not the last word in the matter. In fact, it is, and given pluralism, social unity is just not on. The appearance of widespread moral disorientation is thus likely to stay, but it is mere appearance. What is true is only that people are, and will be, heading into different directions.

We do not form, and do not need to form, a moral community, but we do need law for living together in a fruitful way. Law, however, as the tradition of legal positivism taught, does not need a foundation in shared moral convictions. It can rest, in an essentially Hobbesian manner,[13] on people's shared interest in having regulations established and enforced that guarantee, to some extent at any rate, peaceful cooperation. Thus, pluralism is not the enemy of law so understood. This understanding of law was precisely developed to secure its function in modern societies divided by moral disagreement.

It may be asked, though, whether it is not to demand too much of individuals that they find all on their own a sensible path through the complexities of contemporary life—whether we do not have to supply them with a basic provision of moral orientation. Yet "on their own" is ambiguous here. All the experience collected by others and laid down in stories, recipes, doctrines, rules, and so on—learning in all its diversity—is theirs to consult and to use in figuring out a good way to deal with particular situations. In that sense, they are not on their own in finding out what to do. They are on their own in drawing their lessons from what they have heard. That, however, is something no learning can do for them. The learning we receive is just testimony. Judge we must ourselves.

---

[12] John Rawls, "The Idea of an Overlapping Consensus," *Oxford Journal of Legal Studies* 7, no. 1 (1987): 1–25.

[13] Thomas Hobbes, *Leviathan*, ed. A. D. Lindsay (London: Dent, 1914), chaps. 13, 14, 17.

Joy of Discovery—Respect for the Search for Truth—Honesty
The Blessings of a Global Network of Research Universities

Michael Welker

The Confusing Variety in the Search for Truth at Late Modern Research Universities

Can academic research contribute to character building, ethical education, and the communication of values in late modern pluralistic societies? The answers of the contributions in this volume range from strong skepticism to marked affirmation. What they have in common is that they do not reduce academic research to the empirical research of the natural sciences, but rather focus on the German concept of *Wissenschaft*, "which includes social science, jurisprudence, and the humanities as well."[1] The diversity of academic disciplines brings with it various processes of the search for truth and makes the talk of "the one and absolute truth" appear as a "toxic chimera."[2] This diversity calls into question the invocation of the one "continuum of rationality" as well as classical ideas of "the university."[3]

Modern research universities offer a variety of processes of methodically ordered search for truth. They are always looking for "interesting truths"—truths that are often connected with the idea of successful technological, medical, or even military applicability and also promising academic careers (cf. Bittner and Schweiker). According to Schweiker, modern universities formed "intellectual silos, lacking communication with other silos." This argues against the assumption that academic research can be considered a formative force in a broad internal and external ethical and moral orientation.

---

[1] See the contribution of the philosopher Rüdiger Bittner, "Can Academic Research be a Moral Guide?," in this volume.

[2] See the challenge of the mathematician Bernold Fiedler, "Absolute Truth: A Toxic Chimera?," in this book.

[3] This is argued by the theological ethicist William Schweiker in his contribution to this volume, "The Idea of a Research University."

This view is shared only to a limited extent by the contributors to this volume. On one hand, the theoretical physicist Jörg Hüfner explicitly states: "ethical education was not part of my duty"; on the other hand, he clearly recognizes that ethical questions have also strongly pushed into the physicist's horizon, because "the science of physics is not an island, separated from the rest of the world." With respect to character formation and ethical impacts, he underscores the importance of "honesty and potential ethical restrictions to research."[4] Michael Kirschfink takes a similar view in his chapter, "Ethical Considerations in Biomedical Research: Welcome Guidance or Unwanted Restrictions to Scientific Progress?" In scientific research, it is important to prepare students for difficult ethical and moral decisions, even if the general conditions for these decisions can change.

For about thirty years, research universities have worked increasingly against silo formation. More and more international and interdisciplinary collaborative projects are emerging on more or less significant issues that cannot be meaningfully addressed by one discipline alone. The perspective on and of the research personalities and the students is also changing. In all their efforts to achieve scientific objectivity and the obligations to do so, they are seen as participants and actors and thus also as ethically challenged academic researchers.[5]

A particularly impressive example is the development of the research field of law and religion. Research programs on the relationship of these two disciplines—a matter of course for centuries—had become obsolete in modernity. Over the past thirty years, however, research centers, institutes, and programs on the subject of law and religion have developed at fifty universities around the world. John Witte names countless interscientific, political, cultural, and interreligious conditions for this development.[6] It goes hand in hand with questions and expectations regarding contributions to the shaping of human character, ethical education, and the communication of values, especially in late modern pluralistic societies. The ethical impact of academic research is particularly evident in the context of studies of historical and aesthetic complexes of themes that touch on permanently explosive ethical concerns or currently pressing problems. Gary Hauk offers an impressive example.[7]

Whereas the questions of moral impact of academic research were long posed only by conservative religious educational institutions (so Schweiker, University

---

[4] Jörg Hüfner, "The Impact of Science on Ethics," in this book.
[5] So Schweiker in the final section of his chapter in this book. In an impressive metaethical sociological approach, Andreas Glaeser argues that "human beings are *thoroughly* instituted beings," responding to and generating a multitude of institutionalized processes: "Analyzing Actual Existing Ethics: A Hermeneutic-Institutionalist Approach."
[6] John Witte Jr., "The Educational Values of Studying Law and Religion," in this book.
[7] Gary Hauk, "Academic Bondage and Social Transformation: The Case of American Universities and Slavery," in this volume.

of Chicago), a research university with high reputation like the University of Chicago is now developing a Center for Practical Wisdom with the theme, "Character Education in Universities."

"Developing Practical Wisdom and Virtue in Multidisciplinary Academic Frameworks" is the subtitle of the contribution by biologist and theologian Celia Deane-Drummond in this volume.[8] She has been working for years on topics in the dialogue between theology and science and focuses on ethical tasks of theological and scientific research. This interest also applies to the contributions of the Old Testament scholar Andreas Schüle and the New Testament scholar Stefan Alkier. Schüle examines exegetical-historical continuities and discontinuities between biblical classics in the treatment of the theme of creation (Genesis 1:1–31 and Psalm 104:1–30).[9] Alkier asks about Christian identity-building processes in terms of the New Testament and practical theology.[10] Common to all contributions is that interdisciplinary questions also have ethical implications and impulses.

"Truth-Seeking Communities" and "the Multimodal Spirit of Truth"

In numerous dialogues between theology and the natural sciences, John Polkinghorne and I have asked what characterizes "truth-seeking communities" in science and religion. We have come to the insight that the search for truth is, on one hand, the search to condense and consolidate certainties, and also the search to obtain agreement and thus the broadest possible consensus. On the other hand, the search for truth is a search for rational and coherent expertise, which must then be differentiated and deepened. Both approaches—the search for certainty and consensus and the search for coherent expertise—can irritate each other, but this makes the search for truth a dynamic and fruitful process.[11]

The university-organized scientific search for truth investigates truth claims, acknowledges them or falsifies them, and thus delivers proven truth findings until further notice. Due to the mutual control of specialized scientists and the sharp sanctions (for instance, loss of reputation) against presenting untenable truth claims as truth, organized science represents an important defense system

---

[8] Celia Deane-Drummond, "Forming Research Scientists? Developing Practical Wisdom and Virtue in Multidisciplinary Academic Frameworks," may have influenced the Chicago project by her publications and research projects.
[9] Andreas Schüle, "Emergence of Truth: The Interplay of Science and Theology in Genesis 1 and Psalm 104."
[10] Stefan Alkier, "Forming Identity by Scripture," in this volume.
[11] John Polkinghorne and Michael Welker, *Faith in the Living God: A Dialogue* (London: SPCK, 2001; 2nd ed. Wipf & Stock, 2019).

against scientific error and fraud. As Jochen Taupitz, professor of law at Mannheim and Heidelberg, summarizes:

> The self-imposed system of mutual checks and balances is one of the essential characteristics of science and scholarship. Science and scholarship constitute an autonomously corrected system committed to the attainment of knowledge that includes the entirety of the previously acknowledged and accepted findings of humankind that have been critically tested and indeed are perpetually accessible to critical testing. Research as the fundamental methodology of science and scholarship is thus committed to the goal of attaining secured knowledge of the objects of its examinations through methodical and systematic study that in its own turn is similarly accessible to testing.[12]

Through its importance in the education of people who want to take on leadership responsibility in all areas of society, science carries its truth ethos and the spirit of truth into all living conditions. Its heartbeat is the universities, which combine research and teaching worldwide and train qualified future research personnel with examinations and doctorates.[13]

Accuracy, certainty, consensus, coherence, appropriateness, tested and proven claims to knowledge—these are some of the final criteria in the evaluation of truth claims in the context of the search for truth. They carry different weight in different fields of knowledge. I have suggested that these differences help us appreciate the "multimodal spirit of truth,"[14] which is expressed in a plurality of sustainable forms of truth claims. This multimodal spirit includes but surpasses the bipolar spirit displayed in the search for truth through so-called common sense and the simple processes of empirical research, a bipolar spirit which strives for correspondence between exploration of objects and perfection of thought.

The examining, judging, and truth-claiming or truth-claims-rejecting spirit of research is an important, but not the only, part of the organized scientific system. Another area is the lively teaching in exchange with ever new generations of students, but also the communication of enthusiasm for the work of research. Re-

---

[12] Jochen Taupitz, "Das hohe Gut der Wissenschaftsfreiheit: Forschung zwischen Erkenntnisgewinn und Risikoproblem," *Forschung und Lehre* 26 (2019): 446–47, here at 446.

[13] Thus the characterization offered by the jurist Joachim Lege in "Die Herzkammer der Wissenschaft: Das Wissenschaftssystem braucht ein Zentrum, das bahnbrechende Erfindungen mit dem wissenschaftlichen und gesellschaftlichen Konsens vermittelt; Das können nur die Universitäten sein," *Frankfurter Allgemeine Zeitung*, Sept. 19, 2019, no. 4.

[14] Cf. the second and the fifth of my 2019–20 Gifford Lectures: *In God's Image: An Anthropology of the Spirit*, translated by Douglas W. Stott (Grand Rapids, MI: Eerdmans, 2021); in the following I take up some parts of these lectures.

search processes are supported by the effort for a creative, in-depth search for truth. The fact that in modern research universities technological success interests, monetary incentives to raise research funds, and possible career advantages can play an additional role in this process should not allow the passion of the search for truth and the critical and self-critical passion in the verification and control of truth claims to be underestimated.

It has also been observed, and rightly so, that some groundbreaking innovations have occurred not within but outside the organized scientific community. But this does not speak against the high value of a globally organized science system. In a powerful "latent pattern maintenance,"[15] university-organized science holds up the globally institutionalized examination of truth claims, the defense of proven truth claims, and in the process the manifold scientific efforts to achieve new "interesting" and, in various respects, fruitful insights into truth. The importance of this enormous achievement, which cannot be overestimated, usually becomes apparent only in extreme cultural and political crises.

The Ethical Relevance of Respect for Truth

The multimodal spirit of truth has an ethical significance that extends far beyond the realm of science and radiates into the whole of society. The Berlin philosopher Volker Gerhardt considers it a "danger to Western civilization" that the current president of the United States of America consistently disregards truth in an effort to cultivate his own image, claiming to do so, moreover, for the sake of doing what is allegedly economically best for his country. Massive amounts of incorrect information and assertions are sent out into the world in the guise of "truths."[16] Gerhardt also observes, however:

> as desperate as the situation indeed is, this presidential renunciation of truth has accomplished one good thing, namely, bringing to an end within a few weeks the dismissal of truth that for much too long had already been viewed as unsurpassably modern (or even as already "postmodern"). Whereas until the spring of that year [2017] attributing *any* meaning at all to "truth" was considered a sign of unequivocal backwardness, there is now a rush to remove any and all doubt about the indispensability of truth not only in "marches for science," but also in academic circles.[17]

---

[15] See Talcott Parsons, *The Social System* (New York: MacMillan Free Press, 1964), 55–58 and 99.

[16] By July 13, 2020, the *Washington Post* had listed twenty thousand false assertions that Trump had disseminated since taking office in January 2017.

[17] Volker Gerhardt, "In Vergessenheit geraten: Über die Unverzichtbarkeit der Wahrheit," in *Forschung und Lehre* 24 (2017): 754–56, here at 755. Concerning the enormous de-

Gerhardt justifiably insists that people had "underestimated the moral significance of truth while overestimating its metaphysical status." When the will to assert serious and resilient truth claims is abandoned, we lose our moorings in thinking, acting, and interacting. It is precisely the "relativity of the human experience of the world" and the "variety, contrariness, and even enduring irreconcilability of positions that must make us conscious that, indeed, nothing is more urgent now than to hold fast to truth."[18]

"Holding fast to truth" is not a simple operation. It requires dealing with differing and even conflicting truth-claims, developing, differentiating, and qualifying them.

Dramatic Conflicts Between Claims to Truth and the Necessity of their Qualification (the Case of Galileo)

Alfred North Whitehead showed how important it is to qualify statements that claim the truth for themselves in the famous case of Galileo Galilei, a dramatic dispute about the truth:

> Galileo said that the earth moves and that the sun is fixed; the Inquisition said that the earth is fixed and the sun moves; and Newtonian astronomers, adopting an absolute theory of space, said that both the sun and the earth move. But now we say that any one of these three statements is equally true, provided that you have fixed your sense of "rest" and "motion" in a way required by the statement adopted. At the date of Galileo's controversy with the Inquisition, Galileo's way of stating the facts was, beyond question, the fruitful procedure for the sake of scientific research. But in itself it was not more true than the formulation of the Inquisition. But at that time the modern concepts of relative motion were in nobody's mind; so that the statements were made in ignorance of the qualifications required for their more perfect truth. Yet this question of the motions of the earth and the sun expresses a real fact in the universe; and all sides had got hold of important truths concerning it. But with the knowledge of those times, the truths appeared to be inconsistent.[19]

The Inquisition supported the perspective of common sense, to which, in some parts of the world, the children's mnemonic rhyme still applies even today: "The

---

structive power of such a cynical attitude toward truth and accuracy within the weave of politics, the media, and the broader public sphere, see also Romy Jaster and David Lanius, *Die Wahrheit schafft sich ab: Wie Fake News Politik machen*, 2nd ed. (Stuttgart: Reclam, 2019).

[18] Gerhardt, "In Vergessenheit geraten," 756.

[19] A. N. Whitehead, *Science and the Modern World* (Cambridge: Cambridge University Press, 1953; paperback ed. 2011), 227–28.

sun rises in the East, turns South at midday's feast; in the North it's never seen, in the West it sets serene." The Inquisition supported the perspective of sensual certainty, which goes hand in hand with a strong claim to truth: "Everyone can see that the sun rises in the east!" Of course, from today's point of view, there is a certain irony in the fact that the Inquisitors, especially—as representatives of the Christian religion, which, with its claims to truth, such as the belief in the Resurrection, challenges common sense and sensual certainty—strove for just this common sense and sensual certainty in order to strengthen their position and oppose the new scientific findings of astronomy. To this day, as is well known, the church has not recovered from the loss of trust that accompanied its decision at that time—not to speak of its use of violent powers to silence Galileo.

The Galileo case also throws light on the limited power of (sensual) certainty when it comes to seeking and defending truth. The assertion is not tenable

> "that truth is accessible to human beings solely in the mode of *certitude*; ... (one cannot assert that) truth is accessible to us only to the extent that we are fully aware and convinced of the truth. At the same time, such certitude can exhibit widely varying gradations and be accompanied, challenged, and called into question to varying degrees by doubt."[20]

Despite this important restriction, such "*certitudinal* orientation," or the linking of truth to certainty, remains problematic,[21] for a great many acts performed within our conscious lives are sustained by knowledge of truth quite without the more or less explicit elimination of irritation and doubt that allegedly characterizes our sense of certainty.[22] Humans live constantly trusting not only countless "correctnesses" supported by personal certainty but also numerous "correctnesses" supported by proven claims to truth that are not backed by personal certainty. The claims about the degree to which correctnesses have to be proven can vary, leading to their viability being disputed. This applies to the consensus theory of truth, which is based on the fact that a large number of certainties are coordinated with one another. It is also true for the coherence theory of truth, which considers the consistent connection of findings and statements to be necessary for making claims to truth.

---

[20] Wilfried Härle, "Das christliche Verständnis der Wahrheit," in *Wahrheit, Marburger Jahrbuch Theologie* 21, ed. Wilfried Härle and Rainer Preuel (Leipzig: EVA, 2009), 82, 61–89.

[21] Thus Julian Nida-Rümelin, *Demokratie und Wahrheit* (Munich: Beck, 2006), 45, accompanied by the warning that "certitudinalism promotes intolerance," 46.

[22] Cf. Ludwig Wittgenstein's reflections and meditations on the complex weave of presuppositions and conditions that necessarily accompany the notion of certainty, in idem, *Über Gewissheit*, Werkausgabe, vol. 8 (Frankfurt a. M.: Suhrkamp, 1984), esp. 140 ff.

The realization is important that no personal search for truth—but also no scientifically supported search for truth—is able "to claim that it achieves absolute certainty beyond the possibility of any further refinement or correction. Rather, its achievement will be gaining a degree of understanding which is sufficiently insightful in its explanatory character for its acceptance to be something to which it is entirely rational to commit oneself."[23] The "toxic chimera" of the one absolute truth (Bernold Fiedler) must be replaced by the realization of the multimodal spirit of truth in its differentiated individual and institutionalized manifestations.

The great ethical blessing—for society as a whole as well as for individuals—which emanates from globally organized academic research as a critical and self-critical creative search for truth, truth-testing, and truth-defense, should not be underestimated. Such a system combines the organized, tireless search for interesting, illuminating, life-furthering, profitable truths by way of practices and strategies of examining, testing, approving, and refuting truth claims: a huge defense system for the sake of lasting reliability, integrity, and honesty.[24]

---

[23] John Polkinghorne, "The Search for Truth," in *The Science and Religion Dialogue: Past and Future*, ed. M. Welker (Frankfurt a. M.: Lang, 2014), 53–59, here at 53.

[24] I am most grateful to the physicist Jörg Hüfner and the mathematician Bernold Fiedler for their comments on my text.

Part Two
Character and Ethics at the Intersection of Disciplines

Part Two

The Impact of Science on Ethics

Jörg Hüfner

Introduction[1]

Broadly speaking, the topic of this volume is the relationship between science and ethics. Rarely has the preparation of an essay taken up so much of my time and thought as the present one. As a professor of theoretical physics, I taught physics to students, helped them in their research, and pursued my own research. But character formation and ethical education were not part of my duties. Therefore, I had not given much thought to the relationship between physics and ethics. On reflection, however, I identified two areas in which ethical questions might be directly relevant for physicists.

First: honesty. Since science should be the search for truth, honesty is a necessary precondition for any scientific research. Though important in theory, honesty is not an important issue in practice, at least not in physics. To a large extent, scientists are honest, not because they are better people but because their experiments can be repeated and their calculations can be checked. Any cheating is quickly detected.

Second: ethical restrictions to research. In the life sciences, strict rules have to be observed when research involves humans and animals, and research often requires approval by an ethics committee. Since physics deals with inanimate matter, no ethical rules restrict the topics and the methods of research.

I conclude: ethics is not an important issue *within* physics.

---

[1] I thank Michael Welker for inviting me to the roundtable consultation held at the University of Heidelberg in April 2019, where I presented the first draft of this chapter for discussion. The invitation forced me to think about a problem that was completely new to me. While struggling with the matter, I increasingly realized its importance and was captivated by it. I am also indebted to the philosopher Rüdiger Bittner and the economist Malte Faber for many discussions that helped me to further clarify my ideas and formulate this article. Thanks go to Beate Witzler for her English-language edits.

But the science of physics is not an island, separated from the rest of the world. On the contrary, discoveries in physics, chemistry, and the life sciences, together with resulting technical transformations of discoveries into products, continually push and change modern economies and thereby affect and change the way people live and interact. Discoveries thereby may raise new ethical questions. Living conditions have improved tremendously during the last two centuries, at least in the industrialized countries. Yet economic progress does not come without a price. Take the following fictive, but not unrealistic, example. Chemists develop a new herbicide that kills weeds more effectively and thereby enhances crop yields. Yet biologists discover that the herbicide also kills certain kinds of insects. Here is the dilemma: should farmers be allowed to use the herbicide to produce more food, or should the herbicide be forbidden because it seriously damages the ecological equilibrium? Science cannot solve this conflict of values. Rather, it is a challenge for ethical discourse and eventually a case for political decision.

I claim: it is by way of the economic transformations triggered by scientific innovations that science, in conjunction with technology, has an impact on ethics. Negative consequences of scientific innovations call for innovative discourses in order to rethink the traditional ethical value system.

Since I am not an expert in ethical theory, I do not feel competent to discuss the above claim in terms of abstract theory. As a physicist, however, I can report on some realistic examples where discoveries in physics have led to ethical problems. Let me choose two examples, the steam engine and the internet. The steam engine stands at the beginning of the first industrialization, and global warming produced by emitted carbon dioxide (CO_2) is the most pressing ethical issue associated with it. The internet is at the center of the second industrialization, and the resulting possibility of global and secret mass surveillance of the public is a danger to fundamental human rights. Let me begin with the internet, since the associated ethical issue is more traditional.

The Internet and Mass Surveillance

In 1947, three physicists—John Bardeen, Walter Brattain, and William Shockley—who worked in the laboratories of the Bell Telephone Company, invented the transistor. This tiny device, which functions according to the laws of quantum physics, not only was a scientific breakthrough, for which they received the Nobel Prize, but also had a tremendous economic impact. Thousands, even millions, of tiny transistors are built into each of today's computers and other electronic devices, such as mobile phones. The World Wide Web, which allows for the massive exchange of data around the globe, was invented in 1989 by the British engineer and computer scientist Timothy Bernes-Lee, while he was working at the nuclear research center CERN in Geneva, Switzerland. The resulting digital revolution, as it is called, has fundamentally changed our lives: the way we work, communicate, learn, and pass our leisure time. Microchips and the internet have even changed warfare: cyberwar has become a new branch of combat.

"The world's most valuable resource is no longer oil, but data" was a headline of the May 2017 edition of *The Economist*.[2] Everyone wants data: individual hackers steal passwords; companies like Facebook collect and sell customer data; in their fight against terror, governments tap communications. As an example of the latter, consider the system of global surveillance that the U.S. government has built up secretly. We know more about this system than that of other governments, because Edward Snowden leaked some details to the public.

Snowden is an interesting personality. Some consider him a hero of the digital age; others call him a traitor and seek to bring him to court. Snowden was not a scientist but a systems engineer who worked for the National Security Agency (NSA) and the Central Intelligence Agency (CIA) of the U.S. government. His task was to maintain and improve the technical system. It was highly classified work. While he was servicing the system, he gradually learned what the system was used for, as he writes in his autobiography *Permanent Record*:

> "I participated in the most significant change in the history of American espionage—the change from the targeted surveillance of individuals to the mass surveillance of entire populations. I helped make it technologically feasible for a single government to collect all the world's digital communications, store them for ages, and search through them at will."[3]

U.S. security agencies tap into the cables of the internet, analyze all of the through-flowing information, copy it, and then store it. This is the equivalent of opening each letter of traditional mail, analyzing and copying its contents, and then letting it continue on its way to the addressee. The electronic surveillance has tremendous advantages over the manual opening of letters because it is automatic, fast, and invisible—it leaves no traces. Nobody can know whether he or she is spied upon.

Whistleblowing

Snowden is a computer nerd. He dropped out of high school and had no interest in anything other than computers. He became an expert already at a young age.

---

[2] *The Economist,* May 6, 2107, https://www.economist.com/leaders/2017/05/06/the-worlds-most-valuable-resource-is-no-longer-oil-but-data.

[3] Edward J. Snowden, *Permanent Record* (London: Pan Books, 2020), 1.

While he was working for the NSA and CIA, he slowly came to the conclusion that what he was doing was wrong. Not technically wrong, but morally. How did he arrive at this conclusion? What was his moral compass? It was not science or technology that gave him moral guidance because, as he quickly realized, "technology does not have a Hippocratic oath."[4] In technology the words "good" and "bad" mean only that a constructed system works or does not work according to design. In his search for a moral compass, Snowden had to look for help outside his field of competence. He studied the Constitution of the United States with its amendments, such as the Bill of Rights, and came to the understanding that some of its principles seemed to be violated by the agencies for which he was working. What did this mean for him personally?

> "I myself had sworn an oath of service not to an agency, nor even a government, but to the public in support of defense of the Constitution, whose guarantee of civil liberties had been so flagrantly violated."[5]

What should and could Snowden do? He had three choices:
- *Close his eyes.* This is what most people choose. They do the job for which they are hired and ask no further questions as to what their work might be used for.
- *Quit his job.* This would have provided Snowden with a clean conscience, because he would no longer be involved. But the illegal work of the agencies would go on, simply performed by other people.
- *Blow the whistle:* He could draw attention to the illegal practices by informing his superiors in the agency or by going public.

Snowden chose the third possibility. The correct way for him to call attention to the illegal practices would have been to inform his superiors first. But he doubted whether his revelations would be passed on to the top of the organization and eventually to Congress. After all, he was ultimately calling the work of the entire organization into question. He decided, therefore, to go public and to leak classified information about illegal practices in the NSA and CIA. For Snowden this was an act of desperation, since he broke the rules of his job. He was well aware that he risked being tried and sent to jail.

Snowden's hope was that his revelations would create a public outcry, and that eventually Congress would pass a law to stop uncontrolled mass surveillance. Indeed, the information that he leaked led to an intense public discussion and to some action in Congress. Snowden himself was not rewarded for his decision, however; he was persecuted and ended up seeking asylum in Russia.

---

[4] Snowden, *Permanent Record*, 182.
[5] Ibid., 6.

What does this example tell us about the relation between science and ethics? The seemingly innocent invention of the transistor and the internet provided humankind with fantastic possibilities, such as easy communication, but also with frightening possibilities, some of which may remind us of George Orwell's *1984*. How can bad uses be avoided and good ones retained? Science and technology have no "tool kit" to define what is ethically bad or good, nor can they provide advice as to which direction to take. Guidance can come only from a system of accepted values. In the case of global surveillance, this system of values for U.S. citizens is laid down in the U.S. Constitution, whose authority was established by democratic vote long before the invention of the internet. This was the solid ethical ground on which Snowden acted.

Let me turn to my second example.

Industrialization and Global Warming

The year 1776, when the first efficient steam engines began working in commercial enterprises, may be considered the beginning of industrialization. James Watt was not the inventor of the steam engine, but he used scientific methods to improve an earlier model with the aim of making it commercially viable. Watt began his career as a craftsman repairing scientific instruments in a workshop at Glasgow University. There, he profited from contacts with Joseph Black, a professor of physics and chemistry, and the famous economist Adam Smith. In 1769, Watt had obtained the patent for "A New Invented Method of Lessening the Consumption of Steam and Fuel in Fire Engines." To commercialize his invention, Watt entered a partnership with the entrepreneur Matthew Boulton. The new firm of Boulton & Watt was highly successful, and Watt became a wealthy man. Interestingly, the steam engines produced by the company were not sold but leased to customers. The licensing fee was based on the cost of fodder that a customer would save by replacing work horses with the steam engine.

Further advances in the performance of steam engines profited from the close collaboration between scientists, engineers, and entrepreneurs. Physicists like Nicolas Léonard Sadi Carnot, of France, investigated the nature of heat and its relation to energy. Engineers not only succeeded in improving the efficiency of stationary steam engines further but also installed them on ships and rails, thereby revolutionizing transportation. Still today, combustion engines driven by coal, oil, or gas are the main sources of mechanical and electrical energy.

What had been a breakthrough then—namely, a nearly unlimited source of mechanical energy—has become a problem now: humanly produced global warming. Burning coal, oil, or gas produces carbon dioxide, CO_2. This gas and some others are called greenhouse gases, because they act like the windows of a greenhouse in that they let in and trap part of the solar radiation in the atmosphere, thereby heating the surface of the earth. Of course, carbon dioxide had always been in the atmosphere and guaranteed a comfortable temperature on earth to which life has adjusted. (Without any CO_2 in the atmosphere, the temperature on earth would be permanently below freezing.) But the additional carbon dioxide from present human activities poses the problem, because it raises the average temperature on earth and thereby causes a climate change, with serious consequences for the ecological equilibrium.

The physics of the greenhouse effect had been worked out already by Svante Arrhenius, a Swedish physicist and chemist (and 1903 Nobel laureate). In 1896, he published a paper titled "On the Influence of Carbonic Acid [that is, carbon dioxide] in the Air upon the Temperature on the Ground." According to his calculations, a doubling of the CO_2 concentration in the atmosphere would lead to an increase of the mean global temperature on the earth by 3 to 5 degrees Celsius. This estimate was fairly accurate. Using an estimate for the industrial world's energy consumption at his time, Arrhenius calculated that the doubling of the CO_2 concentration would happen only in the very distant future, three thousand years away. Unfortunately, this prediction was totally wrong. According to modern calculations, the doubling may be reached already by the year 2050.

Although detailed predictions of the effects of global warming on life on earth are not possible, scientists generally agree that the rise in temperature will seriously affect the living conditions of a large part of the world's population. Some densely populated areas of today may have to be abandoned because of rising sea levels or desertification. Plants, animals, and people will have to migrate and fight for survival in new habitats. The first indications of this climate change are already visible today, and its full effects are expected around the year 2050, if the concentration of greenhouse gases continues to rise at the present rate. This is just thirty years away. What should we do? What is the ethical basis for our decision-making, and what are our tools?

Ethics for an Endangered Future

The philosopher Hans Jonas was among the first to analyze the ethical problems of the industrial age, though not specifically global warming. In his book *The Imperative of Responsibility: In Search of Ethics for the Technological Age*,[6] he argued for an extension of ethics to cope with the problems that arise from the new economic power that science has given to humankind. In the tradition of Kant's categorical imperative, Jonas formulated an "imperative of responsibility": "Act so

---

[6] Hans Jonas, *Das Prinzip Verantwortung: Versuch einer Ethik für die technologische Zivilisation* (Frankfurt a. M.: Suhrkamp, 1985).

that the effects of your action are compatible with the permanence of genuine human life."[7]

In the discussion following my talk at the workshop in Heidelberg, where I presented a draft of this chapter, Rüdiger Bittner questioned the necessity of a new ethics. Does not Kant's imperative suffice: "Act only according to that maxim whereby you can at the same time will that it should become a universal law"? Indeed, Jonas's imperative is not a new ethical system, but it is Kant's general imperative applied to new goal. People of today should feel responsible for the well-being of future generations and should not live at their expense. What is new about this?

In traditional ethics, such as Christian ethics, the care for future generations does not play an important role. When people care for the well-being of future generations, they mean their children and grandchildren. This particular care is of a more genetic origin than a moral origin; animals care for the well-being of their offspring as well. The natural care by humans or animals does not reach far into the future and is limited to a small number of future generations. No gene makes people feel responsible for the future well-being of humanity at large. This missing gene has to be replaced by moral law. And that is what Jonas develops in his writing. In what follows, I discuss some aspects of global warming in the light of Jonas's imperative.

What conclusions may we draw from Jonas's imperative? Should we significantly reduce the emission of greenhouse gases in order to stop global warming? The processes that involve the production of greenhouse gases are the pillars of present-day economies and are vital for the current standard of living of much of the world—at least in industrialized countries. If the production of greenhouse gases is to be significantly reduced—for instance, by replacing coal, oil, and gas with wind, water, and sunlight—the way people work and live today must change dramatically. The standard of living may even have to go down. Herein lies the basic conflict behind Jonas's imperative: how many current conveniences are people today willing to sacrifice for decent living conditions for future generations? This conflict is not new. Parents have always had to decide how much of their budget should be allocated for their own living expenses and how much should be invested in their children's future.

When I look at the individual behavior of my fellow citizens, at the efforts of my own government in Germany and that of others at the international level, I recognize only very moderate willingness for sacrifice. Although the great majority of my fellow citizens *say* that something needs to be done to stop global warming, they rarely *do* anything. Instead, they continue to drive large cars and fly to faraway places for their holidays. Global warming seems a priority of the German government's agenda, but the current government is not very courageous in pro-

---

[7] Ibid., 36.

posing unpopular actions. This is true for other countries, too. Some governments even justify inaction by casting doubt that global warming originates from economic activities. Why are individual people and governments so little motivated? Why do they speak about the dangers of climate change on an intellectual level, but feel no moral drive for action?

Could one reason be found in the way people perceive the dangers of global warming? I think so. People cannot feel the dangers of future climate change, even if they believe what scientists tell them.

The following example will explain what I mean. When a person drives a car and hurts another person in an accident, the damage is obvious, and the moral and legal responsibilities are clear. On the other hand, the driver of a car emitting greenhouse gases is not hurting any particular person directly. Still, the driver contributes to global warming, which causes sea levels to rise and damages the living conditions of coast dwellers. In general, the driver will never meet the person whose living conditions have been damaged by the driver's greenhouse gases: the "victim" may live on another continent or may not even be born; and the "victim" is not only one person but the world population at large, since the driver's greenhouse gases spread over the entire world. Therefore, the relationship between the perpetrator and the victim is an anonymous one. The victim can neither accuse the perpetrator nor be grateful to someone who does not emit greenhouse gases. As a consequence, our driver will neither feel guilty about the greenhouse gases emitted while driving nor feel an obligation to avoid driving, except that the driver may believe what scientists are saying. Emotionally, there is a significant difference between what people experience and what they are told is true. This may be one reason why people are convinced of global warming intellectually but not emotionally. This difference is important. Ethical actions are best driven by emotions, not by intellectual insight.

To state it clearly: I do not argue against the role of science in climate change. On the contrary! Scientific diagnosis of the situation is indispensable. For this reason, the United Nations has established the Intergovernmental Panel on Climatic Change (IPCC), a group of scientists from various disciplines. They calculate the future development of the world climate under various assumptions about the future emission of greenhouse gases and propose recommendations on how to deal with the imminent danger of global warming. They are the basis for ethical and political discourses about specific measures to be taken.

These discourses are lively and learned, and they happen on all levels: among people, political parties, NGOs, governments, and international meetings. For instance, at the United Nations Climate Change Conference held in Paris, in 2015, 174 countries signed onto a global agreement on the reduction of climate change, but there is not yet a concrete roadmap with trustworthy promises of action to guarantee a sustainable future for humanity.

However, the future is not far off and is not abstract. The future generation is already on earth and impatiently knocking at the door. On "Fridays for Future," pupils skip school on Fridays and demonstrate for a halt to global warming. They have understood the existential threat. It is their future which is at stake.

Summary

The title of this volume points to "the impact of science on character formation, ethical education, and the communication of values in late modern pluralistic societies." Since I have felt unable to address some of the particular aspects of the title, I have chosen a more general title for my chapter: "What is the impact of science on ethics?" As a physicist, my first and spontaneous answer was that physicists study the laws of nature, and ethics are not their business. Though true, this answer is naive. The results of scientific research had and have a tremendous impact on the economy and thereby on people's lives. New conditions of life require new ethical rules. This is the origin of a relation between science and ethics that I have discussed here.

Economic progress usually comes as a mixed blessing, with both welcome and undesired consequences. To define an undesired consequence requires a moral compass, a value system, according to which it is possible to distinguish between good and bad effects. In the case of the global indiscriminate surveillance via the internet, the U.S. Constitution provided such a compass, and a courageous whistleblower initiated political action. Global warming poses an even more complicated case. Its presence and possible effects cannot be established without scientific measurements and calculations. The actions to deal with the danger require a new ethical compass, a responsibility for genuine human life in the future. To attain the goal of a sustainable future for humanity, science and ethics have to work together.

Ethical Considerations in Biomedical Research
Welcome Guidance or Unwanted Restrictions to Scientific Progress?

Michael Kirschfink

1. Introduction—Impact of Medicine and Biomedical Science on Society

Medical "truths" and concepts have a normative power from which hardly any decision concerning the value of human behavior, attitudes, and ways of life remains unaffected. In disputes about right and wrong behavior, medical issues are of outstanding importance. They are preferably used when it comes to particularly controversial value decisions. Medical arguments used in ethical and aesthetic debates are often believed to be superior to arguments of a different kind.[1]

The achievements of biomedical research of the last hundred years have tremendously contributed to the development of humankind, though with great differences in their impact in healthcare systems around the world. Reflecting historical injustices, health disparities continue to be a shame of the civilized world. Inequities in the social determinants of health—such as poverty and healthcare access—and their different impacts on different populations are interrelated and influence a wide range of health and quality-of-life outcomes and risks. To varying degrees, health disparities exist along lines of race/ethnicity and socioeconomic class in all societies.[2] These disparities are currently best exemplified by the coronavirus pandemic, which has overwhelmed health systems all over the world, but with more dramatic consequences in poor countries where medical resources are scarce.[3]

---

[1] Thomas Anz, "Medizinische Argumente und Krankengeschichten zur Legitimation und Durchsetzung sozialer Normen," in *(Nicht) normale Fahrten. Faszination eines modernen Narrationstyps*, ed. Ute Gerhard et al. (Heidelberg: Synchron, 2003), 147-56.

[2] Cynthia M. Jones, "The Moral Problem of Health Disparities," *American Journal of Public Health*, no. 100, Suppl 1 (April 2010): 47-51.

[3] Vicki Xafis et al., "The Perfect Moral Storm: Diverse Ethical Considerations in the COVID-19 Pandemic," *Asian Bioethics Review* (May 2020): 1-19.

Less research attention is given to diseases of the developing world than to diseases of the industrialized West, further increasing inequality in global health. This disparity highlights not only how poorer populations face the greatest burden from disease and disability, but also how this burden receives the least attention through medical research. As a result, global research about diseases tracks the global market for treatment and the focus on countries with patients who are able to pay for care.[4]

The desire to close existing health gaps between the rich and the poor is evidenced by the efforts to assess progress toward achieving the Millennium Development Goals (MDGs).[5] Substantial progress has been made in the first two decades of the new millennium, but in most respects progress has not been as fast as full achievement of the MDGs requires. In 2015, building on the advances of the Millennium Development Goals, the United Nations adopted Sustainable Development Goals, which include an explicit commitment to achieve universal health coverage by 2030. However, enormous gaps remain between what is achievable in human health and the status of global health today, and progress has been both incomplete and unevenly distributed. In order to meet the goal of universal health coverage, a deliberate and comprehensive effort is needed to improve the quality of healthcare services globally.[6] However, assessing the impact of research on scientific, economic, and health outcomes is complex and difficult to measure, as it is affected, for example, by a nonlinear relationship between basic research and innovation, the time lag between discovery and clinical application, and the complexity of scientific and health outcomes themselves.[7]

Biomedical research, aiming to improve medical care and disease prevention, depends on an understanding of physiological and pathological processes or epidemiological findings. Translation from basic science to clinical application usually requires tests in animals. To prove that findings are clinically useful, experiments must finally be performed on human subjects. Although carefully designed, such research entails some risk to the subjects which is justified not by any personal benefit to the researcher or the research institution, but rather by its benefit to the human subjects involved and its potential contribution to human

---

[4] James A. Evans, Jae-Mahn Shim, and John P. A. Ioannidis, "Attention to Local Health Burden and the Global Disparity of Health Research," *PLoS ONE* 9, no. 4 (April 2014): e90147.

[5] Amson Sibanda and Henry V. Doctor, "Measuring Health Gaps between the Rich and the Poor: A Review of the Literature and Its Implications for Health Research in Africa," *Journal of Public Health in Africa* 4, no. 1 (June 2013): e3.

[6] National Academies of Sciences, Engineering, and Medicine, *Crossing the Global Quality Chasm: Improving Health Care Worldwide* (Washington, DC: The National Academies Press, 2018).

[7] Stefano Bertuzzi and Zeina Jamalediddine, "Capturing the value of biomedical research," *Cell* 165 (March 2016): 9–12.

knowledge, to the relief of suffering, or to the prolongation of life.[8] Although the need for biomedical research is undeniable, it should never be conducted at the expense of the life, health, and well-being of other human beings.[9] Thus, society devises measures to protect against abuses. Trust of the society in biomedical science requires continuous attention to the ethical, policy, and social implications of research as well as to the public's concerns and hopes for beneficial outcomes.[10] The ethical notions of beneficence, justice, fairness, and respect for persons (here in terms of autonomy)—fundamental principles of medical practice—are also explicitly connected with biomedical research.[11] Three of these principles were outlined in the Belmont report on the Tuskegee study (1932–72), in which over four hundred African American men were denied treatment to investigate the natural course of syphilis.[12] The fourth principle was later added by Tom Beauchamp and James Childress in their textbook on the principles of biomedical ethics.[13]

Ethics, however, is sometimes misunderstood by researchers as a hindrance to scientific progress. A highly competitive atmosphere in (not only) biomedical sciences creates a constant pressure to produce results and to publish novel findings as a prerequisite to attract funding. As outlined by Jennifer Blair McCormick and her coauthors in their empirical study,[14] life scientists often face barriers to considering ethical and social implications of research because of either lack of awareness, lack of relevance of such concerns, or self-confidence in their ability to resolve such concerns. Scientists are often not keen to engage with ethical issues for several reasons, ranging from feeling that they are not sufficiently trained in

---

[8] C. N. Fokunang et al., "Contribution of Biomedical Research Ethics in Public Health Advances," in *Current Topics in Public Health*, ed. Alfonso J. Rodriguez-Morales (Rijeka, Croatia: Intech, 2013), chap. 26, doi: 10.5772/53695.

[9] World Medical Association (WMA), "World Medical Association Declaration of Helsinki: Ethical Principles for Medical Research Involving Human Subjects," *Journal of the American Medical Association* 310, no. 20 (2013): 2191–94, https://www.wma.net/policies-post/wma-declaration-of-helsinki-ethical-principles-for-medical-research-involving-human-subjects/.

[10] Paul G. Rogers, "Scientists, It's Time to Speak Up," *The Scientist* 17, no. 15 (July 2003): 8.

[11] Angeliki Kerasidou and Michael Parker, "Does Science Need Bioethicists? Ethics and Science Collaboration in Biomedical Research," *Research Ethics* 10, no. 4 (December 2014): 214–26.

[12] National Commission for the Protection of Human Subjects of Biomedical and Behavioral Research, *The Belmont Report: Ethical Principles and Guidelines for the Protection of Human Subjects of Research* (Bethesda, MD: U.S. Government Printing Office, 1978).

[13] Tom L. Beauchamp and James F. Childress, *Principles of Biomedical Ethics* (Oxford: Oxford, University Press, 1994).

[14] Jennifer Blair McCormick et al., "Barriers to Considering Ethical and Societal Implications of Research: Perceptions of Life Scientists," *AJOB Primary Research* 3 (June 2012): 40–50.

ethics, to believing that their scientific work has little to do with ethics, or thinking that others will make ethical decisions and that ethicists often struggle with new technologies.[15]

As in other scientific fields, progress and success in biomedical research are assessed according to professional and objective criteria such as volume of publication in prestigious journals and associated citations, securing research grants, and running a large team. Outside of this system, in society at large, an increasing demand to be informed about recent discoveries and their impact on morbidity and mortality puts the biomedical community under increasing pressure to demonstrate the value and extent of the impact of its labor.[16]

As biomedical sciences rapidly evolved, ethical decisions became more challenging. More recently, new techniques for gene editing–aimed at treating, preventing, and curing diseases through gene editing–are raising important moral questions about their applications in medicine and treatments as well as societal impacts on future generations. An example of this kind of question is raised by CRISPR/Cas9 being considered as a promising therapeutic tool.[17] In November 2018, the Chinese scientist He Jiankui announced that he had "created" the first gene-edited babies–twins designed to be naturally immune to the human immunodeficiency virus (HIV). The news immediately induced international condemnation and a debate over the scientific and ethical legitimacy of He's genetic experiments. He admitted to crossing the red line to test his hypothesis of "rendering these babies HIV-resistant" by using the editing tool CRISPR to delete the CCR5 gene. This gene codes for a receptor in the immune system (lymphocytes), whereas HIV requires this gene to enter human blood cells to infect them and cause AIDS. However, the CCR5 gene is responsible for other biological functions. When its DNA is modified, the impact and any possible collateral damage are only gradually observed by monitoring the babies' development. As a result of the scientific manipulation in this life-size experiment, these Chinese twins are, to state it drastically, genuine human "guinea pigs." The Chinese Academy of Medical Sciences published a letter in *The Lancet* stating that the academy was "opposed to any clinical operation of human embryo genome editing for reproductive purposes."[18] He's work has revitalized a long conversation about the ethics surrounding germline gene editing. A number of issues–those inherent in the tech-

---

[15] Paul Root Wolpe, "Reasons Scientists Avoid Thinking about Ethics," *Cell* 125, no. 6 (June 2006): 1023-25.

[16] Liz Allen, "The Art of Evaluating the Impact of Medical Science," *Bulletin of the World Health Organization* 88 (2010): 4-5.

[17] Françoise Baylis, "Counterpoint: The Potential Harms of Human Gene Editing Using CRISPR-Cas9," *Clinical Chemistry* 64, no. 3 (March 2018); 489-91.

[18] Chen Wang et al., "Gene-Edited Babies: Chinese Academy of Medical Sciences' Response and Action," *Lancet* 393 (January 2019): 25-26.

nologies themselves, as well as scientific hurdles that need to be overcome—must be addressed before initiating clinical trials, to ensure that they are carried out as ethically as possible.[19]

2. From Medical Ethics to Bioethics: Guidelines for an Ethical Framework

Ethical standards in biomedical research have evolved over many centuries through the interplay of historical and political events, social and legal considerations, and continuous medical and technological advances.[20] Historically, the origin of Western medical ethics is contemporary with Socrates (469-399 BCE) and can be traced back to antiquity to guidelines on the duty of physicians, such as the Hippocratic Oath, with its three fundamental maxims: benefit the patient by alleviating his/her needs due to illness; maintain the physician's professionalism and dedication, beyond corruption and personal interest; and respect patient confidentiality, preserving the patient's data and privacy.[21] The Formula Comitis Archiatrorum, written in the fifth century CE, during the reign of the Ostrogothic king Theodoric the Great, is considered the first code of medical ethics. It demands from physicians that they widen and deepen their knowledge and consult with other physicians. During medieval and early modern times, medical ethics came under the significant influence of Islamic scholars, such as Ishaq ibn Ali al-Ruhawi (who wrote the *Conduct of a Physician*, the first book dedicated to medical ethics), Avicenna (the Canon of Medicine), and Muhammad ibn Zakariya ar-Razi (known as Rhazes in the West), but also Jewish thinkers, such as Maimonides, and Roman Catholic scholastic thinkers, such as Thomas Aquinas. These intellectual traditions continued in Catholic, Islamic, and Jewish medical ethics.

A major change in the concept of medical ethics took place in the twentieth century and continues today in our twenty-first-century reconsideration of the attitudes of researchers, doctors, patients, and pharmaceutical companies and public authorities—in part because they often follow different lines of interest. The Nuremberg Code of 1947 laid the first stone of modern biomedical ethics by requiring the voluntary consent of subjects and minimum scientific requirements.[22]

---

[19] Sheldon Krimsky, "Ten Ways in Which He Jiankui Violated Ethics," *Nature Biotechnology* 37, no. 1 (January 2019): 19-20.

[20] Raul Artal and Sheldon Rubenfeld, "Ethical Issues in Research," *Best Practice & Research Clinical Obstetrics & Gynaecology* 43 (January 2017): 107-14.

[21] Beauchamp and Childress, *Principles of Biomedical Ethics*.

[22] Paul Weindling, "The Origins of Informed Consent: The International Scientific Commission on Medical War Crimes, and the Nuremberg Code," *Bulletin of the History of Medicine* 75, no. 1 (February 2001): 37-71.

The code resulted from the trial of physicians who had conducted atrocious experiments on unconsenting prisoners and detainees during the Second World War as revealed at the Nuremberg War Crimes Trials in 1947. Designed to protect the integrity of the research subject, the code defined conditions for the ethical conduct of research involving human subjects and emphasized the imperative of the human subject's "voluntary consent" to research. This code is regarded as the founding document of contemporary research ethics, which emphasizes sound scientific research protocol and consent.

In 1964, the World Medical Association (WMA) took an important further step to reassure society: it adopted the Declaration of Helsinki, most recently revised in 2013, which lays down ethical guidelines for research involving human subjects. It is considered the fundamental document in the field of ethics in biomedical research and has had considerable influence on the formulation of international, regional, and national legislation and codes of conduct.[23]

In the late 1970 s, in view of the special circumstances of developing countries in regard to the applicability of the Nuremberg Code and the Declaration of Helsinki, the Council for International Organizations of Medical Sciences (CIOMS) and the World Health Organization (WHO) undertook a further examination of these matters, and in 1982 issued Proposed International Guidelines for Biomedical Research Involving Human Subjects. The purpose of these guidelines was to indicate how the ethical principles that should guide the conduct of biomedical research involving human subjects, as set forth in the Declaration of Helsinki, could be applied effectively, particularly in developing countries, given their socioeconomic circumstances, laws and regulations, and executive and administrative arrangements.[24] The Universal Declaration on Bioethics and Human Rights, adopted by the United Nations Educational, Scientific, and Cultural Organisation (UNESCO) in 2005, was an important step in the search for global minimum standards in biomedical research and clinical practice. This was the first international legal, though nonbinding, instrument that comprehensively linked human rights and bioethics.[25] As a consequence, research ethics committees (RECs) were established over the past decades to safeguard the welfare, dignity, and safety of research participants, ensuring that ethically approved research is conducted in line with approved protocols, and promoting public confidence in the conduct of human research. Since then, RECs have played key roles in pro-

---

[23] WMA, "Declaration of Helsinki."
[24] Council for International Organizations of Medical Sciences (CIOMS), *International Ethical Guidelines for Health-Related Research Involving Humans*, 4th ed. (Geneva: CIOMS, 2016).
[25] Roberto Andorno, "Global Bioethics at UNESCO: In Defence of the Universal Declaration on Bioethics and Human Rights," *Journal of Medical Ethics* 33, no. 3 (March 2007):150–54.

moting ethical practices in biomedical research and in identifying solutions to ensure that the interests of researchers and society do not take precedence over the rights of the participants.

With a better understanding that diseases are complex and multifactorial, biomedical research has become increasingly multidisciplinary and now includes a wide range of different academic fields and forms of expertise to investigate diseases. Previously, ethics and science collaboration focused on review, oversight, or consultation. Ethics tended to be situated at the periphery of scientific work and was considered only in addressing specific issues at specific times, such as in reviewing a potentially controversial project or solving a particular quandary that had emerged. Nowadays, in the collaboration between ethics and science, ethics is present at all stages and in all parts of the biomedical research process.[26]

This new emphasis has led to the development of a novel discipline of ethics—*bioethics*—which is commonly understood to refer to the ethical implications and applications of all health-related life sciences. In particular, bioethics comprises debates over the boundaries of life (for example, abortion and euthanasia), the allocation of limited healthcare resources (for example, organ donation and rationing of medical treatment), and the right to refuse medical care for religious or cultural reasons. The scope of bioethics continuously has expanded with the development of biotechnology, from manipulation of basic biology through alteration of DNA and protein, to cloning, gene therapy, and human genetic engineering.

The public entrusts the scientific community with the responsibility for undertaking high-quality scientific research. In hand with this responsibility comes the expectation that this research is always done in good faith, with honesty and integrity. This *good scientific practice* represents standards and values to be applied by all researchers throughout their career in biomedical science at any level of practice. A prevailing problem is scientific misconduct, which undermines not only integrity, credibility, and objectivity in research but also trust, both among researchers and in the general public.[27] As published data may directly affect human health, publication ethics is of particular importance in biomedical science. Article 36 of the latest version of the WMA Declaration of Helsinki states:

---

[26] Kerasidou and Parker, "Does Science Need Bioethicists?"

[27] Malhar N. Kumar, "Dealing with Misconduct in Biomedical Research: A Review of the Problems and the Proposed Methods for Improvement," *Accountability in Research* 16, no. 6 (November 2009): 307–30; Ana Marusic et al., "Interventions to Prevent Misconduct and Promote Integrity in Research and Publication," *Cochrane Database of Systematic Reviews* 4 (April 2016): art. no. MR000038.

Researchers, authors, sponsors, editors and publishers all have ethical obligations with regard to the publication and dissemination of the results of research All parties should adhere to accepted guidelines for ethical reporting. Negative and inconclusive as well as positive results must be published or otherwise made publicly available. Sources of funding, institutional affiliations and conflicts of interest must be declared in the publication.[28]

Reports of research not in accordance with the principles of this declaration should not be accepted for publication.[28] In an international survey of knowledge and attitudes about common issues in publication ethics among authors of submissions to twenty research journals, researchers found a large degree of variability in espoused training and perceived knowledge, but also in views about how ethical or unethical different scenarios were. The authors of the survey concluded that ethical standards need to be better articulated and taught to improve consistency of training across institutions and countries.[29]

The German Research Foundation (DFG) in 1998 published recommendations for safeguarding good scientific practice to further research integrity and establish it as an integral part of research and teaching. The recommendations represent the consensus among the member organizations of the DFG on the fundamental principles and standards of good practice, and these organizations uphold the recommendations. These comprehensive guidelines, recently extensively revised,[30] formulate a system of self-regulation which underscores the importance of integrity in the everyday practice of research and provide researchers with a reliable reference to embed good research practice as an established and binding aspect of their work.

---

[28] WMA, Declaration of Helsinki.

[28] Dale J. Benos et al., "Ethics and Scientific Publication," *Advances in Physiology Education* 29, no. 2 (June 2005): 59–74; Mindaugas Broga et al., "Publication Ethics in Biomedical Journals from Countries in Central and Eastern Europe," *Science and Engineering Ethics* 20, no. 1 (2014): 99–109.

[29] Sara Schroter et al., "Biomedical Authors' Awareness of Publication Ethics: An International Survey," *BMJ Open* 8, no. 11 (November 2018): e021282.

[30] Deutsche Forschungsgemeinschaft (DFG), *Guidelines for Safeguarding Good Research Practice. Code of Conduct*, 2019, https://www.dfg.de/download/pdf/foerderung/rechtliche_rahmenbedingungen/gute_wissenschaftliche_praxis/kodex_gwp_en.pdf.

3. The "Participatory Turn" in Modern Biomedicine: A New Role of the Society

Recent years have witnessed a wave of innovation in health technologies driven by new medical breakthroughs, novel scientific approaches, and the rise of digital health technologies. Developments in biomedical research and technology can exert powerful effects on individuals' lives and society's ways of providing health services. Recent advances in genetics are changing the way how we think about kinship, risk of illness, and the ability to intervene in biological processes to change physical characteristics. The possibilities to visualize interiors of the body (for example, by functional Magnetic Resonance Imaging, fMRI) and to analyze biochemical changes inside the body (for example, by microsensors and lab-on-a-chip devices) affect the way we classify and characterize "normal" function and behavior. The ability to grow cells into whole tissues using tissue engineering, or to invent new surgical procedures using telemedicine, will dramatically transform the way therapies are delivered and medicine is practiced.

At the same time, social, political, and economic environments shape the form of innovation by restricting or promoting certain research directions and funding. Consumers or patient-advocacy groups increasingly influence activity in certain research areas, and controversies erupt over innovations that seem to disrupt long-held cultural beliefs. Researchers study the interactions among science, technology, and society, including emerging and unanticipated ethical and social concerns, the implications of changes in the way science is conducted (for example, issues of patenting and commercialization), and implications of new technologies for access and social justice, their possible effect on concepts of race and gender, and effects on clinical and basic research practice.

In *biomedical sciences that aim to translate innovation and stimulating discoveries into new therapies, diagnostics, and prevention strategies with a direct impact on the well-being of society, partnerships are required between public and private sectors.* Individuals and collectives—whether as patients, citizens, or consumers—are participating in new and unprecedented ways in the conduct of biomedical research, health policy, and health practice. Their activities meanwhile comprise a wide spectrum of activities, from monitoring blood glucose levels with a smartphone, to ordering a genetic test kit online, to receiving genetically customized medication, to patients with rare diseases mobilizing online communities of fellow sufferers to run a do-it-yourself (DIY) clinical trial. This participatory turn in health offers a number of new roles to citizens, whether as experimenters, stakeholders, providers of data, research participants, or users. It covers not only the gathering and volunteering of data and the involvement of nonexperts in scientific experimentation and analysis, but also the lobbying efforts of interest groups and public input into research and funding as well as into the formulation and regulation of policies. Citizen involvement manifests at different stages in the process—from upstream interventions in priority setting and funding decisions, to a more direct downstream involvement of citizens and patients in the use and application of medical knowledge and information. These new developments motivated the European Commission in the early 1990s to establish the European Group on Ethics in Science and New Technologies to analyze the ethical implications of new health technologies and citizen participation.[31]

In 2016, the Council for International Organizations of Medical Sciences (CIOMS) released its latest edition of International Ethical Guidelines for Health-Related Research Involving Humans, the universally acknowledged ethical standards in biomedical research.[32] Among the improvements are the relevance assigned to the social value of research and its effects on decision-making and the creation of public policies. The guidelines constitute progress regarding the context and needs of populations in which research will be conducted, with greater community involvement in the different phases of the investigation project, thus allowing communities to access potential benefits of the research. Despite the improved harmonization with scientific, technological, and social changes, and despite the tool that the guidelines provide for researchers and research ethics committees, some topics remain unsolved—for instance, the management of participants' minimal risk and conflicts-of-interest in research, but also the development of research in low-income scenarios.[33]

The implementation and further development of inclusive and reasonable forms of public exchange constitute a central bioethical concern. This is particularly true when bioethics is seen as an area that spans from theoretical considerations and academic teaching to policy advice and even biopolitics. A bioethical position that fails to foster this public exchange and thus avoids confronting different public arguments—including perhaps those based on different cultural histories, relations, and ontological grounds—not only runs the risk of missing important aspects, ideas, and arguments; it also arouses strong suspicion of being indeed one-sided, biased, or ideological—thus illegitimate. Insofar as polemics against the "ethics industry" have to be taken seriously as criticism, it is clear

---

[31] European Group on Ethics in Science and New Technologies to the European Commission (EGE), *The Ethical Implications of New Health Technologies and Citizen Participation*, opinion no. 29 (Luxembourg: Publications Office of the European Union, 2016).

[32] CIOMS, *International Ethical Guidelines*.

[33] Marjorie Borgeat Meza et al., "Council for International Organizations of Medical Sciences (CIOMS) Ethical Guidelines: Advancements and Unsolved Topics in 2016 Upgrade," *Medwave* 18, no. 2 (April 2018): e7208.

that uncritical and poorly founded "expert-centrism" (and its blind spot concerning public understandings of ethics) still exists.[34]

4. The Educational View: Implementing Character Formation and Ethical Education in Biomedical Science

The rapid advances in biomedical science and technology as well as increased societal complexities underpin the importance of morals, values, and ethics and their benefits as they profoundly influence society, science education, and teaching practices. Discussions of bioethical challenges take place in the media, in the academy, and in classrooms, but also in labs, offices, and hospital wards. They involve not just doctors but also patients, not just scientists and politicians but also, finally, the general public.[35]

Article 23 of the UNESCO Declaration on Bioethics and Human Rights underscores the importance of bioethics education, training, and information to gain a better understanding of the ethical implications of scientific and technological developments. It is a repetition to some extent of what the Universal Declaration of 1997 postulated in asking governments to further education and training in bioethics across the board. In this context, therefore, it is of the utmost importance to emphasize the need for those learners who are going to be engaged professionally in the scientific, environmental, or healthcare fields "to be educated in bioethics."[36]

Nowadays, all medical schools teach bioethics, although with large variations in its extent, and while discussions about bioethics have become frequent in most medical journals, there are often barriers to teaching and incorporating what has been taught into daily practice.[37] Recognizing the lack of ethics of some researchers, those engaged in university teaching sometimes ask themselves whether they should consider attempting to transmit, besides theoretical and practical knowledge, the ethical "sense" needed for research, and should make the univer-

---

[34] Silke Schicktanz, Mark Schweda, and Brian Wynne, "The Ethics of 'Public Understanding of Ethics'—Why and How Bioethics Expertise Should Include Public and Patients' Voices," *Medical Health Care Philosophy* 15 (2012): 129–39.

[35] Mohammad Chowdhury, "Emphasizing Morals, Values, Ethics, and Character Education in Science Education and Science Teaching," *The Malaysian Online Journal of Educational Science* 4, no. 2 (2016): 1–16.

[36] Antonio Liras and Alicia Arenas, "Bioethics in Biomedicine in the Context of a Global Higher Education Area," *International Archives of Medicine* 3, no. 1 (June 2010): 10.

[37] Erich H. Loewy, "Education, Practice and Bioethics: Growing Barriers to Ethical Practice," *Health Care Analysis* 11, no. 2 (July 2003): 171–79.

sity a space for ethical learning as well.[38] Education in research ethics should be mandatory for biomedical students and physicians and should be included as a continued longitudinal curriculum in graduate and postgraduate medical education.[39] Good bioethics teaching depends on teachers, mentors, and role models who encourage open discussions that are respectful of multiple viewpoints. Discourses, both in the classroom and in practice, need to consider the partly complicated historical circumstances that led previous biomedical researchers to work on projects that seem so unethical in hindsight.[40] Although teaching bioethics alone will not prevent misconduct, it promotes integrity, accountability, and responsibility in research. In a recent survey of twenty-four U.S. medical schools, a majority of medical students, regardless of demographic and religious characteristics, were shown to be receptive to the role of character development in medical education, supporting the value of curricular reforms that also address issues of character formation in medical education.[41] Preparing medical students for difficult moral decisions is still of utmost importance, requiring continuous discussion of teaching goals to further develop medical curricula.[42]

However, empirical studies on how best to cultivate moral sensibilities and normative reasoning skills into the institutional and individual practices of biomedical scientists and healthcare professionals are still much needed. Educating ourselves about how best to integrate ethics into science and healthcare will be an ongoing challenge.[43]

---

[38] Liras and Arenas, "Bioethics in Biomedicine."

[39] Misti Ault Anderson and James Giordano, "Aequilibrium Prudentis: On the Necessity for Ethics and Policy Studies in the Scientific and Technological Education of Medical Professionals," *BMC Medical Education* 13 (April 2013): 58; Bratislav Stankovic and Mirjana Stankovic, "Educating about Biomedical Research Ethics," *Medicine, Health Care, and Philosophy* 17, no. 4 (November 2014): 541–48.

[40] Barron H. Lerner and Arthur L. Caplan, "Judging the Past: How History Should Inform Bioethics," *Annals of Internal Medicine* 164, no. 8 (April 2016): 553–57.

[41] George B. Carey, Farr A. Curlin, and John D. Yoon, "Medical Student Opinions on Character Development in Medical Education: A National Survey," *BMC Research Notes* 8 (September 2015): 455.

[42] Monika Bobbert, "20 Jahre Ethikunterricht im Medizinstudium: Eine erneute Lernziel- und Curriculumsdiskussion ist erforderlich," *Ethik in der Medizin* 25, no. 4 (2013): 287–300.

[43] Lisa M. Lee, Mildred Z. Solomon, and Amy Gutmann, "Teaching Bioethics," *Hastings Center Report* 44, no. 5 (September 2014): 10–11.

Academic Bondage and Social Transformation
The Case of American Universities and Slavery

Gary S. Hauk

Introduction: Unearthing the Past to Redeem the Future

The past two decades have focused the light of scholarship on a subject often alluded to by historians but rarely examined in depth until recently—the significant role of chattel slavery in the establishment and operation of American colleges and universities before 1865. In this new century, books, articles, conference proceedings, and institutional self-studies have deconstructed generations of oral history, received tradition, and unexamined cultural values in both the southern and the northern United States. The truth thus unveiled tells, among other reasons for regret and sorrow, a story of academic eminence built with the capital of a slave economy; great American universities have in many instances grown from seeds planted by men and women who enslaved, bought, and sold other human beings.[1] At the same time that the academy has supported this current schol-

---

[1] Brown University set the pace for institutional self-examination in 2003: see "Report of the Brown University Steering Committee on Slavery and Justice," https://www.brown.edu/about/administration/institutional-diversity/resources-initiatives/slavery-justice-report. For other examples, see the later report of the Georgetown University Working Group on Slavery, Memory, and Reconciliation, https://www.georgetown.edu/news/georgetown-shares-slavery-memory-and-reconciliation-report-racial-justice-steps/; and the extensive work of the University of Virginia President's Commission on Slavery and the University, https://slavery.virginia.edu/.

For more comprehensive history, see especially Craig Steven Wilder, *Ebony and Ivy: Race, Slavery, and the Troubled History of America's Universities* (New York: Bloomsbury, 2013), a detailed study of how America's oldest and now most-elite higher educational institutions benefited from slavery; and Leslie M. Harris, James T. Campbell, and Alfred L. Brophy, eds., *Slavery and the University: Histories and Legacies* (Athens: University of Georgia Press, 2019), a collection of essays growing out of the first national conference on the topic, held at Emory University in 2011. See also Stephen Smith and Kate Ellis, "Shackled

arly work, campuses have wrestled with the legacy of statues, buildings, and other named spaces that honor the memory of slave-owning or egregiously racist founders, presidents, professors, and alumni. Meanwhile, many cities, states, townships, and private organizations have removed or renamed memorials stained by association with slavery or the legacy of apartheid laws.[2]

The universities that have undertaken this self-examination are not alone in touting their commitments to the pluralistic ideals of diversity, equity, and inclusion; most American universities, from the oldest to the newest, underscore such principles.[3] These commitments and the broader social activism for justice and reform point to a recognition that the modern, pluralistic democracy of the United States can no longer countenance the values of a society that relied on enslaved labor before the American Civil War or the legally mandated separation of the races during the subsequent Jim Crow era. It is not always clear whether the academy is shaping or being shaped by widespread social concerns about racial justice, reparations, and what Charles Taylor has called "the politics of recognition."[4] It is not always clear whether academic research is helping to transform social values or, in the other direction, whether national debates have turned the attention of academic research toward these topics. Perhaps the influence flows both ways.

Yet there is no question that the academic life of an earlier period did significantly shape the cultural and personal values of the day. Antebellum colleges and universities in the United States—those established before the Civil War—had a profound impact in forming Americans' religious, philosophical, and scientific understanding of racial identity and slavery. Books of history and political science

---

Legacy: History Shows Slavery Helped Build Many U.S. Colleges and Universities," American Public Media Reports, September 4, 2017, https://www.apmreports.org/story/2017/09/04/shackled-legacy.

[2] See, for example, "Confederate Monuments Are Coming Down," *New York Times*, updated August 28, 2017, https://www.nytimes.com/interactive/2017/08/16/us/confederate-monuments-removed.html?smid=fb-share&fbclid=IwAR0 aBVWJFEka6 m8 L7053QrFGYdrHWe3gz5VsApvKCZozxGsU6AW8Gv-c0cY. See also Southern Poverty Law Center, "Whose Heritage? Public Symbols of the Confederacy," publication of the Southern Poverty Law Center, February 1, 2019, https://www.splcenter.org/20190201/whose-heritage-public-symbols-confederacy.

[3] The website of the Office of Diversity, Equity, and Inclusion at Emory University, for example, says that the name of the office "is more than a name, it is a spirit. We remind each other daily not only what our laws call for but also what Emory's strong collective spirit of fairness demands. We respect the dignity and worth of each human being in our community and support the sharing of different values and perspectives."

[4] Charles Taylor et al., *Multiculturalism and the Politics of Recognition: An Essay* (Princeton, NJ: Princeton University Press, 1994).

written by early nineteenth-century academics laid the foundation for an argument that slavery was inherent to human society. Works of biblical interpretation and moral philosophy written by professors built a structure of righteous justification of slavery. And in case there was any doubt about the rightness of "the peculiar institution," biological scientists stepped forward with conclusive "evidence" of a hierarchy of races to demonstrate the suitability of one race for dominance and the inevitability of another for servitude. These scholarly works trained the thinking of generations of college students and permeated the outlook of both highly educated and poorly educated citizens beyond the gates of campuses in both the north and the south.

This chapter explores these mirror examples of academic influence on social mores at opposite ends of nearly two centuries of development. At the more distant end, beginning in the 1830 s, a number of eminent scholars and authors essentially reduced to rubble the Enlightenment edifice that was the home of the autonomous, free individual, and they replaced it with a plantation big house and its outcroppings of slave quarters. Half a century after the American colonies had won their independence on the principle that "all men are created equal," the philosophical underpinnings of that enterprise had been knocked out and replaced by more pernicious assumptions that pervaded American society. That pervasive view of race—elaborated and sharpened by academics of the early nineteenth century—still unfortunately informs many contemporary conversations about social justice. It is also the subject of much current scholarship about the role of slavery in early American universities.

At the more recent end of this historical development, scholars observe that the founders of the American republic declared their equality and independence while simultaneously leaving millions of men and women in anything but equality and independence. Our current watchwords of diversity and inclusion signal the aim of educational institutions to rectify—indeed, atone for—this hypocrisy and to lead society to a fuller embrace of those founding ideals.

Curiously, the history of Emory University offers a case study for each end of this historical spectrum. The antebellum college was tightly entangled with and supportive of the institution of slavery, while the modern university strives to instill in its students, faculty, and staff the values of a more universal and progressive humanity. The first two sections of this chapter explore the impact of Emory College and other antebellum colleges and universities as they fostered and extended the ideological basis of chattel slavery. The third section discusses the attempt of Emory University to transform its community through an examination of that earlier history. The concluding observations pose serious questions about the potential impact of current scholarship on the formation of social values and individual character 250 years after the birth of the American republic.

Setting the Stage for the Academic Shaping of a Slave Society

The early years of Emory College offer insight into the role of antebellum colleges in forging an increasingly intransigent ideology that would lead to civil war. From its founding in 1836 until its temporary closing in 1861, when many of its students and some of its faculty members left to fight for the seceding Confederate States of America, little Emory College both influenced and exemplified the role of the academy in deepening entrenched southern attitudes about race and slavery. Some background about Emory may help illuminate this point.

When Methodists founded the college in the town of Oxford, Georgia, they had one overt reason for doing so—and perhaps one unstated reason as well. The ostensible reason was the relative absence of educational opportunity in the state. Only one institution of higher education existed in Georgia before 1830—the University of Georgia, chartered in 1785. The legislative act that created that state university expressed the conviction that education shapes the morals of a people. The charter of the state university notes that the "happiness of free governments" and "civil order" as well as "public prosperity ... very much depends upon suitably forming the minds and morals of their citizens." Law and punishment alone will not exert this kind of influence, which "can be claimed only by religion and education." For the good of "national prosperity" and to "support the principles of religion and morality," the leaders of society should have as their primary aim the instruction of youth, "that by instruction, they may be moulded [sic] to the love of virtue and good order."[5] Such language was not unusual for the time, as similar rhetoric appears in some of the first state constitutions of the young republic and in earlier documents that laid out the governance of the thirteen British colonies.[6]

Much the same philosophy guided the leaders of religious denominations in Georgia, who feared that the state-supported university would undermine the religious discipline and conviction of the faithful. For this reason, in 1833 Georgia Baptists founded Mercer University, and in 1835 Presbyterians founded Oglethorpe University. Not to be outdone, in 1836 the Methodists founded Emory College, now part of Emory University. An 1834 document prepared by three prominent Georgia Methodists laid out the primary reasons for the founding of the college—to ensure that "the youth who has grown up under our [Methodist] ministry and institutions" will continue in the faith rather than "become an infidel

---

[5] Charter of the University of Georgia, http://dlg.galileo.usg.edu/cgi-bin/ebind2html.pl/reed_c01?seq=25 m, p. 17.

[6] See, for instance, the Constitution of Massachusetts (1780), part 1, art. 3, and part 2, chap. 5,

and a profligate."⁷ The Georgia Methodists aimed to see to the moral development of young people and the continuation of certain social and religious values as well as education for leadership in society.

The very namesake of Emory College points to the moral and educational purposes of the founders. They named their new institution for a Methodist bishop from Maryland, John Emory, who had brought significant educational credentials to his work as a church leader. He had gained a classical education under private tutors and at Washington College, in Maryland. He had also studied law and gained admission to the bar in Maryland at the age of nineteen before deciding on a career in the ministry. He had helped to establish Wesleyan University in Connecticut and served until his death in 1835 as chair of the board of trustees of Dickinson College in Pennsylvania. As founding editor of the *Methodist Magazine and Quarterly Review*, he wrote extensively about the value of education, the ideal college curriculum, the standards of collegiate administration, and subjects ranging from poetry to music to the classics.⁸ He also presided over the annual conference of the Georgia Methodists in 1834, when the idea of a Methodist college in the state was first proposed. So his death in a carriage accident in December 1835, just as the Georgians of his denomination were planning that new college, provided a coincidental reason to memorialize him in an appropriate way.

At least one scholar, however, has surmised that a less overt reason for naming the new college for Bishop Emory may have been his stance against the growing abolitionist movement among northern Methodists.⁹ John Emory was the scion of one of the largest slaveholding families in the state of Maryland. He himself owned slaves, despite the antislavery principles of the founders of Methodism and the regulations in early American Methodism prohibiting clergy from owning slaves.¹⁰ (Just as the country itself had reached a compromise on slavery while creating the U.S. Constitution, so the Methodist Episcopal Church had reached accommodation on the issue, and enslavement of African Americans by Methodist clergy was common.) Moreover, Bishop Emory achieved prominence as a spokesman against growing abolitionist sentiment in the northern United States. Like many slaveholders, including George Washington and Thomas Jefferson, he

---

[7] Report of James O. Andrew, Stephen Olin, and Elijah Sinclair to the Conference, January 13, 1834, Georgia Conference Minutes, Methodist Episcopal Church South.

[8] John Emory, "Extracts from Mr. Emory's Contributions to the *Methodist Magazine and Quarterly Review*," in Robert Emory, *The Life of the Rev. John Emory, D.D.* (New York: George Lane, 1841), 335-75.

[9] Mark Auslander, *The Accidental Slaveowner: Revisiting a Myth of Race and Finding an American Family* (Athens: University of Georgia Press, 2011), 130.

[10] John Emory's will provided for the manumission of his slaves after his death: Last Will and Testament of John Emory, testated January 2, 1836, Baltimore County Registry of Wills, 436-37, Maryland State Archives. Cited in Auslander, 347n3.

regretted the institution of slavery and wished for its eventual demise. His letters and journals express his abhorrence of slavery. Nevertheless, he thought that abolition would leave an uneducated and unprepared people adrift in society, where they would founder and sink. (Left unspoken, of course, was that abolition also would completely disrupt the economic flourishing of the white society that relied on slave labor.)

Bishop Emory expressed his views most forcefully and articulately in a publication that gained wide acclaim in 1835. In a letter to the Methodist ministers of New England,[11] Emory and his fellow bishop Elijah Hedding (from the state of New York, which by then prohibited slavery), outlined many of the arguments against abolition that would crystallize over the next two decades, in part through the scholarship of professors at Emory College and other southern colleges and universities.

First, Emory and Hedding begin by noting the "disturbance" in New England on the question of immediate abolition, while they express happiness that "a majority of our members and friends" disapprove of this "agitation." Feeling the need to address a "pastoral letter" to the New England conferences, the bishops first note that the U.S. Constitution—they assume all will agree—reserves to each state "the exclusive control of its internal and domestic affairs." This reference to the authority of individual states within the union is essentially the states-rights argument—honed and broadcast in part by law school professors—that would grow in importance through the 1840 s and 1850 s and would lead to secession of the southern states from the Union.

Second, the bishops point out that abolitionists advocate the immediate liberation of enslaved persons without compensation to slaveholders,[12] yet the northern states owe much of their wealth to the slave trade and to manufacturing that continues to rely on the raw materials produced by the slaveholding south. This apparent hypocrisy of the north would also become a favorite weapon in the rhetorical arsenal of academic defenders of slavery over the next two decades.

Third, the bishops refer to the history of slavery during the Roman Empire, which demonstrates the impracticability of immediate emancipation; enslaved African Americans, once emancipated, would not have access "to the rights of citizenship, or even to amalgamation" into society that freed Roman slaves enjoyed, because the U.S. Constitution made no provision for the citizenship of freed

---

[11] John Emory and Elijah Hedding, "To the Ministers and Preachers of the Methodist Episcopal Church within the New-England and the New-Hampshire Annual Conferences," reprinted in Robert Emory, *The Life of the Rev. John Emory,* 279–84.

[12] Through the Slavery Abolition Act of 1833 (section 24), Great Britain had freed the slaves in its Caribbean and African colonies while compensating the slaveholders for their loss of assets. The act is available online: http://www.irishstatutebook.ie/eli/1833/act/73/enacted/en/print.html.

slaves.[13] This argument would stiffen into the conviction that the mixing of races in American society must be avoided, and reams of academic prose would bolster that conviction.

Finally, while the bishops acknowledge that "the New Testament Scriptures" and "the preaching or practice of our Lord or his apostles" were never "intended to justify the condition of slavery," they also assert that the Bible furnishes no example for the kind of wholesale manumission urged by abolitionists. The argument from scriptural example—conveniently overlooking the Exodus and God's wholesale freeing of the enslaved Hebrews in Egypt—would become a prominent feature of academic pronouncements before the Civil War.

All of these arguments advanced by Bishop Emory and Bishop Hedding would be taken up and echoed by scholars and teachers to help form the character and moral philosophy of thousands of southerners before the Civil War. In textbooks, lectures, public speeches, and sermons, influential faculty members and college administrators reshaped the political ethos of an entire population. Thus, eighty years after fighting a revolutionary war over *the natural law principle* that "all men are created equal," the American south was prepared to fight another war over the conviction that the enslavement of four million human beings was *justified by natural law*.[14] This turn from the Enlightenment to a "scientific" rationalization of an economy and a way of life was navigated with the help of the academy.

The Subject of Slavery in Classroom, Text, and Scholarly Discourse

One of the influential voices of the South in defense of slavery was that of Augustus Baldwin Longstreet, the second president of Emory College, who served from 1840 to 1848. Longstreet was a newspaper publisher, judge, clergyman, and author, whose collection of short stories titled *Georgia Scenes* had made him famous.

---

[13] The U.S. Constitution does not use the words "slave" and "slavery" but alludes to the institution by circumlocution and euphemism. Nevertheless, a kind of summation of the argument against "amalgamation" was the decision by the U.S. Supreme Court in *Dred Scott v. Sandford* (1857). Chief Justice Roger Taney, writing the majority opinion, asked, "Can a negro, whose ancestors were imported into this country, and sold as slaves, become a member of the political community formed and brought into existence by the Constitution of the United States, and as such become entitled to all the rights, and privileges, and immunities, guaranteed by that instrument to the citizen?" The court said no. See Dred Scott v. Sandford 60 US 393 (1857), https://www.law.cornell.edu/supremecourt/text/60/393, here quoting from par. 22.

[14] *Alfred L. Brophy traces this development in "Proslavery Political Theory in the Southern Academy," in Harris, Campbell, and Brophy, Slavery and the University, 65–83, at 70–72.*

As president of Emory, Longstreet twice became embroiled in controversy over slavery. The first instance grew out of Methodist Bishop James O. Andrew's ownership of slaves. Bishop Andrew, who lived near the Emory College campus, was serving as president of the college's board of trustees in 1844, when the quadrennial national conference of the Methodist Episcopal Church occasioned an intense conflict over slavery.

John Wesley, the founder of Methodism, had opposed the slave trade and slavery. The leaders of Methodism in the American colonies and then the new United States also opposed slavery, and they wrote prohibitions against slave ownership into the church's official *Discipline*. Yet Methodism increasingly turned a blind eye to the institution of slavery through the first decades of the republic. Following the book of Romans, Methodists conceded the government's right to promulgate laws—including laws perpetuating the bondage of one race by another. Thus, for many Methodists, slavery was legally permissible; the only moral questions concerned treatment of the enslaved, and preachers exhorted slaveholders to treat enslaved persons with compassion.

By 1844, however, growing abolitionist sentiment in the church led to a rancorous debate over the issue of slavery and the church. Meeting in New York City that year, the Methodist general conference became consumed by Bishop Andrew's ownership of slaves. At the end of a month of argument, northern delegates moved that Bishop Andrew should resign. Southern delegates—led by Emory College trustees and faculty—made a countermotion that the church should divide into slaveholding and nonslaveholding branches, and the next year, Emory College faculty and administrators helped to form the slavery-endorsing Methodist Episcopal Church, South. Emory president Longstreet was thick in the middle of this debate and at the birth of the new southern church.[15]

The second way in which Longstreet became closely associated with slavery in the mind of the South was through *A Voice from the South*, a book he published in 1847, while he was president of Emory College. Comprising ten letters written as if from the state of Georgia to the state of Massachusetts, the thirty-seven-thousand-word volume is an extended argument not in defense of slavery but against the hypocrisy of the north. Longstreet points out that during the time when Georgia prohibited slavery (from its founding as a colony in 1733 until 1750), New England profited handsomely from the slave trade. Now, having built an economy increasingly dependent on industrial mills that employed what Longstreet calls "white slaves" (poorly treated millworkers, predominantly women) the north has had a change of heart about slavery while not changing its heart about "negroes,"

---

[15] The Methodist Episcopal Church, South, through its dozens of small liberal arts colleges and eventually three universities (Vanderbilt, Southern Methodist, and Emory), would perpetuate many of the intellectual biases of the antebellum society well into the twentieth century, when the southern and northern churches reunited in 1939.

whom it excludes from its society in various ways. (Ohio, for instance, outlawed slavery in 1802 but also barred immigration by blacks). The book is a closely argued—some might say tedious—but rhetorically adept attempt to justify the growing sectional divide between the south and the north. The book also advanced views about the U.S. Constitution and states' rights that would undergird arguments for secession.

For eight years, therefore, Emory College, its students, and its faculty members looked to their highly regarded president for guidance on religious, moral, political, and social matters. That he was a leader in the south and a prominent voice in the growing sectional divide in the nation was a matter of pride for the college and its surrounding community. His intellectual, spiritual, and rhetorical authority helped make Emory College a center of Methodist influence in the south, even as the little college struggled financially to keep its doors open.

Longstreet, however, did not speak alone. His successor as president, George Foster Pierce, had served as president of what is now Wesleyan College, in Georgia, and had spoken vehemently in defense of Bishop Andrew and slavery at the 1844 church conference. Elected as a bishop in 1854, while serving as Emory's president, Pierce became the preeminent leader and voice of Southern Methodism. In a book titled *Incidents of Western Travels* (1857), Pierce laid out some of his thoughts about the appropriateness—even the necessity—of expanding slavery into the western territories of the United States.[16]

Among the faculty at Emory, William Sasnett, the professor of "mental and moral sciences" as well as ancient languages and English literature, regularly lectured about slavery—not only its constitutional legitimacy and its economic necessity but also its moral rightness and, indeed, its Christian imperative. One of his lectures was recorded in the diary of an Emory student in March 1858—a student named George Lovick Pierce Wren. Born in 1836, the year of Emory's founding, Wren was named in honor of both George Foster Pierce, who already had achieved renown by then for his eloquence, and Pierce's well-known clergyman father, Lovick Pierce.

In his diary, young Wren records Professor Sasnett saying, "In the first place, slavery is right per se." Sasnett argued, moreover, that many slaves brought to America as "heathens" have become Christian, and therefore slavery serves to advance the work of God. Such is the inferior nature of the enslaved race, further-

---

[16] George F. Pierce, *Incidents of Western Travel: In a Series of Letters* (Nashville, TN: E. Stevenson and F. A. Owen, 1857). In his narration of events he witnessed in Kansas, Pierce describes proslavery forces there as law-abiding and desirous of peace, contrary to "the partisan misrepresentations of the Northern press," while he views the depredations of abolitionists as the source of misery, death, and destruction: 189-91, https://books.google.com/books?id=FZw-AAAAYAAJ&printsec=frontcover&source=gbs_ge_summary_r&cad=0#v=onepage&q&f=false.

more, that their governance by the superior white race is necessary for their "guidance, support, and protection."[17]

As Patrick C. Jamieson notes in commenting on this diary entry, lectures like Professor Sasnett's represent the way in which southern educators not only inculcated a worldview into their students but also sought to influence the broader society in which those students soon would become leading citizens:

> "Emory College did more than shape the lives of the few thousand students and professors who lived and studied in Oxford before the Civil War. Its faculty developed, elaborated, and propagated numerous arguments to explain and justify the peculiar institution, placing the college at the forefront of the proslavery defense."[18]

Three years after writing this entry in his diary, G. L. P. Wren enlisted in the Confederate army and prepared to lay down his life for the southern way of life, including slavery. He survived the war and named his first son Robert Lee Wren in honor of the foremost general of the Confederacy, Robert E. Lee.

The administrators and faculty members of Emory College certainly were not alone or even necessarily the most effective educators in defining the moral and cultural values of generations of young men, who would graduate from college to lead their society as clergymen, legislators, teachers, businessmen, and everyday citizens. Books, pamphlets, lectures, and journal articles by a significant roster of southern educators advanced a proslavery philosophy on the basis of economics, sociology, and history as well as the developing pseudoscience of racial hierarchy.

These academics included Thomas Roderick Dew, a nationally prominent intellectual and professor of history, metaphysics, and political economy (and later president) at the College of William and Mary, where Thomas Jefferson had been educated.[19] Dew gained attention for his commentary on a number of issues, from tariffs and banking to women's suffrage, but his lasting reputation rests on his *Review of the Debate in the Virginia Legislature of 1831 and 1832*.[20] Following the

---

[17] George Lovick Pierce Wren, Diary, March 1858, MSS 249, Stuart A. Rose Manuscript, Archives, and Rare Book Library, Emory University.

[18] Patrick C. Jamieson, "Making Their Case: Religion, Pedagogy, and the Slavery Question at Antebellum Emory College," in Harris, Campbell, and Brophy, *Slavery and the University*, 99-113, at 100.

[19] For a biographical account, see "Thomas R. Dew (1802-1846)," *Encyclopedia Virginia*, https://www.encyclopediavirginia.org/Dew_Thomas_R_1802-1846#start_entry. For Dew's scholarly influence, see Jody L. Allen, "Thomas Dew and the Rise of Proslavery Ideology at William & Mary," *Slavery and Abolition* 39, no. 2 (2018): 267-79. See also Brophy, "Proslavery Political Theory in the Southern Academy," 67-69.

[20] Thomas R. Dew, *Review of the Debate in the Virginia Legislature of 1831 and 1832* [Richmond: T. W. White, 1832], repr. ed. (Westport, CT: Negro Universities Press, 1970).

Nat Turner slave rebellion in 1831, Virginia legislators considered a number of proposals for the gradual elimination of slavery in Virginia. Dew not only recorded these discussions but also commented extensively on them. Like John Emory and others, Dew shows in this work the conflicted views of slaveholders. He recognizes that slavery offends Christian principles, while he claims that slavery was instituted by God. He acknowledges the horrors of the slave trade while asserting that Africans benefited from Christianization. Like Augustus Longstreet at Emory, Dew points to what he considers the foisting of slavery on the south by the British and New England slave trades. Yet he also advances the theory that while slavery in general was wrong, enslavement of Africans was acceptable because of their inherent inferiority. He opposes emancipation because American blacks were unfit for freedom and could not live among whites, yet he opposes colonization of freed slaves to Africa because of the cost. Dew thus articulated and reinforced views that would become widespread in both northern and southern states in the ensuing decades.

(By a curious twist, a descendant of Dew—the distinguished Civil War historian Charles B. Dew—grew up in Virginia believing in the myth of the Lost Cause of the Confederacy, including the whitewashed notion that slavery had nothing to do with the Civil War, which was supposedly all about states' rights. Charles Dew admits to being "stunned" to learn from his academic research that the rhetoric of defending human slavery pervaded not only the speeches of Confederate leaders during the lead-up to the war but also every Confederate state's articles of secession, which named slavery as the cause of disunion.[21])

Albert Taylor Bledsoe, a professor of mathematics at the University of Alabama and later at the University of Virginia, used to weave into his lectures on astronomy and calculus his observations on slavery, abolition, and liberty. In 1856 he published *An Essay on Liberty and Slavery*.[22] Though published by a mathematician, the work was no amateur production but was what one recent scholar has called "the most extensive philosophical treatment of slavery ever produced by a Southern academic."[23] In this book, Bledsoe ranges across the disciplines of philosophy and law with deep knowledge of the works of Thomas Hobbes, John Locke, William Blackstone, Edmund Burke, William Paley, Thomas Macaulay, and others. His arguments against abolition and for slavery amount to demonstrating that freedom and public order for one portion of the population (white)

---

[21] Charles B. Dew, *Apostles of Disunion: Southern Secession Commissioners and the Causes of the Civil War* (Charlottesville: University Press of Virginia, 2001).

[22] Albert Taylor Bledoe, *An Essay on Liberty and Slavery* [Philadelphia: J. B. Lippincott, 1856], https://archive.org/details/essayonlibertysl01bled/page/n5/mode/2up.

[23] Alfred L. Brophy, *University, Court, and Slave: Pro-Slavery Thought in Southern Colleges and Courts and the Coming of the Civil War* (New York: Oxford University Press, 2016), 89.

depended on the legal, proper, and naturally right restriction of freedom for a portion of the population that was unfit for freedom (black).[24]

About forty-five miles from Emory College, another academic, Thomas R. R. Cobb, helped to establish the Lumpkin Law School at the University of Georgia, in Athens. One of the most learned lawyers in the state, Cobb produced a massive treatise on the law of slavery. His book, *An Inquiry into the Law of Negro Slavery in the United States of America*, marshalled legal, historical, and scientific arguments to defend slavery.[25] The work quickly became a cornerstone of legal education in the South and influenced judicial decisions long after emancipation and the end of the Civil War. In 1898, more than three decades after the war, no less a figure than Oliver Wendell Holmes Jr. wrote an opinion that Cobb would have approved. Holmes was the chief justice of the Massachusetts Supreme Court and soon (1902) would be appointed to the U.S. Supreme Court. A case before the Massachusetts court posed the question whether the marriage of two slaves in Virginia before the Civil War was now legally binding. Holmes, who had fought during the war to save the Union and abolish slavery, oddly relied on the law of property as Cobb had applied it four decades earlier to slavery: enslaved persons were property and could not legally marry. By the time of Holmes's decision, Cobb was dead —killed while leading Confederate troops at the Battle of Fredericksburg in December 1863—but his intellectual influence lived long after him.[26]

Other influential southern academics included James Philemon Holcombe, professor of law at Jefferson's University of Virginia, who explicitly reversed Jefferson's principle of equality by arguing that people are born unequal and must earn equality, for which Africans were unfit; Henry St. George Tucker, professor of law at William and Mary, who taught that slavery was consistent with natural law; George Frederick Holmes, who taught history, political economy, and ancient languages at several prominent southern institutions before serving as the first president of the University of Mississippi and later a professor at the University of Virginia, where he wrote in support of slavery and states' rights; and William Porcher Miles, professor of mathematics at the College of Charleston (South Carolina) and later one of the "Fire-Eaters" bent on secession.

Possibly the most perniciously durable academic work produced before the Civil War comprised the published scholarly conclusions of scientists who advanced the notion of racial hierarchy. This school of scientists sought to explain,

---

[24] Brophy, "Proslavery Political Theory in the Southern Academy," 70-71.
[25] Thomas R. R. Cobb, *An Inquiry into the Law of Negro Slavery in the United States of America* [1858], repr. ed. (Athens: University of Georgia Press, 2012). For a biographical summary, see "Thomas R. R. Cobb (1823-1862)," *New Georgia Encyclopedia*, https://www.georgiaencyclopedia.org/articles/history-archaeology/thomas-r-r-cobb-1823-1862.
[26] Paul Finkelman, "Thomas R. R. Cobb and the Law of Negro Slavery," *Roger Williams University Law Review* 5, no. 1 (1999): 75-115, at 112-15.

among other phenomena, the existence on one continent of people descended from European, African, and Native American stock. These biologists, paleontologists, and ethnologists included the world-famous Louis Agassiz, of Harvard University, who in the 1840 s and 1850 s proposed a theory of polygenesis, or the belief that human variety is owing not to descent from a single source (as in the biblical Adam and Eve or a geographically specific tribe) but from different, independent sources, each with its own attributes and qualities—Asians in Asia, Africans in Africa, and so on. The American School, as it came to be called, included Samuel George Morton, a professor of anatomy at the University of Pennsylvania, president of the Academy of Natural Sciences, and, in the view of many, the first physical anthropologist. His extensive study of hundreds of human skulls led him to conclude that white Europeans were superior to all other human races, and his publications helped to solidify antebellum (and enduring) convictions of white supremacy.[27]

Agassiz and Morton laid the foundation of racial profiling. Other scientist/scholars built the rest of the temple. They included George Gliddon, an Egyptologist whose work helped ignite American interest in Egypt. Gliddon learned from Morton and published several books with him, but Gliddon's best-known treatise was one he published with Josiah Clark Nott, an anthropologist and professor of surgery at the Medical College of Alabama. Nott and Gliddon published *Types of Mankind* (1854), a landmark work that advanced the theories of Morton, and they later collaborated on a follow-up, *Indigenous Races of the Earth* (1857). These two works extended and elaborated studies that Nott had been publishing for two decades already.[28]

The American School held that cranium size determines intelligence and other capabilities, and that research demonstrates a hierarchy of human capacity ranging from Africans at the bottom to Europeans at the top.[29] In retrospect, these views appear to be the crackpot maunderings of misguided and biased researchers. But apart from their theories of polygenesis, much of their other work made

---

[27] Morton's collection, reputed to be the largest gathering of human crania, is curated at the University of Pennsylvania Museum, in Philadelphia.

[28] For more on the way antebellum legal and political theory drew on the work of Gliddon and Nott as well as Cobb, see Brophy, "Proslavery Political Theory in the Southern Academy," 73-76.

[29] Friedrich Tiedemann, a German anatomist, conducted studies similar to Morton's at about the same time and arrived at different conclusions—that while a larger cranium might house a more complex and intelligent brain, the average crania of whites differed not at all from the average crania of blacks, and that the belief in the intellectual inferiority of blacks was founded on racial prejudice. See "A New Take on the 19th-Century Skull Collection of Samuel Morton," *Penn Today*, October 4, 2018, https://penntoday.upenn.edu/news/new-take-on-infamous-Morton-skulls.

substantial contributions to scholarship that still has value. More significantly, their books, teaching, and public lectures on polygenesis had a profound impact on Americans' attitudes about race throughout the country—then and still. The historian Robert A. Smith concludes that "the activities of these scientists and intellectuals was the first serious attempt by American science to offer support for social policy, and also the first attempt by contemporary American society to justify its actions based on scientific evidence."[30]

Sadly, the impact of scholars at Emory College and similar antebellum institutions throughout the American south—as well as influential scholars in the north—would linger well into (and beyond) the twentieth century. Their impact endured in Jim Crow laws that separated white and black citizens in public spaces in the south—from restaurants to theaters, schools, buses, and even drinking fountains. The legacy of racial pseudoscience and its related defenses of slavery would linger in the north as well, where prejudice, hardened by false information about the races, would lead to social (sometimes legally mandated) segregation in New York, Boston, Chicago, Philadelphia, and Detroit, as well as smaller cities and towns in between. The thinking of those nineteenth-century academics still informs the beliefs and, more to the point, the behavior of many Americans nearly two hundred years later.[31]

The perdurance of these attitudes, along with their influence on character formation and moral judgment throughout society, raises the question whether a reverse kind of influence may emerge from current scholarship. The next section of this chapter takes up that question and examines the effort of one university to "transform community" through academic research.

---

[30] Robert A. Smith, "Types of Mankind: Polygenism and Scientific Racism in the Nineteenth Century United States Scientific Community (MA thesis, Pittsburg State University, 2014), 6, https://digitalcommons.pittstate.edu/cgi/viewcontent.cgi?article=1136&context=etd.

[31] See Tom Jacobs, "The Idea of Racial Hierarchy Remains Entrenched in American Psyches," *Pacific Standard*, January 22, 2015, https://psmag.com/books-and-culture/study-suggests-racial-hierarchy-remains-entrenched-americans-psyches-87225. Notoriously, Adolf Hitler and German National Socialism drew on American racial "science" and eugenics as well as on the American notion of Manifest Destiny and the history of genocide against American Indians. See Alex Ross, "How American Racism Influenced Hitler," *The New Yorker*, April 30, 2018, https://www.newyorker.com/magazine/2018/04/30/how-american-racism-influenced-hitler.

Taking Another Look through the Lens of History

Like nearly all colleges and universities in the South before 1960, Emory University enrolled primarily white students through most of the twentieth century.[32] Students from Asia—principally Korea, Japan, and China—were admitted to Emory College as early as the 1890 s because of Methodist missionary work in those countries. But state law prohibited private, tax-exempt schools from enrolling both white and black students. To do so would mean losing the tax exemption on endowment income and incurring multimillion-dollar tax burdens on institutional budgets. By the late 1950 s, however, the civil rights movement and a number of judicial and legislative measures at the federal level began to open the door for African Americans to enter state universities in the south, and private universities soon broke down legal barriers to allow them to enroll black students as well.

Opening the door, however, did not necessarily mean making people feel at home. At Emory, for example, the first African American student enrolled in the fall of 1962, but seven years later African American students were protesting the absence of African American faculty members and administrators, the perceived paucity of library resources focused on black history and literature, exclusion from social fraternities and sororities, and a curriculum devoid of courses in the study of African American history and culture. These and other grievances amounted to an indictment of the university for admitting black students but continuing business as usual, leaving blacks feeling treated as second-class citizens.

Responding to a set of demands by black students in 1969, the university administration began to address what it called "the status of minorities." In 1971 Emory College opened the first black studies program at a private university in the south (that program is now the Department of African American Studies). A universitywide presidential commission established in 1979 enlisted the perspectives of a range of faculty, staff, and students to remove obstacles to inclusion and understanding. Appointment of eminent black faculty members and creation of programs for recruiting and retaining minority students attracted increasing numbers of black undergraduate and graduate students. Important collaborations were established with the historically black colleges in Atlanta. By the early 1990 s, Emory had recorded the highest percentage increase in black student enrollment of any top university in the country during the previous decade and had

---

[32] Exceptions were historically black institutions founded for freed African Americans after the Civil War—colleges like Morehouse, Spelman, Clark, and Morris Brown (all in Atlanta), and universities like Howard, Dillard, and Tuskegee. The Atlanta institutions were prohibited from enrolling white students.

a higher percentage of African American students (nearly 10 percent) than any of the other top twenty-five U.S. universities.[33]

Despite these efforts, however, occasional incidents would shatter the apparent racial amity on campus. Someone would wear a Confederate uniform to a fraternity party. A white student would dress in blackface for Halloween. Somewhere a racial slur would appear scrawled outside a black student's dorm room. After each incident, black and white members of the campus community would spill onto the main quadrangle in protest, the university administration would investigate and perhaps discipline someone, there would be vows to work harder in creating a more inclusive institution that values the humanity of each individual equally, and in time the dust would settle and life would move on—until the next racist incident occurred. Then the cycle would begin anew.

In 2005, the university decided to try to interrupt this apparently fruitless cycle of pain, apology, reflection, and status quo followed by more pain, apology, and reflection. The method of interruption would be scholarship—academic research, teaching, and publication.

The impetus for this decision was an especially troubling incident two years earlier. A highly regarded white faculty member in Emory College unthinkingly had used "the n-word"[34] while making a metaphorical point in a departmental meeting. Although an African American professor was present, no one in the meeting raised an objection to the use of the racial slur. Although the offending faculty member later apologized for using the term and never sought to justify it, the untenured African American faculty member publicly questioned the commitment of the department to racial diversity. Soon the campus was embroiled in angry protests and public forums. Outrage about perceived racism marched across the quadrangle once again.

Two faculty members recognized this old pattern: offense prompts outrage, followed by institutional apology and return to normal until the next offense. Many campuses have experienced the same pattern through the years, almost like a liturgical calendar. Wanting to break the pattern and perhaps lead the community to actual change, history professor Leslie Harris and journalism professor Catherine Manegold decided to try to lead Emory in charting a different path. They suggested turning anger into education. An apology for an offense is certainly appropriate. But when the racial climate on a campus remains unaddressed, or

---

[33] Data from *The Journal of Blacks in Higher Education* (Summer 1995), as reported by Jody Cressman, "Black Enrollment at Emory Outpaces Top Competitors," *Emory Report*, November 6, 1995, http://www.emory.edu/EMORY_REPORT/erarchive/1995/November/ERnov.6/11.6.95higher.edu.html.

[34] I use the standard euphemism here, but for a full account of the history and impact of the word, see Randall Kennedy, *Nigger: The Strange Career of a Troublesome Word* (New York: Pantheon Books, 2002).

when the community lacks the good will and courage to meet the challenges of change, dramatic action may be necessary.

Harris and Manegold proposed that Emory should look more deeply into the sources of the racial language, the racial stereotypes, and the history of race that undergird the way Americans relate to each other across racial lines. Harris, an African American scholar of slavery, and Manegold, a white, award-winning journalist—invited the university to examine its racial history and put it all on record. Only through such scholarship, they reasoned, would subsequent generations of students and others understand where their often-subconscious impulses and half-articulated beliefs come from, and only through understanding would they be able to effect transformation. The notion was almost psychotherapeutic in its intention—dredge up the past to understand the present and move into a healthier future.

Thus, beginning in the fall of 2005, the Emory University administration poured more than $5 million into what it called the Transforming Community Project (TCP). Over the next five and a half years, more than two thousand students, faculty members, staff members, and alumni of the university participated in eight-week-long seminars devoted to a carefully devised curriculum that examined the history of slavery, racism, and their impact on America's national psyche. Workshops taught students how to use the archives to research the particular history of Emory. Seminars and retreats examined the psychology of unconscious bias and ways to be aware of it in oneself and others. Public lectures, journal articles, and blog posts shared the findings from all of this research. The capstone of the project came in February 2011, when Emory hosted the first national conference on the topic of slavery and universities. The proceedings from this conference appear in the volume *Slavery and the University: Histories and Legacies*.[35]

Similar efforts have been undertaken at other universities. All of these activities owe a great deal to South Africa's Truth and Reconciliation Commission and other examples of truth-seeking communities pursuing the transformation of social values, mores, and modes of engagement.[36] Some of these activities make explicit their aim of changing ethical perspectives. As Ruth Simmons, president of Brown University, said in launching that university's study of its relationship to human enslavement, "What better way to teach our students about ethical con-

---

[35] See note 2.

[36] The first such commission in the United States was the Greensboro, North Carolina, Truth and Reconciliation Commission. See Spoma Jovanovic, *Democracy, Dialogue, and Community Action: Truth and Reconciliation in Greensboro* (Fayetteville: University of Arkansas Press, 2014). See also "Truth and Reconciliation," Beloved Community Center website, https://belovedcommunitycenter.org/truth-reconciliation/. A list of other universities studying slavery, especially as it relates to their own institutional history, is available at https://slavery.virginia.edu/universities-studying-slavery/.

duct than to show ourselves to be open to the truth, and to tell the full story?"[37] What better way to promote the individual values of truth-telling and forgiveness and the social value of reconciliation?

While I know of no empirical studies that demonstrate the effectiveness of these efforts—even the Emory project did not follow-up with a statistical survey of attitudinal change—the legacy of such programs continues. The University of Virginia (UVA), for example, has established a program titled Teaching Race at UVA that is explicitly modeled after the Emory Transforming Community Project (the assistant vice provost who established the UVA program had participated in the Emory project while teaching at Emory in 2008). The UVA program is also a direct response to white supremacist activities at UVA and Charlottesville, Virginia, in 2017.[38]

Nevertheless, some institutional changes have resulted from such projects. At Emory, the TCP led to the proposal that the board of trustees should apologize for the institution's antebellum entwinement with slavery, when all of the trustees and faculty members and many of the students were slaveholders. In January 2011, the university trustees issued such a statement of regret. In it, they underscored the difference between the social values of the founders of the institution and the values of the institution today:

> Emory acknowledges its entwinement with the institution of slavery throughout the College's early history. Emory regrets both this undeniable wrong and the University's decades of delay in acknowledging slavery's harmful legacy. As Emory University looks forward, it seeks the wisdom always to discern what is right and the courage to abide by its mission of using knowledge to serve humanity.[39]

Encapsulated in this statement is the hope, if not the certainty, that the work of the academy as a truth-seeking institution will transform it and, thereby, the larger society into which the academy sends graduates as leaders in every walk and vocation.

---

[37] "Shackled Legacy," https://www.apmreports.org/story/2017/09/04/shackled-legacy.
[38] For the story of the Charlottesville protest by white nationalists, see https://time.com/charlottesville-white-nationalist-rally-clashes/.
[39] Minutes, Board of Trustees, Emory University, January 13, 2011, Stuart A. Rose Manuscript, Archives, and Rare Book Library, Emory University.

Conclusion

This chapter has asked whether Lord Acton was right when he said that "history is not a burden on the memory but an illumination of the soul."[40] History is more than facts and a chronicle of "one damn thing after another."[41] At its finest, history is a path toward social and personal enlightenment—if we wish to take it. There may be no better therapeutic for the soul of American society in the twenty-first century than coming to understand the history of how a nation dedicated on paper to the self-evident truth that "all men are created equal" continually compromised that truth and rationalized its opposite. The same may be said of individuals—that undertaking this journey through history is necessary for illuminating the darker assumptions, biases, and half-truths by which we live. The same may be said of institutions.

Several important questions still remain. To what extent, if any, has historical research into the origins and existence of slavery in American colleges and universities illuminated the souls—the current values—of those institutions today? Has this kind of study actually transformed institutional values to fit those institutions for a pluralistic society? Or has it merely replaced an earlier form of ethical imperialism—one that insisted on the superiority of one race over another—with a modern, equally intolerant kind of ethical tyranny, a kind of political correctness that threatens to erase much of the history of that earlier ethos? Is there evidence that such historical study shapes individual character in ways that give persons more emotional resilience, intellectual generosity, and moral imagination? Does such study ever really transform community? And does any of this have any impact on the moral commitments of members of the broader society beyond the campus? Does it illuminate any soul?

At many universities, the answer to that first question, about the illumination of current institutional values, seems to be yes—such study does reveal the way certain institutional practices have sometimes allowed the persistence of values inconsistent with a diverse community, and institutions must change those practices to both signal and effect changes in value. The University of Mississippi now prohibits the longstanding practice of waving Confederate battle flags at sporting events, so as to remove a symbol of a slaveholding society, and Washington and Lee University, where Robert E. Lee served as president during the last years of

---

[40] John Emerich Edward Dalberg Acton (First Baron Acton), *Lectures on Modern History* (London: Macmillan, 1899), Appendix 1, par. 4, https://en.wikisource.org/wiki/Lectures_on_Modern_History/Appendix_1.

[41] This definition of history is often attributed to either Arnold J. Toynbee or Max Plowman, both of whom actually said something similar while pointedly disagreeing with it. But the saying has antecedents as a definition of life. See https://quoteinvestigator.com/2015/09/16/history/#note-12001-1.

his life, has removed Confederate battle flags from the university chapel that bears his name.[42]

Questions remain, however, about the efficacy of historical research in transforming cultural values and shaping moral commitments. In the decade since the Emory trustees issued their statement of regret for the institution's "early entwinement with slavery," the university has continued to experience occasional episodes of community anger over racial insensitivity, often the result of thoughtlessness more than deliberate viciousness. Expressed values may change, but human fallibility seems ineradicable. Meanwhile, American society has been riven by increasingly fraught and sometimes violent racial incidents, including the murder of eleven black church members in Charleston, South Carolina, by a white supremacist who explicitly sought to start what he called a "race war," and including the death of a young woman at the hands of a white supremacist during a rally of anti-Semitic white supremacists in Charlottesville, Virginia. Surveys indicate that a large plurality of U.S. citizens are unaware that slavery was the principal cause of the American Civil War.[43] The battle flag of the slavery-defending Confederate States of America still flutters in the front lawns and from the vehicles of many American citizens in the north as well as the south.[44]

As I write, in July 2020, the United States has been gripped by waves of protests sparked by the particularly callous murder of an unarmed black man by a white police officer—just one in a long series of deaths of unarmed blacks by white police and self-styled civilian vigilantes. The chant of "black lives matter" is countered frequently by the dismissive chant that "all lives matter," as if white Americans have experienced, to the same degree as blacks, a history of lynching, racial profiling, housing discrimination, unwarranted seizure of property, denial of voting rights, and other legacies of viewpoints imbued more than a century and a half ago. Sadly, it is clear that the impact of scholars from an earlier time, when the racial attitudes of the country were hardening, is still felt in powerful and perni-

---

[42] In July 2020, the faculty of Washington and Lee University voted to petition the board of trustees to drop the name Lee.

[43] Pew Research Center, "Civil War at 150: Still Relevant, Still Divisive," https://www.people-press.org/2011/04/08/civil-war-at-150-still-relevant-still-divisive/; Lauren Camera, "Students Aren't Learning about Slavery," *US News & World Report*, February 1, 2018, https://www.usnews.com/news/education-news/articles/2018-02-01/students-dont-know-slavery-was-a-central-cause-of-the-civil-war-report-shows; Southern Poverty Law Center, "SPLC: U.S. Education of American Slavery Sorely Lacking," https://www.splcenter.org/news/2018/01/31/splc-report-us-education-american-slavery-sorely-lacking.

[44] Bristow Marchant, "3 Years Later, Confederate Flag Casts Shadow Again over SC State House," *The State*, July 10, 2018, https://www.thestate.com/news/politics-government/article214555950.html.

cious ways. One can only hope that current academic research will have the kind of therapeutic impact on campus culture—and the broader American society—that organizers of the Transforming Community Project sought.

The Educational Values of Studying Law and Religion

John Witte Jr.[1]

Over the past three decades, a major new field of study in law and religion has emerged in the academy, now involving more than fifteen hundred scholars around the globe. These scholars are studying the religious dimensions of law, the legal dimensions of religion, and the interaction of legal and religious ideas and institutions, methods and practices–historically and today, at home and abroad. From different perspectives, these scholars have shown that religion gives law its spirit and inspires its adherence to ritual, tradition, and justice. Law gives religion its structure and encourages its devotion to order, organization, and orthodoxy. Law and religion share such ideas as fault, obligation, and covenant and such methods as ethics, rhetoric, and hermeneutics. They also balance each other by counterposing justice and mercy, rule and equity, discipline and love. It is this dialectical interaction that gives these two disciplines and two dimensions of life their vitality and their strength. Without law at its backbone, religion slowly crumbles into shallow spiritualism. Without religion at its heart, law gradually devolves into empty, and sometimes brutal, formalism.

In the United States, the study of law and religion has drawn a substantial scholarly guild of some four hundred American law professors and many more scholars from the humanities and social sciences. More than 120 American law schools now have at least one basic course on religious liberty or religion-state

---

[1] This chapter reflects work in progress on a volume tentatively titled "The Religious Vindication of Law." It draws in part on my earlier writings, each with more detailed documentation: *God's Joust, God's Justice: Law and Religion in the Western Tradition* (Grand Rapids, MI: Wm. B. Eerdmans, 2006); *Christianity and Law: An Introduction* (Cambridge: Cambridge University Press, 2008); "The Interdisciplinary Growth of Law and Religion," in *The Confluence of Law and Religion: Interdisciplinary Reflections on the Work of Norman Doe*, ed. Frank Cranmer et al. (Cambridge: Cambridge University Press, 2016), 247–61; "The Study of Law and Religion in America: An Interim Report," *Ecclesiastical Law Journal* 14, no. 3 (2012): 327–54; and "Afterword," in *Leading Works in Law and Religion*, ed. Russell Sandberg (London: Routledge, 2019), 197–205.

relations as part of their basic legal curriculum, and some schools also offer courses in Christian canon law, Jewish law, Islamic law, and natural law. Many legal scholars now include serious consideration of law and religion materials in their treatments of legal ethics, legal history, jurisprudence, law and literature, legal anthropology, comparative law, family law, human rights, and other basic law courses. Two dozen American universities have interdisciplinary programs or concentrations in law, religion, and ethics, several with specialty journals, websites, and blogs. And more law-and-religion scholars work in university departments of religion, philosophy, political science, history, anthropology, and regional studies. The American Academy of Religion, the American Political Science Association, the American Anthropological Association, and the Society of Christian Ethics now all have dedicated programs or sections on law and religion.

Around the globe, some fifty centers, institutes, and programs in law and religion have popped up on university campuses—in Europe, sub-Saharan Africa, Latin America, Australia, New Zealand, India, Indonesia, Hong Kong, and South Korea. These groups are further integrated by international and regional consortia of law-and-religion study and by dozens of periodicals and blogs. More than seventeen hundred books on law and religion were published in English alone worldwide over the past twenty-five years. Several new book series and concentrations in law and religion are now on offer from major publishers at Ashgate, Brill, Cambridge, Catholic, Eerdmans, Mohr Siebeck, Notre Dame, Oxford, Routledge, and Springer. The study of law and religion is no longer just the hobbyhorse of isolated and peculiar professors principally in their twilight years and suddenly concerned about their eternal destiny. It is no longer just the preoccupation of universities that were explicitly founded on Christian, Jewish, Muslim, or other religious premises. Religion now stands alongside economics, philosophy, literature, politics, history, and other disciplines as a valid and valuable conversation partner with law.

The Historical Flow and Ebb of the Study of Law and Religion

The modern study of law and religion is, in no small measure, a return to millennium-old forms of education. When the first Western universities were founded in the eleventh century, the faculties of theology, law, and medicine were dominant. Together, these three faculties were thought to provide a complete education about the soul, mind, and body respectively. In preparation, younger students were first trained in the seven liberal arts—the trivium of grammar, logic, and rhetoric, and the quadrivium of geometry, arithmetic, astronomy, and music. The best students then went on for advanced study in theology, law, or medicine, sometimes in combination. It was common for law students to earn at least a dual doctorate in the canon law of the church and the civil or common law of the state—the *doctor iuris utriusque* on the Continent, the LLD in England and its colonies. It was also common for advanced students to combine the study of law with the study of theology. Indeed, bishops, deans, abbots, and other church leaders customarily had legal training alongside their theological formation. And many judges, law professors, and other legal professionals were ranking ecclesiastics.

Until the eighteenth century, this interlacing of legal and theological education and professional life was considered normal for Western societies that routinely established Christianity as the state religion by law. As part of these religious establishments, Catholic hierarchs and, later, Protestant rulers chartered most of the major universities and professional guilds of the West. They further licensed the professors, clergy, and jurists, and in return expected their allegiance and defense of the locally established church and state. In 1667, German polymath Gottfried Leibniz could still say easily that in his day, "theology is a certain species of jurisprudence," and "law remains in no small part a handmaiden of theology."[2] In 1676, England's chief judge, Sir Matthew Hale, could declare confidentially from the King's Bench that "Christianity is part of the common law."[3] In 1780, American jurist and future President John Adams could still write into the preamble of the Massachusetts Constitution that the people of his state

> "acknowledg[e] with grateful hearts, the goodness of the Great Legislator of the Universe, in affording us, in the course of his Providence, an opportunity ... o[f] entering into an Original, explicit, and Solemn Compact with each other; and of forming a New Constitution of Civil Government for ourselves and Posterity; and devoutly imploring His direction in so interesting a Design."[4]

---

[2] Gottfried Wilhelm Leibniz, *Nova methodus discendae docendaeque iurisprudentiae* [1667], in Christopher Johns, *The Science of Right in Leibniz's Moral and Political Philosophy* (London: Bloomsbury, 2013), 149-50, and in *The* New Method of Learning and Teaching Jurisprudence According to the Principles of the Didactic Art Premised in the General Part and in the Light of Experience, trans. Carmello Massimo de Iuliis (Clark, NJ: Talbot Publishers, 2017), 121-24. I am grateful to Eric Enlow for introducing me to these insights. See Eric Enlow, "Mosaic Commands for Legal Theology," Journal of Law and Religion 32, no. 1 (2017): 26-32.

[3] *Taylor's Case*, 1 Vent. 293, 86 Eng. Rep. 189 (K.B. 1676). See the continued use of this legal adage in Stuart Banner, "When Christianity Was Part of the Common Law," *Law and History Review* 16, no. 1 (1998): 27-62.

[4] Reprinted in Francis Thorpe, ed., *The Federal and State Constitutions ...*, 7 vols. (Washington, DC: Government Printing Office, 1909), 3:1888-89. For further such sentiments in early American constitutional law, see John Witte Jr. and Joel A. Nichols, *Religion and the American Constitutional Experiment*, 4th ed. (New York: Oxford University Press, 2016).

From the mid-eighteenth century onward, this centuries-long integration of law and theology gradually broke down under mounting new pressures. Strong new Enlightenment philosophical attacks on traditional Christian teachings, together with violent attacks on churches and their clergy in some quarters, shook Western Christendom to its foundations. New constitutional reforms, starting in America, led to the legal disestablishment of religion and to separation of church and state and *laïcité* movements in many Western lands. Comprehensive legal codification movements, starting on the Continent, transformed Western state laws and separated these laws from many traditional religious, moral, and customary norms and institutions. New secular universities, both public and private, sprung up throughout nineteenth- and twentieth-century Europe and the Americas devoted to scientific methodology, free academic inquiry, and rigorous debate about all subjects. New (social) scientific and sometimes skeptical forms of religious study became ever more acceptable in state universities—and in the United States led to strong divisions between public state schools and universities and private religious schools, colleges, and seminaries. New positivist theories of knowledge separated higher education into growing numbers of increasingly specialized forms of exact, humane, and social sciences, each with its own language, methods, literature, libraries, faculty, and students, and each equipping professional specialists for the workplace. The proverbial "renaissance man," and now woman—praised for wide learning in various fields, including the classic liberal arts, theology, law, and medicine—gave way to the scientific and technical specialist.

These modern movements undercut the traditional prestige and integration of theology and law in the Western academy. Theology, once the proud "queen of the sciences" that produced the coveted clerical leaders of society, was slowly reduced to just another discipline in the university, yielding ministers with shrinking cultural privilege and intellectual prerogative. Religion is now "a separate department of knowledge," Thomas Jefferson wrote in 1815, alongside physics, astronomy, law, government, economy, business, and medicine. Preachers are the specialists in religion, who must devote their professional time and energy to soulcraft alone and not bother with other matters beyond their ken. "Whenever, therefore, preachers, instead of a lesson in religion, put them off with a discourse on the Copernican system, on chemical affinities, on the construction of government, or the characters of those administering it, it is a breach of contract, depriving their audience of the kind of service for which they were salaried."[5] Church historian Brooks Holifield has documented the "irresistible secularization" and "decline" of authority of theology and the clergy that followed from such early

---

[5] Thomas Jefferson to P. H. Wendover (draft), March 13, 1815, *The Papers of Thomas Jefferson*, Retirement Series, vol. 8, *1 October 1814 to 31 August 1815*, ed. J. Jefferson Looney (Princeton, NJ: Princeton University Press, 2011), 340–43, https://founders.archives.gov/documents/Jefferson/03-08-02-0270-0002.

sentiments, even in religiously observant modern America: "[P]riests and ministers no longer have the control over education, the voice in government, or the moral monopoly" they enjoyed in earlier centuries. "They no longer formulate legal enactments, discipline the merchants, dominate the printing presses, or regulate the universities as they did.... On many matters, clergy appear to have ceded jurisdiction to physicians and psychiatrists, social workers and sociologists, scientists and the gurus of technology."[6]

The study of law, too, became more narrow, specialized, and isolated in the later nineteenth and twentieth centuries. In both Europe and North America, legal education became focused on local national law rather than the entire legal system viewed in full intellectual context. In Europe and England, law became an undergraduate department, with apprenticeships to follow for budding lawyers. In the United States, legal study was sequestered into new, separate professional schools, often at the edge of campus and heavily focused on legal practice. By the early twentieth century, most Western legal academies adopted a philosophy of legal positivism that reduced the study of law to the concrete rules and procedures "posited" by the political sovereign and enforced by the courts. While many other institutions and practices might be normative and important for social coherence and political concordance, they were considered beyond "the province of jurisprudence properly determined."[7] This narrowing of legal study eventually caused a "spiritual crisis," a "crisis of morale" within the legal profession, Yale law school dean Anthony Kronman lamented in 1993: "the collapse" of the traditional "set of values that prizes good judgment above technical competence and encourages a public-spirited devotion to the law" and allegiance to "wisdom and character as professional virtues."[8] Indeed, Kronman continued in a later book, "under the influence of the modern research ideal, our colleges and universities

---

[6] E. Brooks Holifield, *God's Ambassadors: A History of the Christian Clergy in America* (Grand Rapids, MI: Eerdmans, 2007), 3–4. Holifield, however, goes on to warn against exaggerating the cultural and educational authority of religion and the clergy in earlier centuries as well as the modern decline of religion and clerical authority, which he shows still lives on in many traditional and novel quarters in the United States and other Western societies. On the latter, see further Michael Welker et al., eds., *The Impact of Religion on Character Formation, Ethical Education, and the Communication of Values in Late Modern Pluralistic Societies* (Leipzig: Evangelische Verlagsanstalt, 2020).

[7] John Austin, *The Province of Jurisprudence Determined* (London: John Murray, 1832).

[8] Anthony Kronman, *The Lost Lawyer: Failing Ideas of the Legal Profession* (Cambridge, MA: Harvard University Press, 1993), 1–3. See also Mary Ann Glendon, *A Nation under Lawyers: How the Crisis of the Legal Profession Is Transforming American Society* (Cambridge, MA: Harvard University Press, 1999).

[altogether] have expelled this question [of what living is for] from their classrooms, judging it unfit for organized study."[9]

In this modern academic environment, the traditionally vibrant interdisciplinary study of law and religion was reduced to a tiny boutique area of scholarship at best. Until 1990, most Western universities had, if any, only a specialist or two in law-and-religion study sprinkled among the faculties of history, divinity, law, politics, or anthropology and focused mostly on religious laws, church-state relations, and religious freedom. Even these small scholarly lights seemed to be fading as university campuses remained under the thrall of the secularist hypothesis that the spread of reason and science would slowly eclipse the sense of the sacred and restore the sensibilities of the superstitious. Liberalism, Marxism, and other new critical philosophies were regnant on many university campuses, including in law schools. Even divinity schools and seminaries were arguing that "God is dead" and organized religion is dying.

No longer! Over the past three decades, another great awakening of religion has broken out—now global in its sweep, vast in its diversity, and sometimes frightening in its power. Even if the Global North now features more nones, neins, and nyets on organized religion than ever before, the Global Middle and South have seen powerful new upsurges of old and new religions. Globalized media, migration, marketing, and mission work have brought these religions, and their special needs and challenges, to the Global North and West, too. In its newly awakened form, religion has presented the Western academy with a whole alphabet of new challenges that now occupy our global headlines—Apostasy, Blasphemy, Conversion, Defamation, Evangelism, Fundamentalism, Genocide, Hate Crimes, Immigration, Jihad, Klansmen, Liberalism, Migration, Neopaganism, Ostracism, Polygamy, Queer Rights, Refugees, Shari'a, Theocracy, Universal Rights, Value-Voters, Warfare, Xenophobia, Yazidis, and Zealotry.

Over the past three decades, the Western world has also seen a new great awakening of law. The fall of the Berlin Wall and the collapse of the Soviet Union; the strengthening of the European Union and the Council of Europe; the consolidation and expansion of many branches of the United Nations; the new democratic movements in former colonial and authoritarian regimes in Africa and Latin America—all these seismic legal and political movements since the 1980 s have triggered intense and innovative new forms and forums of constitutional ordering and lawmaking. Legal campaigns against terrorism and jihadism have further tested both the strength and the limits of international law and domestic law in Western democracies. Strong new anticorruption campaigns of late have again been mounted to shore up the rule of law and constitutional democracy against strong new populist authoritarianism in the United States, Mexico, Brazil, Poland,

---

[9] Anthony Kronman, *Education's End: Why Our Colleges and Universities Have Given up on the Meaning of Life* (New Haven, CT: Yale University Press, 2008).

Hungary, and elsewhere in the West. And a vibrant new global-law movement has emerged to address pressing challenges like massive human rights violations, genocide, arms trafficking, refugees and migrants, sex trafficking, global disease, hunger, famine, poverty, global political and economic corruption, global climate and environmental challenges, and major (bio)technological issues—all of which are beyond the capacity or power of any national law or even international law to address fully.

This new legal awakening, like the new religious awakening, has forced the Western legal academy to abandon its narrow positivist views of law. Legal scholars have come to see that law is much more than simply the rules and procedures of the state and how we apply and analyze them. Law is also an inherently human and communal enterprise—a living system of legislating, adjudicating, administering, obeying, negotiating, litigating, and other legal conduct not only within the state but also within churches, colleges, corporations, clubs, charities, and other nonstate associations. Law and legal behavior, moreover, are exercised out of a complex blend of concerns, conditions, and character traits variously shaped by nature, class, race, gender, persuasion, piety, charisma, faith, virtue, and more. To be properly understood, therefore, law must be studied and taught in context and in conversation with sundry other disciplines: economics, politics, literature, history, science, medicine, philosophy, psychology, anthropology—and notably, too, religion and theology.

Mapping the Modern Field of Law and Religion

This legal awakening was the birthing process of modern interdisciplinary legal studies. And out of this movement, the modern study of law and religion has re-emerged in the Western academy. Today, it has become increasingly clear—as it was in prior centuries—that law and religion are two universal solvents of human living, two interlocking sources and systems of values and beliefs that have existed in all axial civilizations. Law and religion, Justice Harry Blackmun once wrote, "are an inherent part of the calculus of how a man should live" and how a society should run.[10] To be sure, the spheres and sciences of law and religion have, on occasion, both converged and contradicted each other. Every religious tradition has known both theonomism and antinomianism—the excessive legalization and the excessive spiritualization of religion. Every legal tradition has known both theocracy and totalitarianism—the excessive sacralization and the excessive secularization of law. But the dominant reality in most eras and cultures is that law and religion stand in a dialectical harmony, constantly crossing over and

---

[10] Harry A. Blackmun, "Foreword," *The Weightier Matters of the Law: Essays on Law and Religion*, ed. John Witte Jr. and Frank S. Alexander (Atlanta, GA: Scholars Press, 1988), ix.

cross-fertilizing each other. Every major religious tradition strives to come to terms with law by striking a balance between the rational and the mystical, the prophetic and the priestly, the structural and the spiritual. Every legal tradition struggles to link its formal structures and processes with the beliefs and ideals of its people.

These points of crossover and cross-fertilization are the special province of the interdisciplinary field of law and religion. How do legal and religious ideas and institutions, methods and mechanisms, beliefs and believers influence each other—for better and for worse, in the past, present, and future? These are the cardinal questions that the burgeoning field of law and religion has set out to answer. Nine major themes now dominate the academic study of law and religion.

First, by far the largest body of scholarship in law and religion is devoted to issues of religious freedom and religion-state relations in national and international contexts. This topic will continue to dominate the field in the foreseeable future. In the United States, this is in part the law of the First Amendment guarantees of no establishment and free exercise of religion and related statutes. In other Western lands, these questions are topics of special constitutional provisions, concordats, treaties, statutes, regulations, and cases. Several international human rights instruments also include religious-freedom norms, not least the 1950 European Convention, the 1966 International Covenant on Civil and Political Rights, and the 1981 UN Declaration on the Elimination of All Forms of Intolerance and of Discrimination Based on Religion and Belief.

The legal, theological, cultural, and personal issues arising under such provisions are perennial and profound. How to manage religious pluralism and protect religious and cultural minorities—particularly groups like Jews, Muslims, Jehovah's Witnesses, Bahai's, and Indigenous peoples, who often bring charges of private and state-based discrimination. How to define and set limits on religious and antireligious exercises and expressions that cause offense or harm to others or elicit charges of blasphemy, defamation, or sacrilege. How to adjudicate challenges that a state's laws run directly counter to a party's core claims of conscience or cardinal commandments of faith. How to balance private and public exercises of religion, including the liberty of conscience of one party to be left alone and the free exercise right of another to proselytize. How to balance conflicts between the rights of parents to bring up their children in the faith and the duties of the state to protect the best interest of the child. How to discern the proper place of religion in public, state schools, and the proper place of government in private, religious schools. How to protect the distinct religious needs of prisoners, soldiers, refugees, and others who do not enjoy ready access to traditional forms and forums of religious worship and expression.

Many issues of religious freedom also involve religious groups, for whom the right to organize as a legal entity with juridical personality is itself often the most critical first issue. But here, too, myriad other questions have reached national high courts and international tribunals: How to negotiate the complex needs and norms of religious groups without according them too much sovereignty over their members or too little relief from secular courts in the event of fundamental rights violations by religious officials. How to balance the rights of religious groups to self-determination and self-governance with the guarantees of freedom from discrimination based on religion, gender, culture, and sexual orientation. How to balance competing religious groups who each claim access to a common holy site, or a single religious or cultural group whose sacred site is threatened with desecration, development, or disaster. How to protect the relations between local religious communities and their foreign coreligionists. How to adjudicate intra- or interreligious disputes over property, contracts, or torts that come before secular tribunals for resolution. How to determine the proper levels of state cooperation with and support of religious officials and institutions in the delivery of child care, medical services, disaster relief, or humanitarian aid. How to define the lines of cooperation and jurisdiction between religious and political officials over fundamental institutions like the family, school, and charity that have both spiritual and secular dimensions for many citizens.

Second, and related, various scholars now focus on the (contested) place of religion and religious freedom in the pantheon of human rights. Several leading critical scholars today—jurists, historians, anthropologists, political theorists, and philosophers alike—argue that religion is too dangerous, divisive, and diverse in its demands to be accorded special protection. Claimants to freedom of conscience unfairly demand the right to be a law unto themselves, to the detriment of general laws and to the endangerment of other people's fundamental rights and legitimate interests. Institutional religious autonomy is too often just a special cover for abuses of power and forms of prejudice that should not be countenanced in any organization—religious or not. Claims of religious liberty are too often proxies for political or social agendas that deserve no more protection than any other agenda. Religion, these critics thus conclude, should be viewed as just another category of liberty or association, with no more preference or privilege than its secular counterparts. Religion should be treated as just another form of expression, subject to the same rules of rational democratic deliberation that govern other ideas and values. To accord religion any special protection or exemption discriminates against the nonreligious. To afford religion a special seat at the table of public deliberation or a special role in the implementation of government programs invites religious self-dealing.

By sharp contrast, a number of leading scholars argue that religion is a cornerstone of human rights, and that religious freedom is indispensable to constitutional order. Even in today's liberal societies, committed to policies of secularism, neutrality, or *laïcité*, religions still help to define the meanings and measures of shame and regret, restraint and respect, responsibility and restitution that a human-rights regime presupposes. Religions help to lay out and tie down the fundamentals of human dignity and human community, and the essentials of human nature, human capacities, and human needs upon which human rights are built. Moreover, religious organizations stand alongside the state and other institutions in helping to implement and protect the rights of a person and community—especially at times when the state is weak, distracted, divided, cash-strapped, transitioning, or corrupt. Religious communities can create the conditions (sometimes the prototypes) for the realization of civil and political rights of speech, press, assembly, and more. They can provide a critical (sometimes the principal) means of education, healthcare, childcare, labor organizations, employment, and artistic opportunities, among other things. And they offer some of the deepest insights into duties of stewardship and servanthood that lie at the heart of environmental care and the rights of nature. Several detailed empirical studies, Brian Grimm writes in a recent summary of this literature, have shown that the protection of "religious freedom in a country is strongly associated with other freedoms, including civil and political liberty, press freedom, and economic freedom, as well as with multiple measures of well-being"—less warfare and violence, better healthcare, higher levels of income, and better educational and social opportunities, especially for women, children, the disabled, and the poor.[11] By contrast, where religious freedom is low, communities tend to suffer and struggle, and protection of human rights dramatically declines across the board.

Third, the internal religious legal systems of the great world religions have also captured growing attention in law-and-religion scholarship—and worries, too, in some quarters. Each of these world religions—especially Christianity, Judaism, and Islam—has long had its own internal legal specialists. But their particular legal topics are now becoming more mainstream in departments of law, religion, sociology, history, and anthropology in research universities and in societies worldwide, with growing new attention to the place of law in various Asian and Indigenous traditions as well. Cambridge University Press, for example, has inaugurated a series of fresh studies on law and Christianity, Judaism, Islam, Hinduism, Buddhism, Confucianism, and Indigenous religions. Other books are beginning to emerge offering intra- and interreligious perspectives on discrete legal topics—human rights, family law, constitutionalism, private law, and more.

A major new issue that many Western democracies are now facing squarely is the place of faith-based laws, tribunals, and dispute resolution in secular legal regimes. How much deference do secular authorities owe to these religious authorities? How much involvement may secular authorities have in the adjudication of religious disputes and questions that come before them for resolution? These new questions join older questions about more overt state establishments

---

[11] Brian J. Grim, "Restrictions on Religion in the World: Measures and Implications," in *The Future of Religious Freedom: Global Challenges*, ed. Allen D. Hertzke (New York: Oxford University Press, 2013), 86, 101.

of forms of Christianity, Judaism, Islam, Shintoism, Confucianism, and other faith traditions. How do modern nations square their state establishment or privileging of one faith with the universal human-rights claims to religious freedom and equality for all?

Fourth, a small library of books has also emerged documenting the contributions of the world's religions and their religious legal systems to the secular legal systems around them, both historically and currently. Part of this inquiry concerns the exportation, transplantation, or accommodation of discrete internal religious rules or procedures into secular legal systems. But more of this inquiry concerns the influence of religious ideas and practices on the complex doctrines of public, private, penal, and procedural law of the state. In the Western tradition, numerous historians have documented the successive influences of Christianity on Roman law, Germanic law, medieval and early modern canon law, civil law, and the common law, and the eventual colonization of these efforts throughout the world. Similar work is now being done on the cross-cultural legal influences of the laws of Judaism, Hinduism, and Confucianism, and especially the tremendous influence of Islamic law on the secular laws of the current fifty-seven Muslim-majority states and their political predecessors. The reality in many parts of the world, including in the secular West, is that religious ideas and institutions, norms and practices are part of the foundation and infrastructure of the positive laws of the state.

Fifth, as part of these last two points, a large body of literature has grown around the perennially contested issues of law, religion, and family life. Three new questions are now attracting a great deal of new scholarly attention. The first question concerns the growing contests between religious liberty and sexual liberty. May a state require a minister to marry a gay or interreligious couple, a medical doctor to perform an elective abortion or assisted-reproductive procedure, or a pharmacist to fill a contraceptive prescription, when those required actions run counter to those parties' core claims of conscience or the central commandments of their faith? May a religious organization dismiss or discipline an official or member because of their sexual orientation or practice, or because they had a divorce or abortion? These are major points of contestation and litigation on both sides of the Atlantic and with likely implications for the field of global law and religion. A second question concerns religiously based polygamy. For nearly two millennia, the West has rejected polygamy, calling it a capital offense from the ninth to the nineteenth centuries. These issues are back, with various Muslims, Fundamentalist Mormons, and traditional religions and cultures in Asia and Africa pressing their case for toleration, if not recognition, of polygamy on grounds of religious freedom, sexual autonomy, domestic privacy, and equal protection. This issue, too, has triggered a small avalanche of writing.

A final question in this subfield of law, religion, and family concerns the growing call by religious minorities to opt out of the state's family-law system and into their own religious legal systems. This is raising a lot of hard legal and cultural questions: What forms of marriage should citizens be able to choose, and what forums of religious marriage law should state governments be required to respect? How should religious minorities with distinct family norms and cultural practices be accommodated in a society dedicated to religious liberty and self-determination, and to religious equality and nondiscrimination? Is legal or normative pluralism necessary to protect religious believers who are conscientiously opposed to the values that inform modern state laws on sex, marriage, and family? Doesn't state accommodation or implementation of a faith-based family-law system run the risk of higher gender discrimination, child abuse, coerced marriage, unchecked patriarchy, or worse, and how can these social tragedies be avoided? Won't the addition of a religious legal system encourage more forum shopping and legal manipulation by crafty litigants involved in domestic disputes, often pitting religious and state norms of family against each other? Does the very state recognition, accommodation, or implementation of a religious legal system erode the authority and compromise the integrity of those religious norms? Isn't strict separation of religious norms and state laws the best way to deal with the intimate questions of sex, marriage, and family life? These hard questions are generating a great deal of important new scholarship. Comparable complex work is addressing the issues of law and religion surrounding education, charity, poor-relief, immigration, environmental care, sex trafficking, warfare, torture, terrorism, and more.

Sixth, natural-law theory is becoming a topic of growing interest again, having once dominated patristic, medieval, and early modern Catholic, Protestant, and Enlightenment thought before giving way to modern legal positivism. The renaissance of natural-law theory in some Western academies began already in the mid-twentieth century. The horrible excesses of Nazi Germany and Stalinist Russia catalyzed the modern international human-rights revolution, which defined and defended the natural-rights protections of human dignity and the natural-law limits on state power. The rise of Catholic social teachings and the monumental reforms of the Second Vatican Council in 1962–65 together gave further powerful impetus to Catholic natural-law theories. A number of Jewish, Protestant, Eastern Orthodox, and Muslim scholars are now also resurrecting the rich natural-law teachings of their own traditions and developing new natural-law theories to address fundamental legal questions today in terms that others with different faith traditions can appreciate. All of these groups have found interesting overlaps with the burgeoning scholarship in religion and science that is exposing the natural foundations of human morality and sociability. Natural-law theory, while still controversial, is becoming a promising new arena of interreligious and interdisciplinary dialogue.

Seventh, natural-law arguments often inform a related area of continued importance in the study of law and religion: the topic of legal ethics, both by itself and in comparison with theological ethics, business ethics, medical ethics, and more. Legal and theological ethicists have long recognized the overlaps in form and function of the legal and religious professions. Both professions require extensive doctrinal training and maintain stringent admissions policies. Both have developed codes of professional ethics and internal structures of authority to enforce them. Both seek to promote cooperation, collegiality, and *esprit de corps*. There are close affinities between the mediation of the lawyer and the intercession of the cleric, between the adjudication of the court and the arbitration of the consistory, between the beneficence of the bar and the benevolence of the diaconate. Ideally, both professions serve and minister to society. Both professions seek to exemplify the ideals of calling and community. Nonetheless, there can be strong tensions between one's legal professional duties and personal faith convictions. What does it mean to be a Christian, Jewish, Muslim, Hindu, or Buddhist lawyer at work in a secular legal system? These topics have attracted a small cluster of important new scholarship.

Eighth, this last question—about the place of the religious believer in the legal profession—has raised the broader question of the place of overt religious arguments in legal discourse altogether. This is in part an epistemological question: whether legal and political argumentation can and should forgo religious and other comprehensive doctrines in the name of rationality and neutrality. In America, this is also in part a constitutional question: whether the First Amendment prohibition on establishment of religion requires that all laws be based on secular and neutral rationales in order to pass constitutional muster. In the heyday of secular liberalism and strict separationism in the twentieth century, it was common to insist that all political debates sound in terms of rationality and neutrality. Today, a number of scholars have argued that religious and other comprehensive doctrines are essential parts of an enduring legal and political morality.

Finally, questions of law and religious language, have also raised broader questions about the overlaps between legal and theological interpretation, translation, and hermeneutics. Legal historians have long been intrigued by the overlaps between the scholarly methods used to interpret the Bible and a constitution, a code and a creed, a consistory judgment and a judicial opinion. The rise of modern literary theory and of form-critical methods of biblical interpretation has heightened this scholarly interest in how to discern the original meaning and understanding of authoritative texts. And with the rise of globalization and the study of global law and world religions, a number of jurists have become keenly interested in the questions of translation, transplantation, and transmutation of legal and religious ideas across cultural, disciplinary, and denominational boundaries.

Summary and Conclusions

In the past three decades, religion has defied the wistful assumptions of the Western academy that the spread of Enlightenment reason and science would slowly eclipse the sense of the sacred and cure the sensibilities of the superstitious. Religion has also defied the evil assumptions of twentieth-century Nazis, fascists, and communists alike that gulags and death camps, iconoclasm and book burnings, propaganda and mind controls would inevitably drive religion into extinction. Religion has proved to be an ineradicable condition of human lives and communities—however forcefully a society might seek to repress or deny its value or validity, however cogently the academy might logically bracket it from its legal and political calculus. A new great awakening of religion is upon us, demanding attention from many quarters, not least from the Western academy.

In the past three decades, law, too, has moved beyond the skeptical and cynical attacks of its critics, not least law professors themselves. In the heyday of critical legal studies in the last century, legal skeptics assailed much that seemed sound, settled, and even sacred in the law. They dismissed legal doctrine as malleable, self-contradictory rhetoric. They depicted the law as an instrument of oppression and exploitation of women, of minorities, of the poor, of the different. They derided the legal system for its promotion of the economic and political purposes of the powerful and the propertied. This assault from within the law, and especially from within the legal academy, eventually sparked a spiritual crisis of the legal profession. It forced legal professionals to reform laws that did cause injustice but also compelled them to return to the fundamentals of a just and sound legal order. This return to legal fundamentals has been further spurred by the seismic legal and political challenges of the new millennium, both at home and abroad. Western lawyers and legal academics alike have had to tend with renewed alacrity to the foundational values of rule of law, constitutional democracy, ordered liberty, and orderly pluralism.

This resurgence of focus on the fundamentals of religion and law, separately and together, has been a boon to the Western academy and to Western liberal societies. As the founders of the Western academy saw a millennium ago, religion and law are two universal solvents of human living, two interlocking sources and systems of values and beliefs that have existed, in dialectic tension, in all axial civilizations. Unlike a millennium ago, when law and religion dominated the first Western universities, several other sources and systems of values now command close study, for they provide deep normative coding and direction for persons and peoples to navigate their lives. Included are the normative systems and institutions of families and friendships, markets and economies, charities and schools, science and research, healthcare and security systems, and more.

All of these modern spheres and institutions, however, ultimately need law to guard and guide them. Aristotle saw this already when he wrote:

"Just as man is the best of the animals when completed, when separated from law and adjudication he is the worst of all."[12] American founder James Madison saw it too: "If men were angels, no government would be necessary. If angels were to govern men, neither external nor internal controls ... would be necessary.... [B]ut experience has taught mankind the necessity of auxiliary precautions."[13]

American Supreme Court justice Oliver Wendell Holmes Jr. underscored this reality anew when he wrote: "All the great questions of theology and philosophy [and society and culture] must ultimately come to law for their resolution."[14] Holmes's claim, while provocatively overstated, has merit. While our theologians and philosophers debate questions of the origin, nature, and purpose of life and society, and while our social, cultural, and economic leaders work out the best norms and policies, it is jurists and judges who settle these questions and resolutions in cases and statutes, codes and conventions.

All of these modern spheres ultimately need religion to inspire and instruct them. Religion not only helps interpret "the law written on our hearts" (Romans 2:15) but also helps apply the law written on the books. As Martin Marty has documented, religions deal uniquely with the deepest elements of individual and social life. Religions catalyze social, intellectual, and material exchanges among citizens. They trigger economic, charitable, and educational impulses in citizens. They provide valuable checks and counterpoints to social and individual excess. They help diffuse social and political crises and absolutisms by relativizing everyday life and its institutions. Religions provide prophecy, criticism, and exemplars for society. They force others to examine their presuppositions. They are distinct repositories of tradition, wisdom, and perspective. They counsel against apathy. They often represent practiced and durable sources and forms of community. They provide leadership and hope, especially in times of individual and social crisis. They contribute to the theory and practice of the common good. Religions represent the unrepresented, teach stewardship and preservation, provide fresh starts for the desperate, and exalt the dignity and freedom of the individual.[15] No religion, of course, lives up to all these claims all the time. Some religions never do, and a few even work hard to destroy these goods. But these private and public goods offered by most organized religions argue strongly for the continued study

---

[12] Aristotle, *Politics*, bk. 1, chap. 2, 1253a31–33.
[13] *The Federalist Papers*, No. 51.
[14] Quoted in Albert W. Alschuler, *Law without Values: The Life, Work, and Legacy of Justice Holmes* (Chicago: University of Chicago Press, 2000), 54, 73.
[15] See Martin E. Marty and Jonathan Moore, *Politics, Religion, and the Common Good: Advancing a Distinctly American Conversation about Religion's Role in Our Shared Life* (San Francisco: Jossey-Bass, 2000).

of religion alongside law in shaping character, values, and morality in late modern differentiated societies.

Emergence of Truth
The Interplay of Science and Theology in Genesis 1 and Psalm 104

Andreas Schüle

Science and the Issue of "Impact"

Oftentimes, premodern societies, including the world of antiquity, are also called prescientific societies. While people have always attempted to probe the world in which they lived and to look behind the curtain of what experience taught them, it is a genuinely modern achievement to have established science as an independent system of inquiry and knowledge. Clearly, the title of this volume presupposes this modern development, since it asks about the impact of science on other areas of social life—as, for example, education. The language of "impact" presupposes that science, on one hand, and the realm of values, moral ideas, and visions of the good life, on the other, do not necessarily walk hand in hand; rather, their relationship needs to be negotiated, and the outcome of these negotiations appears to be largely unpredictable. There is no guarantee that, compared to premodern times, scientific knowledge renders a society morally more refined, equips it with better judgment, or helps to provide well-rounded education. The exact opposite is equally conceivable, and one might argue that the current state of large portions of the modern world provides proof that science is not a one-way ticket to salvation.

There is definitely a way of measuring scientific progress over the course of human history. The things we know about the world and what we can do within it have dramatically increased. But things are not quite as obvious in other areas. Has humankind become more humane? Will the longer lives that most of us will be able to enjoy increase only the quantity of life or also its quality, not only for us as individuals but for the communities in which we live? What would be the criteria for asserting that we are in a "better" place than the people of previous cultures and civilizations? Our lives may be more comfortable and, to some extent, more secure, but is that what life is all about?

Turning to my own field, Old Testament and biblical studies, we are clearly not dealing with anything modern. By any of today's standards, the world of the Bible was prescientific. It was not, however, nonscientific. It is a cliché to assume that people back then were caught up in a mythical worldview that kept them essentially naive and under the veil of prejudice and ignorance until, in more enlightened ages, the darkness was finally lifted. If one looks at the world of the Old Testament, one can observe scientific progress in all areas of life: architecture, metal construction, farming, mining, geography, geology, astronomy, and many more ologies. People then did know that the earth wasn't flat, although they could talk about it that way as the world of everyday experience, very much in the same way we do today. They did not have microscopes and telescopes to venture deep into the world beyond human sight, and that may be the most striking difference to modern times. But even without these instruments, the people of antiquity sought, for example, to understand the difference between living things and dead matter, and they were certainly not satisfied by giving prescribed religious answers to probing questions.

In more recent research, scholar across the fields of ancient Near Eastern studies and antiquities have observed an increasing interest in what one might call natural philosophy, beginning roughly in the eighth century BCE. Greece may be the most obvious case, but Mesopotamia and the Levant are also places from which we have textual evidence that new modes of inquiry about the natural/ physical world were developed and tested.[1] If one reads the so-called creation texts of the Old Testament carefully, one can hardly avoid being reminded of certain schools of thought from the Aegean. What may make it sometimes difficult for a contemporary audience to understand these efforts is that the ancient world was guided by an objective that I would call simultaneous progress. By this I mean that changes in one social system were expected to trigger corresponding effects in other social systems as well. Very generally speaking, people were convinced that things they considered to be right or true had to resonate with more than one aspect of social life. It is probably an overstatement when Niklas Luhmann and others have claimed that only the modern world has achieved a sufficient degree of what Luhmann calls "uncoupling."[2] By this he means that different societal systems, at some point, were allowed to roam free, as it were. The ancient world was not as far "behind" in terms of its vigor of inquiry as we sometimes tend to assume. However, while we are familiar and even comfortable with the idea of different and potentially conflicting rationalities and multiple truths, the ancient world was not. For the world of antiquity, scientific progress was somewhat unreal, unreliable, or simply irrelevant, as long as it did not connect with other areas of life; and the same was true, of course, for religious or moral claims, which did not make any sense unless they seemed reasonable from a scientific point of view.

---

[1] Ephraim A. Speiser, "Ancient Mesopotamia and the Beginning of Science," *The Scientific Monthly* 55 (1942): 159–67.

[2] Niklas Luhmann, *Die Gesellschaft der Gesellschaft* (Frankfurt a. M.: Suhrkamp, 1997), 92–120.

Put differently, the expectation was that the various aspects of societal life and human knowledge advance together; and it may be this sense of distinct yet interlocking societal systems that marks in fact the gap between the modern world and the world of antiquity. It would have been confusing to someone from the ancient world to think about how, to use the title of this volume, natural science might impact ethics or religion. The language of impact suggests a level of disconnect and even loss of common understanding, which to avoid was among the primary goals of ancient societies.

Science and Theology in the Old Testament

I will use two texts from the Old Testament that illustrate the mutual discourse between science and theology: the famous account of creation in Genesis 1 and a less well-known, albeit equally important, creation psalm, Psalm 104. As I will try to show, these texts seek to be both scientifically informed theology and theologically informed science. This alone may not be particularly surprising. It is striking, however, that Genesis 1 and Psalm 104 (which, chronologically, may be a century or more apart from each other), differ greatly with regard to their theology and their scientific assumptions about the world. Genesis 1 depicts an ontological hierarchy, moving from dead matter to plants, animals, and finally human beings as images of God. In contrast, Psalm 104 entertains a much more holistic view of the cosmos with a panentheistic deity that sets the rhythm of all life, a view that to some extent even contradicts the notion that humans are any closer to the deity than other entities. It is clear that both the science and the theology behind Psalm 104 are vastly different from the science and theology that inform Genesis 1. But this is precisely what might indicate that there was in fact a very close connection between scientific and theological progress. One would not be true without the other, which in turn meant that neither one could claim truth and superiority over the other.

The Science behind Genesis 1:1–2:3

In narrative form, Gen 1:1–2:3 depicts God as the ultimate cause behind the created world.[3] God brings things into existence and assigns them their respective

---

[3] For recent work on the cosmology of Genesis 1 and the primeval history, see Mark S. Smith, *The Priestly Vision of Creation* (Minneapolis: Fortress Press, 2010); John Walton, *The Lost World of Genesis One: Ancient Cosmology and the Origin Debate* (Downers Grove, IL: InterVarsity Press, 2009); and Gordon Wenham, *Rethinking Genesis 1-11: Gateway to the Bible* (Eugene, OR: Wipf and Stock, 2015).

purposes. All of this occurs in a rather hands-on fashion. God is architect, craftsman, and artisan. So it comes as no surprise that the cosmos that God makes resembles a building under a giant crystal dome. A closer look, however, reveals that God's level of involvement varies across the different works of creation. One pattern seems to be that God simply mandates that something occur in the world. The dry land is supposed to bring forth vegetation (Genesis 1:11–12). Apparently, the assumption is that this does not require any additional effort on God's part. In other cases, however, God is depicted as a craftsman who devises a design for each of his works and makes them accordingly. This is the case with the firmament and the stars as the basic material items relating to time and space (Genesis 1:6–7).

As far as living beings as the actual focus of creation are concerned, there is yet another pattern, which involves a coworking of sorts. First, God commands that the seas bring forth water animals and that the earth produce land animals (Genesis 1:20–21, 24–25). The idea seems to be that earth and water are vital forces with enough creative power to bring forth certain forms of life. While this suffices for plants, it is not quite enough for more complex beings, such as fishes, birds, and land animals. So in these cases God, too, is depicted as the one who actively participates in the creation process. While the text does not go into any details, the context suggests that God commissions the elements to bring forth "raw forms" that then, through God's own doing, become living creatures. Here, God is not so much a craftsman as an artisan who creates not just entities but the wealth of forms, colors, movements, and sounds that everyone readily associates with the animal kingdom.

With the creation of humankind, the priestly text takes a consequential next step because, unlike with plants and animals, God is now presented as the only creative source responsible for the occurrence of human beings. There is no calling on the primordial elements to assist in the making of humans; rather, God calls upon himself or his heavenly assembly ("Let us make ...": Genesis 1:26) to create humankind. This is consistent with what we know about the making of divine images in ancient Mesopotamia, since only the gods themselves could create their cultic images and accept them into their midst.[4]

These distinctions that the priestly text uses for its cosmology establish an ontological hierarchy.[5] The level of involvement on God's part seems to correlate with the importance that the different entities have. Strikingly, Genesis 1 is the only text in the entire Hebrew Bible that establishes such a clear ontological

---

[4] Catherine L. McDowell, *The Image of God and the Garden of Eden: The Creation of Humankind in Genesis 2:5–3:24 in Light of mīs pî, pīt pî and wpt-r Rituals of Mesopotamia and Ancient Egypt* (Winona Lake, IN: Eisenbrauns, 2015).

[5] Andreas Schüle, *Theology from the Beginning: Essays on the Primeval History in its Canonical Context*, FAT 113 (Tübingen: Mohr Siebeck, 2017).

scheme. It is likely that the authors did not find this in their own, traditional ways of thinking about creation, but that they were in dialogue especially with natural philosophy as it emerged in the philosophical schools of the Greek world. This is not the place to go into any discussion about the connections between the Levant and the Aegean around the middle of the first millennium BCE. It is a safe assumption, however, that from a certain point onward, science was used as a vehicle to communicate religious beliefs and belief systems across cultural spaces. Clearly, the authors of Genesis 1 intended to articulate their understanding of the world as created by a single God in ways that resonated with views that apparently were seen as attractive, innovative, and scientifically state-of-the-art. This is a clear example of the conviction that religion and science had to advance together, and that any uncoupling of the two would make them both unreasonable or even untrue.

Psalm 104—a General Overview

Let us turn to another example of a biblical text that demonstrates the same effort to locate science and theology in the same intellectual and spiritual realms. Psalm 104 has received much attention as one of the preeminent creation texts of the Hebrew Bible.[6] Together with Genesis 1–2, Job 38–41, and some passages of Second Isaiah, Psalm 104 seems to have been composed as a text that describes creation from a naturalistic point of view. It develops an understanding of nature in all its complexity, comprising patterns of time and space, matter and living beings, and it ties all of this to the presence of God. While Psalm 104 characterizes God as the maker of all the things in existence, the focus is not so much on the genesis of the world (with the exception of verses 5–9) but, for the most part, on its vitality and the variegated rhythms of life that permeate it: grass grows, birds nest, the wild animals come out at night, humans go about their work during the day. This shift from cosmogony to cosmology might indicate that Psalm 104 was deliberately composed as a continuation of Genesis 1 (and 2).

God and the Elements

The first depiction of God in Psalm 104 presents him as wrapped up in light (verses 1–2):

---

[6] Thomas Krüger, "'Kosmo-theologie' zwischen Mythos und Erfahrung: Psalm 104 im Horizont alttestamentlicher und altorientalischer' Schöpfungs'-Konzepte," in *Biblische Notizen* 68 (1994): 49–74.

> You are clothed with honor and majesty,
> wrapped in light as with a garment.

This is not simply a way of applying garment language to God's outer appearance. The Hebrew word for "garment" here has two semantic characteristics: it is mostly used in connection with a mantle, cloak, or robe, which typically formed the top layer of clothing.[7] The other characteristic is that "wrapping" is oftentimes understood as "concealing," "covering up," or "hiding" (Leviticus 13:45; Ezekiel 24:17, 22; Micah 3:7), the idea being that someone who is "wrapped up" would be only partially visible or not visible at all.[8]

Taken together, these two characteristics indicate that light is an aura surrounding the deity and that light, while a strong indication of divine presence, hides God's inner being from an outside world. Is this more or less a metaphorical expression, meaning that, if one could fathom God, then his appearance would be that of a person wrapped in a mantle of light? Or is "light" here the actual light that permeates the world of creation—the light that everyone can see and feel? This is a pertinent question because in all other cases, verses 2–4 list elements that in fact belong to the empirical world: clouds, wind, and fire. Especially wind and fire as God's servants and messengers are tangible elements and, as such, connect the sphere of divine presence with the natural world as the habitat of plants, animals, and humans. Or to put it differently, where there is light, or wind, or fire, there is also God in the vicinity.

The psalmist, however, is careful not to equate God with these elements. Light is the mantle, fire and winds are the servants, so there is a clear sense that God's own being transcends the elemental and natural world. Yet while this sense of difference is maintained throughout the psalm, it seems clear that Psalm 104 seeks to associate divine vitality with the powers of nature. While this would also be true for Levantine weather and storm gods, Psalm 104 goes a crucial step beyond this paradigm. While the God of Psalm 104 is in charge of watering the ground from below and above, he is also the god of the basic elements, even before the created world emerges. This omnipresence does not even exclude those elements that other cosmological accounts assign to the hostile spheres that tend to resist divine governance: water and darkness (cf. Genesis 1:1–3).[9]

---

[7] The root is not used in connection with shirts, skirts, or other garments that belong to the bottom layer and would typically have immediate skin contact (1 Samuel 28:14; Isaiah 59:17).

[8] In negative contexts, "wrapping" can be used to depict someone who is completely covered over with shame and disgrace (Psalms 71:13; 89:45; 109:29).

[9] There are only very subdued traces of such a cosmological antagonism, because God "rebukes" the waters (verse 7) so that they withdraw from what is about to become arable land. However, a single word or gesture seems to be enough to put the waters in their

God's "Spirit"

It is certainly no coincidence that at the end of its cosmological account, Psalm 104 culminates in hymnic praise of God as the one who not only establishes the conditions of life but also gives and takes life (verses 29–30).

> When you hide your face, they are terrified;
> When you take away their breath/spirit, they die and return to their dust.
> When you send out your breath/spirit, they are created and so you replenish the face of the earth.

These verses begin in a manner not unfamiliar from other psalms. The hiding of the face is a motif that frequently occurs in lament psalms to express grief (Psalms 10:1; 69:17). When God hides, life deteriorates. The setting for the notion the God hides his face is typically the temple cult. The temple is the place where God's face can be "seen," although seeing might be a metaphorical expression for perceiving the presence of God, rather than seeing an actual physical appearance.

Psalm 104 takes up this language but also immediately translates it into a different setting. The way in which divine presence and absence are now perceived is the giving and taking away of "breath" or "spirit" (the Hebrew word can have both connotations), as that which enlivens animals and humans living. There is a sense of ultimate dependence, because, according to Psalm 104, all living beings are not just dependent on God's care, they also know that life is something that they have received rather than something that they own. Life is sustained by food and water, but life itself is something that God gives and withdraws. This giving and taking is certainly not anything that Psalm 104 sees as something that God decides for each living entity. As part of the natural order, the movement of spirit is something that we, today, might call the natural life span.

There are, however, some exegetical problems here that may at least be mentioned. It is not entirely clear how God's own spirit relates to the one that humans have. According to verse 29, God takes away the spirit of the living beings. This statement points to a familiar concept in ancient Near Eastern anthropology that humans (rather than animals) consist of two components, a material body and a pneumatic life substance that symbiotically coexist until a person dies. The assumption was that a physical body alone would not be sufficient to reach the level of a living organism. This requires another component that permeates the physical structure and infuses it with life.

---

place. In the case of darkness, there is no potential for chaos at all anymore. Rather, God creates darkness so that there is night for the wild animals to hunt (verse 20).

Looking only at verse 29, one would be led to assume that Psalm 104 is indebted to this common understanding of life and death in the ancient Near East.[10] Such a concept would work quite well in the case of Psalm 104, because spirit then would be among the things that God provides for his creatures to be able to live. Verse 29 would then be a fitting conclusion to verses 27–28: God nourishes his creatures with "good things," which they gather up when given. In the same way, God gives spirit and takes it away again when the lifespan of an entity comes to a close.

Verse 30, however, adds a crucial layer to this familiar scheme. Here, it is explicitly God's own spirit that God "sends out" to replenish/make new the face of the earth. Exegetes have always sensed a certain tension between this verse and verse 29. It is not altogether transparent how the human spirit relates to God's. This tension has led exegetes to omit either verse 29 or verse 30 as a secondary addition. While this tension may in fact be due to literary growth, one should not jump to redaction criticism too quickly. It is at least conceivable that "spirit" in verses 29 and 30 means two different things. Verse 29, as just noted, delineates the binary anatomy of a living being. Verse 30, on the other hand, aims at something far more comprehensive: when God sends out his spirit, living beings are "created." The Hebrew root *bārā* (to create, one of the key terms in Genesis 1) is used only once in Psalm 104, precisely to describe the work that God's own spirit does.[11] This use of particularly poignant language suggests that God's spirit creates everything that pertains to life—physical bodies, life forces, and the rhythm of life itself. God's spirit is responsible for the ebb and flow of life, for living and dying, or, in the words of verse 30b, the spirit "replenishes the face of the earth."

Understood in this way, Psalm 104 is, in fact, an update of traditional creation language.[12] In its own way, it underscores what is also crucial in Genesis 1: there is only one God as the origin of everything that is. There are also differences, however: in Genesis 1, God is depicted as a fairly hands-on craftsman and artisan who fashions the material universe, as well as the world of plants and living entities. Yet while all of creation is God's work, nothing in it—with the exception of humankind—is associated with God's own being. This is where Psalm 104 goes a crucial step further. Through his spirit, God permeates the world as the very essence of life.

---

[10] Annette Krüger, "Himmel–Erde–Unterwelt: Kosmologische Entwürfe in der poetischen Literatur Israels," in *Das biblische Weltbild und seine altorientalischen Kontexte*, FAT 32, ed. Bernd Janowski and Beate Ego (Tübingen: Mohr Siebeck, 2001), 65-83.

[11] Hermann Spieckermann, *Heilsgegenwart: Eine Theologie der Psalmen*, FRLANT 148 (Göttingen: Vandenhoeck & Ruprecht, 1989), 21-49.

[12] See, in greater detail, Pierre Auffret, *Note sur la structure littéraire du Psaume 104 et ses incidences pour une comparaison avec l'hymne à Aton et Genèse 1* (Strasbourg: Université des sciences humains de Strasbourg, 1982).

In a variety of ways, Psalm 104 presents itself as the boldest of all creation texts by associating God so closely with the world of creation. For a parallel, one might think of Isaiah 55:10–11, where it is the "word" of God that goes out, enters into the world, accomplishes its task, and returns to God. One does find images from nature here (the word is compared to snow and rain), and in fact, some of the imagery of Isaiah 55 is reminiscent of the language in Psalm 104. There is a sense of the deep and profound impact that God's mediated presence can have on the physical (and intellectual) world. However, Psalm 104 makes a much stronger claim than Isaiah 55, because the spirit not only exercises God's will but is also a part of God's own being that resides in every living entity.

If one now combines verses 29–30 with verses 2–4, the unique theology of Psalm 104 is cast in sharp relief. The creator is closely associated with the elements that make up the fabric of the material word—wind, fire, water—and even with life itself. Since there is no other text in the Old Testament that pushes creation theology in a similar direction, it is likely that Psalm 104 should be seen as in dialogue with natural philosophies of the time. As in Genesis 1, there is no way of knowing what exactly inspired Psalm 104's perception of the divine being within nature. But one can at least point to the pre-Socratic schools and their emphasis on the elements, beginning with Thales of Miletus down to Empedocles, who provided perhaps the most influential account of the four elements (earth, air, water, and fire), and who even associated the elements with the high gods of Greece.[13]

However, Psalm 104, which starts out as a traditional hymn but in fact presents itself as a piece of natural philosophy, does not merely mimic the spirit of the time, as it were. By embracing scientific and philosophical positions, it also defends certain key beliefs of early Jewish religion: a monotheistic world view and the prohibition of idols. As closely as God is associated with the elements, Psalm 104 establishes and maintains careful distinctions: light is (only) God's garment, the clouds are his vehicle, and the winds and fire are his servants.

In both Genesis 1 and Psalm 104, the dialogue between science and theology is certainly a way of negotiating potentially conflicting truth claims. However, these texts also testify to an enormous amount of intellectual creativity and even playfulness. One would not do these texts justice if one thought of them as attempts to establish dogma. Rather, the interplay of scientific and theological ideas and conviction opens up a sphere of imagination and insight that neither theology nor science could have achieved on its own ground.

---

[13] See the excellent entry on Empedocles in the *Stanford Encyclopedia of Philosophy*, https://plato.stanford.edu/entries/empedocles/.

Forming Identity by Scripture

Stefan Alkier

The Interplay of Signs

Before learning to speak, children already inhabit semiotic worlds. The individual's encyclopedic knowledge is built up not only by verbal language but also by the development of semiotic abilities in the mother's womb. These abilities include the recognition of rhythms, sounds, and movements. After birth, touch, smell, taste, and sight develop. Yet the flexibility of verbal language and its communicative as well as cognitive performance give it pride of place in the appreciation of the various sign systems used by humans, at the expense of researching the semiotic complexity of human perception and thinking abilities. This privileging of language in turn has led to a narrowed view of the synesthesia of oral and written communication. The phenomena of human communication and culture have tended therefore to be viewed too one-sidedly from the perspective of an idealized and, at the same time, isolated verbal language creation. However, both the poststructuralist critique of the logocentrism of Western intellectual history and semiotic research since the end of the 1960 s especially have abandoned the specific efficiency of other sign systems and the medial complexity of culture and have led to a more complex view of the connection between oral and written verbal language with other sign systems.

In the course of increased sensitivity to the meaning of (primarily) nonverbal semiotic objects, such as paintings, clothing, sculptures, buildings, city maps, and so on, research into material objects and their significance for the formation of cultures has also advanced in biblical studies. Archaeological research plays a key role here if it is prepared to reflect theoretically on its semiotic foundations and to overcome its precritical attitude toward its objects.[1]

---

[1] See Stefan Alkier and Jürgen Zangenberg, "Zeichen aus Text und Stein. Ein semiotisches Konzept zur Verhältnisbestimmung von Archäologie und Exegese," in *Zeichen aus Text und Stein. Studien auf dem Weg zu einer Archäologie des Neuen Testaments*, Texte und Arbeiten zum neutestamentlichen Zeitalter 42 (Tübingen: Francke, 2003), 21–62. Also: Ian

Intermedial research within the framework of a categorically, semiotically anchored study of the New Testament takes coins, tombs, temples, statues, and other material phenomena as signs, which are subject to the same formal conditions as all signs. In doing so, however, such research takes the specific possibilities and limits of the different media into account, without playing them off against each other or assigning them to ontological hierarchies. Signs made of stone are no less real than texts. Shards do not directly transport their interpreters into the past any less than characters. All signs contribute to the opening up of reality if they are interpreted appropriately, and no sign has an ontological priority.

Only if culture is understood as the intermedial interaction of different sign systems, functioning within the biophysical basis of human senses and the objects perceived by them, can the formatting of culture—to which religions contribute significantly with their sign products and receptions—be adequately researched. Intermedial research deals with effects of meaning that arise from the interplay of different media. One should speak of intermediality only if there is an interest in researching the effects of meaning that arise through the relationship of at least one medium with another medium that is different from it—namely, effects that neither of the two media opens up on its own. This paradigm of intermediality works in both directions. The sense potential of both media is changed by the intermedial reference. Since, however, a medium maintains or can be related not only to one but to many other media, intermediality has to do with the exploration of the decentralization of meaning through the interplay of different media. Meaning is rarely centered in only one of the sign systems but emerges in the interplay of a variety of media.

Additional sign systems must also, however, be identified. Haptic signs feel the world and even enable blind people to read by means of their sense of touch. The sense of taste and smell form the biophysical basis of other sign systems. All senses are involved in the everyday use of signs. The interaction of the senses forms the biophysical basis of all sign use. The senses are organs of perception that make communication possible in the first place. Without them, no signs can be formed, and we owe the plurality of human sign production and reception to them. People can think without verbal language, but not without signs.

All signs need a material body that the senses can grasp. Only what can be perceived can assume a sign function. However, the various senses do not work in isolation from each other. Rather, the senses are at work simultaneously in every act of perception that forms a sign, even if one or the other sense is always in the foreground.

Hodder, *Reading the Past: Current Approaches to Interpretation in Archaeology*, 2nd. ed. (Cambridge: Cambridge University Press, 1991).

If, for example, reading a book engages the eyes, it also involves the sense of touch. The hands touch the pages to turn them. Books have an aroma, which one can experience particularly acutely in libraries with old books. It is not uncommon to experience a certain taste when reading. Even posture plays a role in reading. Working with a book at a desk requires a different posture than reading a comic in the bathtub.

Cornelia Funke has explored the synesthesia of signs in her novel *Tintenherz*. The character Meggie, like her father, Mo, has the ability to read figures and objects from books and to transport them into her own world when they are read with all her senses:

> "Since she could think, she remembered this movement—when he took a book in his hand, stroked it almost tenderly over the cover and then opened it, it was as if he opened a box filled to the brim with treasures never seen before."[2]
>
> "'Taste every word, Meggie,' Mos's voice whispered in her mind, 'Let it melt on your tongue. Taste the colors. Do you taste the wind and the night? The fear and the joy? Taste it, Meggie, and everything comes to life.'"[3]

Because of the biophysical conditions of any sign use, epistemological, hermeneutical, and didactic conceptions must take into account these complex semiotic foundations of any symbolic process. Although the various types of signs can and must be explored in their respective ways of functioning, the work of semiotic analysis and understanding is not finished with this task. The world in which people live is opened up by the synesthetic use of sign systems through various media. Not only culture,[4] understood as the world shaped by human beings, but also nature is opened up by means of signs.[5]

Characters and pictograms can therefore be distinguished on the basis of their respective specific sign systems, but to play them off against each other misunderstands their common semiotic basis. All signs are subject to formal conditions, which are discussed as the grammar, logic, and rhetoric of signs in the categorial semiotics of Charles Sanders Peirce.[6] While structuralist and poststructuralist semiotics remain committed to the binary sign model of Ferdinand de

---

[2] Cornelia Funke, *Tintenherz* (Hamburg: Dressler, 2003), 532. In English, *Inkheart*, trans. Anthea Bell (New York: Scholastic/Chicken House, 2003).

[3] Ibid., 539.

[4] See Umberto Eco, *A Theory of Semiotics* (Bloomington: Indiana University Press, 1976), 28–31.

[5] See Carl R. Hausman, *Charles S. Peirce's Evolutionary Philosophy* (Cambridge: Cambridge University Press, 1997).

[6] See James Jakób Liszka, *A General Introduction to the Semeiotic of Charles Sanders Peirce* (Bloomington: Indiana University Press, 1996).

Saussure, categorial semiotics—mediated among others by Charles Morris and Umberto Eco[7]—works with the triadic sign model that Peirce formed on the basis of his category theory. Therefore, categorial-semiotic exegesis understands texts as sign contexts whose intratextual, intertextual, and intermedial relations must be examined syntagmatically, semantically, and pragmatically. Approached this way, biblical studies receive a sound theoretical basis. New Testament research becomes the study of the production and reception of early Christian sign contexts under the conditions and realities of the contemporary world and communicative practices that the early Christians inhabited.[8]

Make Stories

The acquisition of verbal language is necessarily a creative process. It introduces one to a universe of innumerable text worlds, all of which are somehow linked or at least connectable, but in an unmanageable and ultimately uncontrollable way. Parents, siblings, grandparents, uncles, aunts, girlfriends, friends, educators tell stories about their own birth and the course of their own lives, but they also tell stories about family members or friends who have already died, and even stories of events or people from before they were born. Children learn to live with language from the very beginning by engaging with stories which, to a large extent, form their own identity. They hear fairy tales and sing songs in equal measure. Picture books, audio books, television, and streaming services tell completely different stories that take place in worlds that look different, and to which others and other things belong than the people and things of the everyday world the children have experienced. Exciting, strange, uncanny worlds of adventure from different times and places belong, like children's own everyday world, to the developing encyclopedia of preschool and primary school children, who only gradually learn to distinguish fantastic worlds from their own world of experience. Not only stories from the children's own experience in the real world but also all stories that become theirs in the process of reception from foreign cultures and their own culture have an identity-forming effect. This phenomenon applies not only to the Passover narrative in Judaism or the parables of Jesus in Christianity, but also

---

[7] See Umberto Eco, *Lector in Fabula. Die Mitarbeit der Interpretaton in erzählenden Texten* (Munich: Hanser, 1987).

[8] See Stefan Alkier, "Neutestamentliche Wissenschaft—Ein semiotisches Konzept," in *Kultur, Politik, Religion, Sprache—Text. Wolfgang Stegemann zum 60. Geburtstag*, Kontexte der Schrift, 2nd ed., ed. Christian Strecker (Stuttgart: Kohlhammer, 2005), 343-60; as well as the extended translation in Stefan Alkier, Richard Hays, and Leroy Huizenga, eds., *Reading the Bible Intertextually* (Waco, TX: Baylor University Press, 2009), 223-48.

to stories about superheroes, whenever children, adolescents, and adults are especially affected by them.

"Stories create images."[9] This is true not only when artists translate characters to other media, such as paintings, sculptures, or films. Rather, every reading of a story creates a cinema in the mind. The question of the relationship between text and image arises not only on the level of intermedial research but also in intratextual work, because reading is far more than the passive juxtaposition of abstract signs. This highly complex cultural technique demands creativity, deductive thinking, and cultural knowledge, and in this way the universe of discourse of the text opens up. The term "universe of discourse" refers to the world of the text, which sets and presupposes it.[10]

Due to the economy of signs, however, texts do not say everything that is necessary for the constitution of the universe of discourse required for the act of reading. Readers always have to bring encyclopedic knowledge that they have already acquired to the task of rendering the signs with imaginary images. The less cultural knowledge one brings to the task, the more difficult it is to build a coherent whole out of abstract signs. The more such encyclopedic knowledge one has, the more differentiated and pleasurable the production of meaning in reading will be.

The text's universe of discourse is significantly opened up by the encyclopedic knowledge of the reader. This knowledge, in turn, is acquired and extended in a differentiated way through the reception of narrated stories. Written stories continue to form an essential repository of cultural knowledge.

The economy of stories is not the only reason their characters cannot say everything. The boundaries of their media also require economy. Thus, stories can describe the sound of a voice and even indicate the way in which a character speaks. Stage directions in the text editions of plays supply necessary information for rendering such aspects of a story. They direct the imagination of the readers. They cannot, however, produce the sound of the voice themselves. Texts do not speak. Speech requires the voice of actors or the voice created by each reader in imagination. Reading is an act of creation guided by written signs.

---

[9] Stefan Alkier and Stefanie E. Karweick, "'So hab' ich Jesus ja noch nie erlebt!' Die so genannte 'Tempelreinigung' in der sechsten Klasse einer Realschule," in *"Man hat immer ein Stück Gott in sich." Mit Kindern biblische Geschichten deuten*, Jahrbuch für Kindertheologie Sonderband, vol. 2: *Neues Testament*, ed. Gerhard Büttner and Martin Schreiner (Stuttgart: Calwer Verlag, 2006), 150–67, at 150.

[10] See Stefan Alkier, *Wunder und Wirklichkeit in den Briefen des Apostels Paulus. Ein Beitrag zu einem Wunderverständnis jenseits von Entmythologisierung und Rehistorisierung*, Wissenschaftliche Untersuchungen zum Neuen Testament 134 (Tübingen: Mohr Siebeck, 2001), 74–79.

A sign alone does not yet make a text: *"The signs always stand in relation to other signs, they never exist alone*, except from a purely theoretical point of view."[11] Even a mere juxtaposition of signs does not result in a text. A collection of signs creates the impression of a coherent whole only if these signs have been or can be organized syntagmatically, semantically, and pragmatically in such a way as to generate meaning.

> For us, textuality is not an inherent property of verbal objects. A producer or a recipient regards a verbal object as text if he believes that this verbal object is a coherent and complete whole that corresponds to an actual or assumed communicative intention in an actual or assumed communication situation. A text is—according to semiotic terminology—a complex verbal sign (or a verbal sign complex) that corresponds to a given expectation of textuality.[12]

This definition of "text," by the text theoretician János Petöfi, may appear cumbersome, but it allows texts to be examined on the basis of semiotic foundations both with regard to their "system-immanent construction" and with regard to their function in the respective production or reception contexts. Such an approach can mitigate the dispute between diachronic and synchronic methods, as well as that between the absurd text-theoretical and semiotic playing-off of concepts and questions that regard texts as autonomous aesthetic objects over against those that are interested in reconstructing the emergence of text. The opposition of text-intentional and reader-centered exegesis also proves to be an unnecessary battle that is not sufficiently reflective about textual theory.

Reading produces meaning if it can coherently construct the structure of the signs (syntagmatics), if it can assign the meaning function of the individual signs to this structure (semantics), and if it creates a relationship between text and reader (pragmatics). Reading produces different interpretations depending on how readers structure a text and relate the individual characters to each other (syntagmatics), on which properties of a character are deemed meaningful—highlighted/blown up or downplayed/narcotized (semantics), and on how the readers can be impacted by or inscribed in the text (pragmatics).

These are the basic conditions for successful reading. By "successful reading" I mean "only" reading that leaves a text with the feeling of hanging together as a meaningful, coherent whole. Only when this feeling comes about can "the pleas-

---

[11] Ugo Volli, *Semiotik. Eine Einführung in ihre Grundbegriffe*, UTB Sprachwissenschaft 2318 (Tübingen: UTB, 2002), 79.

[12] János S. Petöfi, "Explikative Interpretation. Explikatives Wissen," in *Von der verbalen Konstitution zur symbolischen Bedeutung—From Verbal Constitution to Symbolic Meaning*, Papiere zur Textlinguistik 62, ed. János S. Petöfi and Terry Olivi (Hamburg: Buske, 1988), 184-95, at 184.

ure of the text" (Roland Barthes) develop.[13] This textual satisfaction is essentially due to the joyful experience of one's own creativity, which is able to create imaginary worlds from abstract signs. Reading not only trains the faculties of the imagination but also entails an operation of abstract thinking and an exercise in logical development.

Reading educates in many ways. Readers are directors, set designers, and actors all in one person. Reading is a highly complex cultural technique that must be taught and learned. Reading is the meaningful collection and arrangement of abstract signs by means of their connection to a homogeneous whole, which is more and different than the sum of its signs. Reading does not simply happen and is by no means child's play. A young reader's preference for media that are less textual and more image oriented certainly becomes comprehensible when one considers the complex degree of difficulty involved in the act of reading. At the same time, however, one will certainly have to refrain from giving in to this desire prematurely. The technique of reading opens up worlds because it trains creativity, reasoning, and memory in equal measure. To give in to the desire for more readily accessible images without hesitation, instead of patiently practicing the demanding and creative cultural techniques of reading, deprives pupils of the opportunity to train their imagination in the art of accessing the imaginary synesthesia of intermedial sign systems, an art that can protect them from an overly passive engagement with cultural life. The rejection of biblical texts in religious education at school is probably to a large extent not specifically a problem of Bible reading per se, but rather an expression of the more general problem of pedagogical negligence in the teaching of reading competence.

With reading competence, however, comes the ability to imagine abstract characters. The characters become audible and visible. The world of text is created in front of the inner eye and ear of the reader. Readers not only see foreign worlds, worlds that they would not otherwise encounter, but are also enabled to view their own world with different eyes and ears. They can hear, see, taste, touch, and smell the world in new and fresh ways.

Identity Formation as a Procedural Task

More recent research on identity[14] has shown that questions and concepts of collective and individual identity must first be differentiated. For reasons of space,

---

[13] Roland Barthes, *The Pleasure of the Text* (New York: Hill and Wang, 1975).
[14] Cf. Burkhard Liebsch, *Prekäre Selbst-Bezeugung. Die erschütterte Wer-Frage im Horizont der Moderne* (Weilerswist: Velbrück, 2012); Jürgen Straub, "Identität," in *Handbuch der Kulturwissenschaften*, vol. 1, *Grundlagen und Schlüsselbegriffe*, ed. Friedrich Jaeger and Burkhard Liebsch (Stuttgart: J. B. Metzler, 2004), 277–303. Erhardt Güttgemanns, following

I cannot engage the problems and perspectives of collective identity. With regard to the concept of personal identity, we can no longer assume a "self" that "remains the same because of any possible constants of 'something.'"[15] The formation of personal identity is better thought of as a process, an ongoing task,

> without it being possible to identify an identical core of the self. To seek for a core identity means in any case to bring into play misleading substantialist ideas of who we are, that is, ideas oriented towards paradigmatic accounts of selfhood. Following Kierkegaard and Heidegger, on the other hand, it is emphasized that we are not, rather we happen into selfhood, a selfhood that continually experiences itself as radically liable to being questioned.[16]

This "event" of selfhood takes place as "active ... constituting performances of a subject caring for itself."[17] These active performances constitute the self by preventing the person from disintegrating into different selves without thereby denying the differences of these various selves:

> "Identity can aptly be conceptualized as the paradoxical ambition of the 'unity of one's differences,' whereby no active 'synthesis of the heterogeneous' can lead to the abolition or elimination of these differences."[18]
>
> This "concept of identity revolves around the permanent 'paradox' of a unity that is inconclusive, divisive, intangible, and above all at the same time is permanently aspired to and continually unachieved."[19]

Jacques Lacan's interpretation of Freud, brought this emphasis into the exegetical debate: see Erhardt Güttgemanns, *Fragmenta semiotico-hermeneutica. Eine Texthermeneutik für den Umgang mit der Heiligen Schrift*, Forum Theologiae Linguisticae 9 (Bonn: Linguistica Biblica, 1983), 263–312. In the context of developing practical theological theory, see Henning Luther, "Identität und Fragment. Praktisch-theologische Überlegungen zur Unabschließbarkeit von Bildungsprozessen," *Theologia Practica* 20, no. 4 (1985), 317–38; Henning Luther, "'Ich ist ein Anderer.' Die Bedeutung von Subjekttheorien (Habermas, Levinas) für die Praktische Theologie," in *Praktisch-theologische Hermeneutik. Ansätze–Anregungen–Aufgaben, Henning Schröer zum 60. Geburtstag*, ed. Stefan Alkier, Ralf Koerrenz, Harald Schroeter, Dietrich Zilleßen (Rheinbach-Merzbach: CMZ, 1991), 233–54. Regarding the philosophical debate, see Manfred Frank, Gérard Raulet, and Willem van Reijen, eds., *Die Frage nach dem Subjekt* (Frankfurt a. M.: Suhrkamp, 1988).

[15] Straub, "Identität," 285.
[16] Liebsch, *Prekäre Selbst-Bezeugung*, 315.
[17] Straub, "Identität," 285.
[18] Ibid., 280.
[19] Ibid., 280.

That having been said, the event of selfhood does not take place in an interior space that is shielded from the encounter with others. Rather, it takes place in front of and in the eyes of others. The event of the self "is radically dependent on being able to show itself as witnessed, without ever being able to provide a (recognizable) proof of who it is."[20]

Personal identity does not, therefore, develop as an inner possession in abstraction from others. Rather, identity is formed via the mimesis of others and their signs, gestures, and glances. Only by imitation can one testify to oneself that one is a self, both before oneself and before others. This mediation of identity through communication by means of signs is therefore constitutive not only for collective but also for personal identity:

> There is a peculiar, paradoxical relationship between both dimensions of identity. I would like to formulate this in the form of two theses that seem to contradict each other: 1. An "I" grows from the outside to the inside. That is to say, it builds on its participation in the interaction and communication patterns of the group to which it belongs, and on its participation in the self-image of the group. The "we" identity of the group thus takes precedence over the "I" identity of the individual, or: identity is a social phenomenon or "sociogenic." 2. Collective or "we" identity does not exist outside the individuals who constitute and carry this "we." It is a matter of individual knowledge and consciousness.[21]

Thus, the social component necessary for the formation of each personal identity and the formation of the social identity from the collection of individuals that constitute it can and must be considered together. Additionally, one can see more clearly that the generation of these identities through sign processes—processes that individuals do not invent but find already operating in the social contexts they inhabit—is, with all the long-standing differences of individual identities, already inscribed in those very social contexts.

The philosopher and literary theorist Mikhail Bakhtin considered this sign-mediated, communicative condition of all identity formation primarily with a view to verbal communication and has stated:

> It is all the more astonishing that the philosophy of the word and linguistics have especially taken into consideration this artificial, conditional state of the word detached from dialogue and considered it to be the normal state (although the primacy of dialogue over monologue is often enough declared). The dialogue was merely examined as a compositional form of speech construction, but the inner dialogicity of the word

---

[20] Liebsch, *Prekäre Selbst-Bezeugung*, 316.
[21] Jan Assmann, *Das kulturelle Gedächtnis. Schrift, Erinnerung und politische Identität in frühen Hochkulturen* (Munich: C. H. Beck, 1992), 130f.

(in replica as in monological utterance), which permeates its entire structure, its semantic and expressive layers, remained almost unnoticed …. The word is born in dialogue as its living replica; it acquires its form in the dialogical interaction with the foreign word in the object. The design of the object by the word is dialogical. But the inner dialogicity of the word is by no means exhausted in this. Not only in the object does the word meet another foreign one. Each word is directed towards an answer, and none can escape the profound influence of the anticipated word of the replica. This is how every lively dialogue takes place.[22]

The inscription of the language of others in the formation of the child's own identity not only takes place in the child's language acquisition. It remains a constitutive[23] element of every self-relationship through the inescapable dialogical integration into private and public communication by means of all sign media, even when the foreign sign becomes a sign of self, when the foreign word becomes one's "own word":

[T]he differentiation between one's own and a foreign word, between one's own and foreign thoughts begins quite late. When the work of independent, examining and selecting thought begins, above all there occurs a separation of the inwardly convincing word from the authoritarian and imposed word and from the mass of indifferent words that do not touch us …. In the everyday life of our consciousness, the inwardly convincing word is half its own and half foreign. Its creative productivity consists precisely in the fact that it awakens an independent thought and an independent, new word, that it organizes the masses of our words from within and does not remain in an isolated and immovable state. It is not so much interpreted by us as it develops freely, it adapts to new material, to new circumstances, it illuminates itself reciprocally with new contexts. In addition, it takes up an intense interaction and struggle with other internally convincing words …. The meaning structure of the inwardly convincing word is not complete, it is open, it can open up completely new possibilities of meaning in every new, dialogizing context.[24]

Mikhail Bakhtin expresses this thought conceptually with the aesthetic-anthropological concept of dialogicity. This is significant for the conception of a sustainable concept of identity precisely because it does not give up understanding identity in essentialist terms as a stable core or essence in the interior of a person. Rather,

---

[22] Michail M. Bachtin [Mikhail M. Bakhtin], *Die Ästhetik des Wortes*, ed. Rainer Grübel (Frankfurt a. M.: Suhrkamp, 1979), 172 f.

[23] Ibid., 238: "selbst der dürrste und platteste Positivismus kann das Wort nicht neutral, als Ding traktieren und ist gezwungen, nicht nur *über* das Wort, sondern auch *mit* dem Wort zu sprechen, um zu dessen ideologischen Sinn vorzudringen, einem Sinn, der einzig dem dialogischen—Bewertung und Antwort einschließenden—Verstehen zugänglich ist."

[24] Ibid., 232.

such an approach lets the permanent dependence on the gaze and the sign formations of others be thought of as communicative, semiotic dynamics of identity-building processes. Thus, this approach also enables conceptual, semiotic connections between the concepts of personal and collective identity, both to be recognized as interdependent and to be distinguished.[25]

That verbal signs are by no means the only signs that play a role in the processes of identity formation may already have become clear from what has been written so far. The basic tripartite structure of each sign, which enables something to stand for something else in certain respects, allows all interpretation processes and all communication to be understood as a sign process.

Personal and collective identity formation can thus be understood as dialogical sign processes,[26] in which the identity of a person or a collective is always at stake, has to be expressed anew, and is also redesigned if forced to by contingent events or other chronotopic, political, economic, or emotional changes in constellations. "The self is not a principle; and it does not control itself like a sovereign by its own strength and power."[27] Persons and collectives have no control over them-

---

[25] Ibid., 168: "Sprachphilosophie, Linguistik und die auf ihnen beruhende Stilistik lassen jene spezifischen Erscheinungen im Wort fast völlig außer Acht, die durch seine dialogische Orientierung inmitten fremder Aussagen innerhalb derselben Sprache bestimmt werden (der ursprünglichen Dialogizität des Wortes), durch die Orientierung unter anderen, 'sozialen Sprachen' im Rahmen derselben Nationalsprache und schließlich unter anderen Nationalsprachen." Ibid., 225 f.: "Das Thema vom sprechenden Menschen ist im Alltag von großem Gewicht. Auf Schritt und Tritt ist im Alltag von jemandem, der spricht und seinem Wort die Rede. Man kann geradezu sagen: im Alltag wird am meisten über das gesprochen, was andere sagen,–man übermittelt, erinnert, erwägt, erörtert fremde Wörter, Meinungen, Behauptungen, Informationen, entrüstet sich über sie, erklärt sich mit ihnen einverstanden, bestreitet sie, beruft sich auf sie usw. Wenn man den Bruchstücken eines rohen Dialogs auf der Straße, in einer Menge, beim Anstehen, im Foyer usf. genau zuhört, dann hört man, wie oft die Wörter 'sagt er,' 'sagt man,' 'sagte er' sich wiederholen."

[26] See Wolfram Ellenberger, *Das Werden des Menschen im Wort. Eine Studie zur Kulturphilosophie Michail M. Bachtins*, Legierungen 5 (Zürich: Chronos, 2009), 70: "Jede Realisierung des Bezugs auf Erfahrenes, auch der auf eigene Denk- bzw. Erfahrungsprozesse, ist nach Volosinov zeichenvermittelt. 'Die Selbstbeobachtung ist das Verstehen des eigenen inneren Zeichens... Ein Zeichen kann nur mit Hilfe eines anderen Zeichens erhellt werden.' Zwischen interindividuell-öffentlicher und innerlich-selbstadressierter Zeichentransformation besteht damit, aus psychologisch-methodischer und philosophischer Sicht, kein *qualitativer* Unterschied mehr. Und dies gilt umso mehr, als die Ausbildung des individuellen Bewusstseins als Ergebnis einer durch den Prozess der sozialen Interaktion geprägten Zeichenaneignung von 'außen' nach 'innen' konzipiert wird. Die Zeichen, aus und mit denen ein Selbst wird, sind die Zeichen anderer."

[27] Liebsch, *Prekäre Selbst-Bezeugung*, 316.

selves, they do not have their future at their disposal, nor do they know their present, let alone their past in its entirety. Rather, they perceive these things themselves as excerpts, perspectively, within the limits of their chronotopic point of view. They cannot really know who they are, for they do not know who they will have been.

This constitution of identity, which encompasses all dimensions of time, already points to the fact that identity must be thought of not as substantial but as a dynamic process of interpretation, which refuses to allow persons and collectives to take a complete look at themselves. They remain withdrawn from themselves because neither persons nor collectives can have direct access to themselves. Both depend on a permanent, ongoing task of interpretation, which concerns not only them but also the constellations in which they live—their time.

> "Man cannot simply leave time as it is (that is, as it meets him directly). For he experiences it as a break-in of unforeseeable events in his interpreted world—in short, as a change of his world and of himself, which he suffers and to which he must behave because he is not yet sufficiently related to his actions."[28]
>
> Identity in relation to time means precisely the extent of coherence in the temporal change of human self-relations that people need in order to be able to act in a meaningful or culturally oriented way. Identity holds self-awareness and self-design as the duration of one's own ego or we together in such a way that the experience of suffering, of being at the mercy of contingency and of death, can be endured and overcome by action that is both normatively motivated and experience-supported.[29]

Because people have no overall/complete view of their own history, and even less so of that of their collectives, they live in the necessity of making themselves the object of interpretation. They do not remember every moment of their lives, they reassess moments of experience in the current constellation, and they imagine a future that, due to the contingency[30] of life, will never be as expected. This temporal structure of identity-formation processes leads to a gain in freedom only when the limits of one's own point of view are accepted and used productively: "Identity implies the ability to distance oneself (for example, in the form of self-irony), to engage in self-reflection and self-criticism."[31] Identity is subject to the

---

[28] Jörn Rüsen, "Die Kultur der Zeit. Versuch einer Typologie temporaler Sinnbildungen," in *Zeit deuten. Perspektiven–Epochen–Paradigmen*, ed. Jörn Rüsen (Bielefeld: Transcript, 2003), 24 f.

[29] Ibid., 31.

[30] Ibid., 25: "Kontingente Geschehnisse sind unvermutet, plötzlich, unverhofft, ereignishaft. ... Kontingente Zeiterfahrungen müssen gedeutet werden, weil sie Einfluss auf das Leben der jeweiligen Subjekte nehmen."

[31] Straub, "Identität," 281 f.

constraint of self-distancing. This is so because the self changes under the conditions of changing constellations and unpredictable events and thus has to understand itself anew again and again, if it does not want to be torn apart but wants instead to assert itself by means of a self-relationship that can be revised.

Christian Identity-Building Processes as Rethinking with Scripture: The Sermon on the Mount as a Test Case

The assumption of this constraint on a permanent formation of identity opens up possibilities of self-development that are not owed purely to the constraints of repetition, but that actually enable new thinking, rethinking. The basic message of Jesus in the Gospels is therefore: *Metanoeite*, "Rethink!" Rethinking is possible because who we are is not essentially fixed but will emerge through the respective self-expression in the course of life. Only then will we know who we will have been. Christian identity-building processes aim to prove to those who engage in them that they will have become children of the merciful and just God of Israel, the God who raised the crucified Jesus of Nazareth from the dead. This Christian identity, however, cannot be thought of as property, but only as a precarious gift and a task of self-interpretation.[32]

In the conflict-laden dialogue, not only are each person's own testimonies presented, but there is also an ongoing dispute as to what the testimony of belonging to a "we" should look like. This is why those who gather under a certain "we" not only argue long about the constitution of that we but also demonstrate concern for third parties who apparently are not involved at all. What belongs (or not) to a Christian or a Jew or a Muslim is discussed not only by Christians, Jews, and Muslims within their collectives. Such examples of the negotiation of collective identity and the conditions of belonging to it become apparent precisely in the necessity to struggle again and again for the fact that identity is not an object possessed by a subject—whether in the singular or in the plural—but an interpretation that must always be newly formed. Identity is not a substance but a sign process. This is precisely what one can learn from the Sermon on the Mount (Matthew 5–7).

---

[32] See Stefan Alkier, "Die Bergpredigt als ermutigende Anweisung zur prekären Selbst-Bezeugung der Kinder Gottes," in *Subjekt werden. Neutestamentliche Perspektiven und politische Theorie*, Theologische Bibliothek Töpelmann 162, ed. Eckart Reinmuth (Berlin: De Gruyter, 2013), 237–50. Also: Kristina Dronsch, "'Ihr seid Zeugen' (Joh 15,27). Die johanneische Figur des Zeugen in subjekttheoretischer Sicht," in Reinmuth, *Subjekt werden*, 195–212; Eckart Reinmuth, "Subjekt werden. Zur Konstruktion narrativer Identität bei Paulus, Johannes und Matthäus," in Reinmuth, *Subjekt werden*, 251–84.

The Sermon on the Mount is not a guideline for a happy life. It is not an instance of life counseling that aims for the optimization of endorphin release. It is not a lifestyle program that can help one squeeze all the happiness possible out of one's own life. It does not tick with a capitalist logic that capitulates to the economic and political constraints that generate injustice. It is rather a guide that will get one into difficulties and conflicts that will by no means always end well. The sermon calls us to follow a life path that exposes us to threats and even deadly violence. It calls one to the task of following Jesus Christ. His life path in his vulnerable, pain-sensitive body of flesh and blood—a body like that of any other human being or animal—came to a horrible end. He was a victim of individual and institutional guilt and violence. His end was determined by others.

When Jesus, in the macarisms of the Sermon on the Mount that we call the Beatitudes, speaks of those who are poor in spirit, humble, sorrowful, gentle, hungry and thirsty for justice, merciful, pure in heart, committed to peace and persecuted for justice, he knows what he is talking about, because all of this applies to him as he is portrayed in the medium of the Gospels. The conditions he identifies as blessed are fully understood only in light of the path he walked. Jesus is not someone who speaks of these things and then gets through life without himself experiencing them. He does not seek for his own private happiness and does not hope for a streak of luck in the game or at work. In all situations, he proves himself to be a child of God, someone who walks consistently with God through his entire life, a way of life that does not always make him happy.

But to what extent can those addressed in the Beatitudes (Matthew 5:3–12) consider themselves happy or blessed? Under what conditions can the poor in spirit, the disfranchised, the persecuted, the hungry, and the thirsty hear the encouragement of the Beatitudes not as diabolical cynicism but as powerful promises that reorient their self-determination and allow them to say for themselves, even in view of the physical experiences of hunger, injustice, and violence, "I have experienced plenty of blessing"?

We find macarisms, or blessings, not only in the Sermon on the Mount but also in various forms in ancient Judaism and also outside the Judeo-Christian literature. With Goldberg, one can ideally distinguish two types of macarisms: "(1) The ethical behavioral macarism. This praises people because of their behavior or actions, whereby blessing is justified by the consequence of these actions (wages). (2) The personal macarism, the praise of man for the happiness which is given to him, implying the cause of this happiness (just doing)."[33] Hans-Dieter

---

[33] Arnold Goldberg, *Erlösung durch Leiden. Drei rabbinische Homilien über die Trauernden Zions und den leidenden Messias Efraim (PesR 34.36.37)* (Frankfurt a. M.: Selbstverlag der Gesellschaft zur Förderung judaistischer Studien, 1978), quoted in Martin Hengel, "Zur matthäischen Bergpredigt und ihrem jüdischen Hintergrund," *Theologische Rundschau* 52, no. 4 (1988): 327–45, at 332.

Betz distinguishes among religious, secular, and satirical macarisms. A worldly macarism, for example, can be found in Jesus ben Sirach 25:8: "Blessed [*makarios*] is the man who lives together with an intelligent woman." A religious macarism opens the book of Psalms:

> "Blessed is he that walketh not in the counsel of the ungodly, nor walketh upon the way of sinners, nor sitteth where the mockers sit, but hath pleasure in the law of the Lord, and pondereth his law day and night" (Psalm 1:1).

As an example of an ironic macarism, Betz cites Eth Hen 103:5–6: "Blessed are the sinners, they have seen good all their lives. Now they have died in happiness and wealth."[34] Blessing and its justification are coordinated in all these macarisms. This becomes particularly clear in Psalm 1, which says of someone who meditates on God's law, "He is like a tree planted by streams of water, which bears its fruit in his time, and its leaves do not wither. And what he does shall prosper."

Precisely this coherence does not apply to the Beatitudes. They are rather paradoxical. Why should one consider someone who is persecuted to be blessed? An ironic interpretation, as in the example of the Enoch quotation, is excluded here. Rather, the blessing stems from the authority of the speaker, who opposes the constraints of factual experience:

> When Jesus at the beginning of the Sermon on the Mount praises the spiritually poor, the suffering, the meek and many others who are "blessed," he contradicts all experiences that say otherwise. One could explicitly formulate the antithetical structure of the Beatitudes in this way: All experience teaches that people hunger and thirst in vain for justice; but I tell you: "Blessed are those who hunger and thirst for justice; for they shall be satisfied."[35]

The Beatitudes can be understood only if one includes their consistent eschatological perspective. The Sermon on the Mount is completely misunderstood if it is thought to be a guide to a happy life. This is so because it refuses to be bound within the limits of a human life span. Rather, it is guided by the conviction that the path of blessing exceeds the limits of what can be experienced in mortal human bodies. The presupposed perspective that makes the paradox of blessing conceivable is the kingdom of heaven, the kingdom of God. This kingdom is not created by human beings, and therefore its limits are defined not by the empirically

---

[34] Hans Dieter Betz, "Die Makarismen der Bergpredigt (Matthäus 5, 3–12): Beobachtungen zur literarischen Form und theologischen Bedeutung: Gerhard Ebeling zum 65. Geburtstag am 6. Juli 1977," *Zeitschrift für Theologie und Kirche* 75, no. 1 (1978): 1–19, at 10.

[35] Manfred Josuttis, "Predigen mit der Autorität der Bergpredigt," *Evangelische Theologie* 57, no. 4 (1997), 445–58, at 451.

expectable or even feasible, but by the creative vitality of the Creator God of Israel. The creative power of God, as already presented in the writings of Israel and then also in New Testament texts, extends beyond the boundaries of the expected. Only from this perspective can the path of discipleship be seen to lead to the same exciting identity that already characterizes the one being followed. The followers remain entirely in their mortal human reality. Yet, at the same time, they do not understand themselves solely on the basis of that reality, but from the reality of God, to whom they bear witness as those who are children of God. What Manfred Josuttis formulated with regard to the disciples also applies to all readers of the Gospel of Matthew who feel themselves addressed by it and who let this Gospel determine their way of life: "Through the Sermon on the Mount the disciples themselves are transferred to a mountain that radiates healing effects."[36]

But this eschatological perspective, made possible by the synesthesia of the written signs, is not simply a future that has nothing to do with the present. Rather, it is regarded as a determination of the whole of reality. That is to say, it is a reality that determines the present, a determination that arises from the conviction that the Creator God of Israel, witnessed to by Jesus, raised the executed Jesus from death and gave him new, eternal life.[37] This eschatological event of crucifixion and resurrection is the exquisite perspective of hope that determines reality for the children of God, those who already now can ask everything of God, as the Lord's Prayer teaches. To live in such a reality is to live with a perspective that extends beyond the experience of the end of life in flesh and blood. However, in this life this perspective remains challenged by the fact that bodies are fragile, existence is dependent on requests. Life is precarious. This perspective can be mediated only by written signs that always also represent fragile, incomplete embodiments of its textures in the material sense that always require interpretation. Thus, the necessity of textual criticism can be seen as a symbol of the fragility of Christian existence.

The Beatitudes characterize this self-understanding, which relies on the need for intentional, repeated requests—that is, it relies on constant prayer directed to God, not on the chance of happiness or good luck. Those who live in this reality outline this self-understanding in an approximate, unfinished way.

The first Beatitude expresses the fundamental attitude of humility, which, in the face of the eschatological expectation of the kingdom of heaven, is placed be-

---

[36] Ibid., 448.

[37] See Stefan Alkier, *Die Realität der Auferweckung in, nach und mit den Schriften des Neuen Testaments*, NET 12 (Tübingen: Francke, 2009); In English: *The Reality of the Resurrection: The New Testament Witness*, trans. Leroy A. Huizenga, foreword by Richard B. Hays (Waco, TX: Baylor University Press, 2013); Cf. Hans-Joachim Eckstein and Michael Welker, eds., *Die Wirklichkeit der Auferstehung*, 2nd ed. (Neukirchen-Vluyn: Neukirchener Verlag, 2004).

fore any further perception. Humility is the basic attitude appropriate to the whole of reality. To be poor in spirit does not mean to have a limited capacity for thinking. Rather, it is an attitude that grasps that one will never be capable of understanding and organizing life in all its dimensions out of one's own considerations. It is the fundamental rejection of the feasibility of reading and living on one's own, and the humble acceptance of the reading and living of God's creatures, who are always dependent on request and gift.

This humble attitude will not necessarily ward off suffering. The precarious self-determination of the children of God does not count on a painless life. However, the suffering experienced will not develop into a dimension of its own, a power that determines one's identity. Rather, it is expected that the God of consolation will effectively end the suffering, as was already announced in the fortieth chapter of the book of Isaiah.

The blessings for the meek and merciful are intertwined with those for the justice-hungry and the peacemakers. The renunciation of armed violence and of any brutality cannot therefore be misunderstood as a passive, submissive, or even masochistic attitude to life. Like Jesus, those who follow him also prove that they are motivated by the longing for a just life in solidarity with God's creatures. They live in ways that show they are committed to this justice. It is precisely this commitment that brings suffering and even persecution. But those who have the humble attitude of the poor in the Spirit know that they do not build the kingdom of God. The kingdom comes as a gift of God, which all who pray the Our Father can ask for with longing and can already experience fragmentarily through the synesthesia of scripture.

In this way of thinking about the divine gift, and not in the hope of happy circumstances, lie the macarisms of the Sermon on the Mount. The word *makarios* does not aim to identify an inner state of mind, one's feeling of happiness. It does not refer to the stoic carelessness of a self-confidence that relies entirely on itself, that needs no one and nothing, and certainly that does not need the foreign words of scripture. Rather, it designates those who are gifted with the gifts of God, those whom Jesus bestows with his first words. The *makarios* indicates their self-determination, which is permanently dependent on their repeated requests to God. The happiness of this self-determination owes itself entirely to the distribution of God's gift, God's Word, even in the medium of fragile signs, whose spirit is clearly recognized by the poor in spirit.

The power that enables the children of God to become a witness again and again comes from prayer. The children of God are creatures acquainted with lamenting, thanking, and beseeching in prayer. Oda Wischmeyer, in her essay on the words of sorrow in Matthew 6:25–34, has put forward the following excellent thesis: "The double certainty that God the Creator is also God the Father and that this God has defined his *basileia* [kingdom] as the horizon of human existence is bearing fruit. To be human is to be privileged and free to live in the *basileia*. God as

Creator makes possible man's search for *basileia*."[38] With this thesis, she answers the question that Jesus's request in 6:33a aims at: "Seek first the kingdom of God and his righteousness." The way of discipleship is one of constant movement, constant seeking, a way whose desired object remains withdrawn from any availability. It cannot yet be grasped, obtained, tamed. Precisely through this nonavailability, the way for God's coming remains open. With this search for the reason that remains withdrawn is linked a search for the justice connected with the kingdom. This seeking fosters a political sense that appears as the aspirated, imagined identity of the children of God, which contributes as such to the constitution of the potential for action among those who feel themselves to be addressed as children of God. In this identity as children of God, which is constituted by the claim of the Sermon on the Mount encountered in the medium of scripture, lies a normative sense of identity that is made possible precisely by the indicative of the promise to be children of God.

The identity of the children of God is witnessed to by their own seeking, a seeking that commits them to the values of the kingdom of God, whose double withdrawal and repeated failures do not contradict their determination. On the contrary, they gain freedom precisely through the awareness of structural deprivation, which unmasks as ideological deception any talk of factual logics rooted only in experience and thus unfolds in evident political effects without slipping into political triumphalism. Therefore, the request expressed in the Our Father is central to Christian existence: "Your kingdom come" (Matthew 6:10a).

When this foreign word and other words of the Bible become one's own words, Christian identity will be formed. The more biblical words they read, hear, see, or sing, the more the readers, hearers, seers, and singers of biblical texts find themselves to be a part of the story of the Bible. The foreign words make sense in one's own world, and one answers with the way one lives one's own life. Life as an answer to the foreign words that become one's own words becomes an intermedial sign of the lively truth of these biblical words. "'Taste every word ... Let it melt on your tongue. Taste the colors. Do you taste the wind and the night? The fear and the joy? Taste it ... and everything comes to life.'"[39]

---

[38] Oda Wischmeyer, "Matthäus 6,25–34. Die Spruchreihe vom Sorgen," *Zeitschrift für die Neutestamentliche Wissenschaft und die Kunde der Älteren Kirche* 85, nos. 1–2 (1994): 1–22, at 4.

[39] Funke, *Tintenherz*, 539.

Forming Research Scientists?
Developing Practical Wisdom and Virtue in Multidisciplinary Academic Frameworks

Celia Deane-Drummond[1]

Scientists often struggle with difficult ethical issues that arise out of their scientific practice, leading to increased attention being paid to professional ethics. Models for such ethical deliberation are generally heavily consequentialist, thus encouraging scientists to make difficult choices just according to cost/benefit calculations, which may lead to tensions with their religious beliefs.[2] While many academic (but also religious) researchers at universities—at least in the United States—will choose to settle in private, religiously founded institutions, a significant proportion will find themselves for financial or other personal reasons in secular organizations. The philosophy of sciences that was once positivistic and narrow in its epistemological claims, which dominated scientific research, is, however, starting to show signs of change. Atheist philosopher of science Thomas Nagel is bold enough to argue that, when it comes to understanding the human place in the cosmos, especially mind and consciousness, a reductionist Darwinian version of science is inadequate to the task; research scientists have to take proper account of the teleological and perhaps even the transcendent.[3]

I argue in this chapter that an active promotion of practical wisdom or prudence and conscience is necessary within scientific practice and education if the different branches of science are going to achieve goals that contribute in a positive way to human flourishing. Further, I claim that theological traditions have

---

[1] Some sections of this chapter are revised versions of material first developed in Celia Deane-Drummond "The Art and Science of Vocation: Wisdom and Conscience as Companions on a Way," in *Vocation across the Academy: A New Vocabulary for Higher Education*, ed. David Cunningham (Oxford: Oxford University Press, 2017), 156–77. A short form of this chapter was first presented in April 2019 at a colloquium in Heidelberg organized by Michael Welker, and I am most grateful for feedback received at that meeting and for the original invitation.

[2] As noted by Bernold Fiedler, "Absolute Truth: A Toxic Chimera?," in this volume.

[3] Thomas Nagel, *Mind and Cosmos: Why the Materialist Neo-Darwinian Conception of Nature Is Almost Certainly False* (Oxford: Oxford University Press, 2012).

something important to add to the current debate about different forms of knowledge and understanding, even in secular contexts. How far and to what extent do different branches of science *also* encourage a broader perspective on knowing and acting that, in theological and philosophical terms, is known as practical wisdom? What role has conscience to play when scientists are integrated into a specific community of research with its own (often unwritten) norms and values?

In a major project funded by the Templeton Religion Trust[4] analyzing the different virtues emerging in the practice of science, a collaborative team of scholars from different disciplines decided to develop some novel methodologies for empirical and qualitative research within biological research laboratories. First, we spent the first three months meeting six hours a week to enable the psychologists in the team to design new psychological measures for assessing different aspects of character formation of scientists in terms of their participation in laboratory life. These measures have been used both in large-scale surveys as well as in face-to-face interviews. The new design took account of a classic, broadly Aristotelian understanding of the virtues, which gives priority to the role of *phronesis*. We also drew on historical and contemporary sources, which, in the case of theology, ranged from Thomas Aquinas to Josef Pieper and Ralph Waldo Emerson.[5] For the field research, we used a mixed-method approach that drew on both ethnographic tools, employed while accompanying scientists as they went about their daily laboratory tasks, and broader-scale survey data. Our collaborative enterprise yielded results that are relevant for the theme of science and character formation.[6] While existing literature has explored virtues in the light of professional formation of scientists as part of what it means to be excellent in science,[7] our

---

[4] Celia Deane-Drummond, Darcia Narvaez, and Tom Stapleford, principal investigators, "Developing Virtues in the Practice of Science," project supported by the Templeton Religion Trust from 2016 to 2019.

[5] Of the numerous publications, two examples are Emily Dumler Winckler, "Can Genius Be Taught? Ralph Waldo Emerson's Genius and the Virtue of Self-Trust," *Journal of Moral Education* 47, no. 3 (2018): 272–88; and Nathaniel Warne, "Learning to See, Again: Rethinking Education, Science and Moral Formation," *Journal of Moral Education* 47, no. 3 (2018): 289–303.

[6] The summary results of our work and culminating conference proceedings are in an open-access text published as Celia Deane-Drummond, Tom Stapleford, and Darcia Narvaez, *Virtue and the Practice of Science: Multidisciplinary Perspectives,* Center for Theology, Science, and Human Flourishing, https://virtueandthepracticeofscience.pressbooks.com/.

[7] Jeanne Nakamura, David J. Shernoff, and Charles H. Hooker, *Good Mentoring: Fostering Excellent Practice in Higher Education* (Oxford: John Wiley & Sons, 2009); Howard E. Gardner, Mihaly Csikszentmihalyi, and William Damon, *Good Work: When Excellence and Ethics Meet* (New York: Basic Books, 2001).

own project, by drawing largely on Aristotelian concepts of human flourishing, allowed us to probe different aspects, such as advancing human knowledge, the good of communities, or creating and appreciating beauty. It also explored the historical aspects of how virtues played out in the emerging practices of scientific research, along with ethnographic, psychological, and theological engagement in a multidisciplinary team. We shared our findings in a number of different publications.[8]

The removal of virtue talk from the language of scientific research is relatively recent in the history of science, which long associated the creation of knowledge with the cultivation of moral virtues.[9] Many of the ancients also believed that study of the natural world enhanced virtue in its practitioners. That idealism was lost by the early twentieth century, when scientists replaced those moral ideals with minimal moral boundaries for professional practice, such as avoiding sexual or other harassment and not fabricating data.[10] Those minimalist professional frameworks usually rely on deontological approaches to ethics. In the past ten years or so, that framework has come under fire, not only through high-profile scandals arising from fraudulent use of data or sexual harassment by senior scientists, but also by work of sociologists and historians who have shown that character and dispositions are integral to how scientists create trust and establish working communities.[11]

Societally Orientated Science and Troublesome Knowledge?

Different disciplines develop their own ways of knowing and specific practices that, according to anthropologist Marilyn Strathern, lead to *fractal* ways of know-

---

[8] For example, Timothy Reilly and Tom Stapleford, eds. "Science, Virtue and Moral Formation," Special Issue, *Journal of Moral Education* 47, no. 3 (2018); Celia Deane-Drummond and Michael Spezio, eds. "Philosophy, Virtue and the Practices of Science 1," Special Issue, *Philosophy, Theology and the Sciences* 5, no. 1 (2018); Michael Spezio and Celia Deane-Drummond, eds. "Philosophy, Virtue and the Practices of Science II," Special Issue, *Philosophy, Theology and the Sciences* 6, no. 1 (2019).

[9] Matthew L. Jones, *The Good Life in the Scientific Revolution: Descartes, Pascal, Leibniz, and the Cultivation of Virtue* (Chicago: University of Chicago Press, 2006). See also Alasdair MacIntyre, *After Virtue: A Study in Moral Theory* (Notre Dame, IN: University of Notre Dame Press, 1984).

[10] Steve Shapin, *The Scientific Life: A Moral History of a Late Modern Vocation* (Chicago: University of Chicago Press, 2009).

[11] Lorraine Daston and Peter Galison, *Objectivity* (Cambridge, MA: Zone Books, 2007); Shapin, *The Scientific Life*.

ing. By this she means ways of knowing that avoid strict divisions between either rational or interpretative, either individual or communal. She uses an analogy from mathematics, the fractal, in which (as in a snowflake, for example) the pattern laid down at an individual level repeats itself and emerges eventually as a complex structure. Strathern argues that there are viable and workable alternatives to what seem to be insoluble dichotomies or dilemmas. In a higher-educational context for both researchers and students, these alternatives may translate into a tension between one's own desire for academic success, on one hand, and society's needs for basic, often more practically orientated skills, on the other.[12]

An example comes from my own experience teaching global bioethics to scientific-research students in a U.S. setting from 2012 to 2018. Some of these students aspired to be health professionals, often with the eventual aim to become doctors in challenging healthcare settings; others eventually wanted to conduct more biologically focused academic research on, for example, the genetics of malaria or other tropical diseases. All had a background in a biological science of some kind, but they all aspired to use their science in ways that would benefit wider society. Many, however, found it very difficult to think outside their scientific discipline in the ways that are demanded by the field of ethics. At the same time, at least some of these researchers recognized that studying and appreciating ethics, including theological approaches, would be crucial in order for them to do the kind of societal work in religious communities in the poorest regions of the world that specifically demanded their attention.

Different disciplines as *societal* organizations also have a powerfully shaping influence on the character formation of individuals, and as students and early researchers are gradually exposed to these worlds, they begin to experience new sources of meaning. In my own experience as a biologist, and in my experience of teaching science students from a range of subject domains, the sense of loyalty that builds among those committed to scientific research is palpable. The laboratory world is its own world, a minisociety all of its own, and the most successful labs are also highly cohesive.[13] So full immersion by researchers and students in these reified yet highly practical investigative worlds serves like a kind of religious formation, including—perhaps surprisingly to those tooled in the humanities—the specific research practices of scientific investigation.[14] Knowledge can-

---

[12] Marilyn Strathern, *Partial Connections* (Walnut Creek, CA: AltaMira Press, 2004). Matthew Crawford discusses the philosophical issues involved in the move away from practices in Matthew Crawford, *Shop Class as Soul Craft: An Inquiry into the Value of Work* (London: Penguin Publishing, 2009).

[13] Bruno Latour and Steve Woolgar, *Laboratory Life: The Construction of Scientific Facts* [1979] (Princeton, NJ: Princeton University Press, 1986).

[14] For a historical account, see Andrew Warwick, *Masters of Theory: Cambridge and the Rise of Mathematical Physics* (Chicago: University of Chicago Press, 2003), especially 114-75.

not be separated from the particular practices that shape that way of knowing.[15] Thus, as Strathern suggests, "People's identities are in part forged in the kind of knowledge practices that different disciplines engender. This is not just in terms of shared bodies of knowledge, but rests in the manner in which material is collected, evidence appraised, work criticized, and results evaluated."[16]

In my own experience of teaching a course on science and values to undergraduates majoring in the natural sciences, the idea that *science is also value-laden* —or even, at least in some respects, socially and historically constructed—comes as both a surprise and an occasion for further questioning. Their immersion within the scientific milieu thus far has been sufficient for there to be little challenge to the cultural assumptions buried within scientific practice. Students or early researchers exposed to subject domains that cut across the humanities and the natural sciences habitually experience disturbances in equilibrium: knowledge gained seems alien and unsettles previously held convictions about what has been assumed to be the case, or what can be termed *troublesome* knowledge,[17] some of which may be related to deeply held and previously uncontested convictions.[18] Such convictions may stem from educational experiences in secular, religious, or familial settings. The point I am making here is that it cuts both ways: there are dogmatic religious communities of formation, but there are also scientific ones, even if scientific communities express their dogma differently. While on the surface scientific research will be open to all kinds of truth claims in contrast to religious forms of knowing, which are often but not inevitably more doctrinaire, the practices themselves and buried assumptions within science are far less frequently challenged. Making the philosophical and value base of a particular science more obvious is troublesome, perhaps even more so than established clashes between science and religion, which may or may not be held up for further historical or philosophical investigation.

---

[15] Marilyn Strathern, "Knowledge Identities," in *Changing Identities in Higher Education: Voicing Perspectives*, ed. Ronald Barnett and Roberto Di Napoli (London: Routledge, 2008), 11–20.

[16] Ibid., 11.

[17] Ray Land, "Crossing Tribal Boundaries: Interdisciplinarity as a Threshold Concept," in *Tribes and Territories in the 21st Century: Rethinking the Significance of Disciplines in Higher Education*, ed. Paul Trowler, Murray Saunders, and Veronica Bamber (London: Routledge, 2012), 175–85.

[18] Marilyn Strathern also compares interdisciplinary work with that of ethnographic disjunctions; both lead to transformative knowledge processes. Marilyn Strathern, "Disciplinary Encounters: Confident Comparisons and Uncertain Exchanges," keynote lecture delivered at symposium on Transfusion and Transformation: The Creative Potential of Interdisciplinary Knowledge Exchange, Institute for Advanced Study, Durham University, July 13–17, 2014.

Troublesome knowledge may have a profound impact on the lives of beginning researchers with respect to the *ways* they know (the epistemic level) and with respect to their sense of being (the ontological level). As a result, it is more than just a platitude to say that both scientific and religious students are often *not the same* as they were before their experience of higher education. In the course of entering into troublesome forms of knowledge, students enter a liminal phase of oscillation between old and emergent knowledge states.[19] Specific studies on the experience of physics students provide evidence for this phenomenon.[20] Students will often feel bewildered or confused when they encounter disjunctions between, for example, the analytical philosophy of science (which seeks to understand presuppositions behind basic scientific concepts) and science itself (which is premised on its representation of an aspect of material reality). Such a disorientation may also happen later on for an academic scientist who is exposed to other disciplines for the first time.

To humanities students first entering scientific ways of knowing, *suspicion* might be the dominant reaction, whereas *skepticism* predominates among science students or early researchers who encounter the very different methods characteristic of the humanities. This is very uncomfortable psychologically, even for those experienced in this kind of work. It is not surprising, then, that undergraduates tend to resist the transformation that such new encounters require. Instead of true learning, they often try to find ways of mimicking the kinds of work done in the field, imitating either the teacher or some other source.[21] If those research scholars and educators are embedded in a highly competitive context, this translates to student experience and may even impact student mental health, which, in the United Kingdom, has taken a downward spiral over the past few decades.[22] Science is not immune from these influences, and the competitive context is likely to be even more pronounced compared with that of the humanities.

---

[19] Jan H. F. Meyer and Ray Land, eds., *Overcoming Barriers to Student Understanding: Threshold Concepts and Troublesome Knowledge* (London: Routledge, 2006).

[20] For an interesting study on this phenomenon, see Ibrahim Abou Halloun and David Hestenes, "The Initial Knowledge State of College Physics," *American Journal of Physics* 53 (1985): 1043–55; and Ibrahim Abou Halloun and David Hestenes, "Common Sense Concepts and Motion," *American Journal of Physics* 53 (1985): 1056–65.

[21] Glynis Cousin, "An Introduction to Threshold Concepts," *Planet* 17 (2006): 4–5.

[22] Luca Morini, "Universities: Increasingly Stressful Environments Taking Their Toll—Here's What Needs to Change," *The Conversation*, March 29, 2019, https://theconversation.com/universities-increasingly-stressful-environments-taking-psychological-toll-heres-what-needs-to-change-97045.

Practical Wisdom

More broadly, there is a clear need for wisdom and practical wisdom in higher education, moving away from the fragmentation and specialization of knowledge to a more holistic environment for learning.[23] This need also applies to research culture: different models for research need to be encouraged to break down the fragmentation in research and allow mutual learning among disciplines as well as growth within them. Cultivating wisdom is related to experiences that come from actual involvement in practices intended to cultivate it. Every educator knows, for example, that practical teaching experience is crucial to the task of teacher training, and this impact of practice can be repeated across different areas of work. Even a theoretical mathematician needs to have some understanding of what it is like to *apply* mathematics; an experimental biologist needs to know what it means in practical terms to design and implement an experiment and analyze the results according to agreed protocols in a scientific community. When researchers come together from different practical experiences and backgrounds, it is possible, with sufficient openness and generosity, to share their wisdom with each other and thus enhance learning and research insights further, reaching a new, deeper level.

How might a researcher or student discern the best possible choice in any given set of complex circumstances where there are many different and competing demands? Prudence or practical wisdom in the classical traditions is concerned with matters of daily life: how to live well. Prudence has three phases—deliberation, judgment, and action. The ability to learn from others, an accurate memory of experience, clear insights about what is the case, and a keen sense of what outcomes may result from particular decisions are all important, even prior to judgment. Judgment involves the use of reason and insight in decision-making in the context of a community. Action follows small decisions to test out a given direction and can also provide confidence in prudential reasoning. So a researcher will need to make minijudgments about what course to take in order to align their training to a particular intention.

---

[23] Celia Deane-Drummond, "The Amnesia of Modern Universities: An Argument for Theological Wisdom in the Academe," in *Educating for Wisdom in the 21st Century*, ed. Darin Davis (South Bend, IN: St. Augustine's Press, 2019), 42–69. Wisdom is defined here as theoretical knowledge of the particular principles of connectedness which serve to shape relationships within a specific tradition; for theologians, such knowledge necessarily includes a relationship with God. Wisdom can exist within a discipline, so scientific wisdom is distinct from historical wisdom, for example. Practical wisdom, on the other hand, is about how wisdom is understood to work in practical terms, and involves deliberation, judgment, and action.

For virtue ethicists, what is called for in a conflict of interest arising from different potential goods is moral wisdom or discernment, so that, as Rosalind Hursthouse asserts, practical wisdom always makes its possessor good.[24] Practical wisdom acts like a mean between extremes, but such wisdom cannot be found in excess. Practical wisdom, or prudence, gives an *accurate* judgment of the relative risk of certain activities and the intellectual merits of a particular case. Prudence differs from art, which is merely about judgment; prudence also includes an active, practical component, leading to action.[25] Prudence in this classic sense is quite different from its common usage in the contemporary sociopolitical sphere, where it is often reduced just to a sense of caution.

If the researcher is also religious, then decisions about which scientific task to pursue are also in response to a perceived relationship with God. And working out who we are—in relationship to others and in relationship with God—is what the classical Thomistic tradition termed the virtue of *wisdom as such*, existing alongside other virtues of speculative reason, namely, understanding and science. This does not mean that there is no wisdom *of a sort* in fields other than theology, but that a theological perspective considers that the highest form of wisdom must inevitably include that relationship. The tradition of natural theology always included other domains of knowledge, so that insights from the sciences represented a form of wisdom that pointed beyond these fields to the divine source of all things in God. God, as Divine Wisdom, provides a measure of what the highest human form of wisdom entails. The speculative intellectual virtue of wisdom is a *relational* term, and inasmuch as it includes an intellectual understanding of the divine, it presupposes faith. For Thomas Aquinas, "wisdom, to which the knowledge of God belongs, is beyond man's reach .... Yet ... wisdom is preferable to all other knowledge."[26]

Is it still possible to make such a bold claim in a secular university? I suggest that it is, in that it reminds its listeners that an ultimate form of wisdom is never attainable, so that compared with the pragmatism of prudence, wisdom as such has to accept that full insight is, in principle, always impossible. That does not mean, however, that humanity should give up the search for wisdom. Further, the possibility of transcendent wisdom can be shared even by those who do not have

---

[24] Rosalind Hursthouse, *On Virtue Ethics* (Oxford: Oxford University Press, 1999), 13.
[25] The common meaning of prudence in contemporary settings, its historical emergence, and its relevance more generally are discussed in Thomas Albert Howard, "Seeing with All Three Eyes: The Virtue of Prudence and Undergraduate Education," in *At This Time and in This Place: Vocation and Higher Education*, ed. David S. Cunningham (New York: Oxford University Press, 2015), 216-34.
[26] Thomas Aquinas, *Summa Theologiae*, vol. 23, *Virtue (1a2ae. 55-67)*, trans. W. D. Hughes (London: Blackfriars, 1969), 1a2ae Qu. 66.5.

an explicit religious belief and can lead to insights beyond the day-to-day decision-making implied by practical wisdom.

In my own contact with secular anthropologists at the University of Notre Dame, for example, theological belief in wisdom has proved fascinating as a topic for further empirical research,[27] as it says something about deep human desires in a way that is missing from the more observational mode of religious studies. Further, new scientific questions about the evolution of wisdom have arisen as a result of this exchange in a way that opens up a different paradigm for human origins from that typically held by evolutionary anthropologists.[28] In this sense, theology has worked to enhance, rather than to inhibit, social scientific research. Students who hold a religious belief, similarly, need to be taught that they do not have to separate their religious beliefs from their experiences in secular subjects, or see the two domains as nonoverlapping *magisteria*; rather, they need to be encouraged to allow their religious and secular commitments to work together in the discernment process.

Prudence can also be distorted and spoiled in all kinds of ways, so that where truths are forgotten, prudence no longer flowers into action but becomes "blocked."[29] The role of the director of research or educator could be viewed as one that helps unblock potential barriers to prudence acting in the lives of the team members. But gaining a sense of what these barriers might be and helping to solve them is a pastoral as well as educational exercise. Hence, in one sense, the virtue of charity even trumps that of prudence—for without charity, prudential decision-making becomes disconnected from its source as rooted in the love of God and neighbor.

Conscience and Judgment

Conscience is perhaps best understood as an inner existential guide to right decision-making and is relevant to research practice regardless of any particular religious belief. The judgment phase of prudence requires not just prior deliberation but also a well-developed conscience.[30] This is particularly relevant for in-

---

[27] Summarized in Celia Deane-Drummond and Agustín Fuentes, eds., *Evolution of Human Wisdom* (Lanham, MD: Lexington, 2017).

[28] Discussed in Celia Deane-Drummond and Agustín Fuentes, eds., *Theology and Evolutionary Anthropology: Dialogues in Wisdom, Humility and Grace* (London: Routledge, 2020).

[29] Thomas Aquinas, *Summa Theologiae*, vol. 36, *Prudence (2a2ae. 47–56)*, trans. by Thomas Gilby (London: Blackfriars, 1973), 2a2ae Qu. 47.16.

[30] I have discussed conscience in relation to freedom and in the context of decision-making in genetics in Celia Deane-Drummond, "Freedom, Conscience and Virtue: Theological Perspectives on the Ethics of Inherited Genetic Modification," in *Design and Destiny: Jew-*

ternal decisions that have to be made even within a discipline, as well as choices about which field of study or type of work to undertake. In the area of conservation, for example, difficult decisions have to be made about which particular species to protect and why.[31] Given the variety of possible options in research, those decisions will also be decisions of conscience. They will include discernment of moral elements about both what the practice entails and the kinds of goods that result from such activity. A researcher may wish to become a theoretical physicist, but she needs to be sensitive to what her conscience is encouraging her to do when she decides how that knowledge might be used. If conscience, desire, and prudence are aligned, an authentic decision will result.

Linda Hogan has pointed out that conscience has come to be associated with what it means to be good morally.[32] From a religious perspective, the biblical tradition normally associates conscience with having *integrity:* a pure heart, a good conscience, and a genuine faith are bound up with one another.[33] But what happens if research is approved by individual conscience but opposes the teaching of the church or violates other moral rules that the researcher considers authoritative? An example in the Roman Catholic tradition might be a decision to work alongside development-aid agencies who distribute condoms to those in AIDS-ridden regions, or a decision to become a medical researcher on embryos. The tension between conformity to church teaching and individual acts of conscience is highlighted by historically diverse interpretations of the theological meaning of conscience.

According to Thomas Aquinas, *synderesis* is the habit of practical reason arising out of natural law—the first principle of which is to do good and avoid evil. Conscience refers to the way those principles, and especially the first principle, are applied in specific circumstances. This means that the rule of *synderesis* is very general; it would miss the point to see conscience as a mere application of rules. Rather, conscience attempts to take a range of factors into account before reaching a particular judgment. I believe that it is this *range* of factors that needs to be encouraged in working out the strategy for research directions.

For Augustine, conscience is never binding where it contradicts God's law. Aquinas resisted this explanation, since he believed that if natural law applies, then to imply that conscience can *knowingly* contradict God's law makes no sense; rather, a decision in a clear conscience will be *viewed* as a decision that leads to the

---

ish and Christian Perspectives on Human Germ Line Modification, ed. Ron Cole-Turner (Cambridge, MA: MIT Press, 2008), 167–200.

[31] Celia Deane-Drummond, *The Ethics of Nature* (Oxford: Wiley-Blackwell, 2004).

[32] Linda Hogan, *Confronting the Truth: Conscience in the Catholic Tradition* (New York: Paulist Press, 2000), 18–20.

[33] An example is 1 Timothy 1:5. These phrases suggest synonymous meanings—that is, conscience is associated with having moral integrity.

good. Furthermore, a law cannot bind a person who is incapable of knowing its precepts. In other words, the conscience follows the good as *perceived* good, so to act against the good is to act against reason, and thus against an act of good conscience. My own inclination is to follow Thomas and encourage researchers to follow their conscience, as long as that is reflected upon with due diligence.

Linda Hogan also points to the practical consequences of what to do with the "whispering of conscience."[34] This, I suggest, is particularly useful for discerning research directions, since envisaging a form of work may encourage the role of conscience as that which encourages us to act: I should do this or I should not do this. When, on occasion, the researcher has the opportunity to engage in particular practices, the role of conscience as witness may apply: I have become involved by trying out a particular path; and, further, conscience affirms what I have done well, or criticizes what I have done badly. All of these different senses of conscience come into play as different research possibilities come into view. In a technical sense, conscience does not direct action; still, in a practical sense, action follows its lead—insofar as the conscience will witness, incite, or confirm particular actions.

Aquinas also suggests that even where a conscience is in error, "every act of will against reason, whether in the right or in the wrong, is always bad."[35] He even goes further than this in suggesting that if the reason believes something to be the will of God, then slighting that reason amounts to slighting God's law. Hence, as indicated above, he does not pitch the divine law *against* conscience in an Augustinian manner; indeed, law and conscience work together. Moreover, a person cannot be held culpable for those errors of conscience that arise out of unavoidable ignorance, but is guilty only of those that arise out of avoidable ignorance.

Nonetheless, a note of caution is warranted in this context. It is all too easy to transpose our modern understanding of conscience onto Thomas Aquinas's position without taking sufficient account of the very severe restrictions in which his own society functioned. Individual human freedom and autonomy were not valued so highly then as they are today. Hence, Aquinas's view could be seen as a refreshing counterbalance to an overriding trend toward hegemony. In addition, his view of conscience was always optimistic about human nature; *synderesis* applied to all human persons, so in this sense all persons are naturally disposed to follow good and avoid evil. This optimistic view of human nature needs rather more qualification in the light of our more contemporary understanding of the ability for self-deception, though of course Thomas did try to take this into account. Finally, having a clear conscience is just one factor to consider in discerning research strategy in university settings.

---

[34] Hogan, *Confronting the Truth*, 9–32.
[35] Aquinas, *Summa Theologiae*, vol. 18, *Principles of Morality: Ia2ae*, trans. Thomas Gilby (London: Blackfriars, 1965), 1a2ae Qu. 19.5.

In many respects, the classical view of conscience was naive in relation to our current understanding of human psychology and sociology of knowing. However, if conscience is situated more clearly back into the tradition as an element of practical wisdom, then the difficulties encountered in fitting together a more holistic understanding of persons and conscience no longer apply.

As I noted earlier, conscience is a useful tool regardless of religious persuasion. It is particularly important where the choices faced by researchers may lead to a sense of conflicting and competing directions—both of which may not be able to be satisfied. Martha Nussbaum believes that such tragic dilemmas have to be *acknowledged* as such, and accepted as unresolvable;[36] but conscience, I suggest, enables priorities to be drawn, at least in a way that enables acceptance. That does not mean that the decision is a painless one, nor that it can merely be brushed off (as Nussbaum describes the alternative to her own account).

If conscience is understood to be the rudder that helps to steer exploration and discernment, then researchers will be more likely to claim those decisions as *their own*, rather than submitting to peer or other forms of pressure. At the same time, the interpretation of conscience in religious or even scientific communities is one which views conscience as shaped by a process of formation. Decisions are complex; they require navigating the expectations of the community, along with individual sensitivity to what is right, as guided by the action of grace in the heart of the believer—"the still small voice."

Conscience is also linked with the idea of making *responsible* decisions, where responsibility implies taking account of the societal impacts of those decisions. An act of conscience should be seen not just as an individual decision but rather as situated in a community that helps to shape conscience and is shaped by perceived decisions of conscience. Different communities will also give higher priorities to the formation of different virtues allied with prudence—including, for example, justice, compassion, temperance, and fortitude. Researchers making

---

[36] Martha Nussbaum claims in an interview that, "[o]ften when you care deeply about more than one thing, the very course of life will bring you round to a situation where you can't honor both of the commitments. It looks like anything you do will be wrong, perhaps even terrible, in some way." Bill Moyers, "Interview with Martha Nussbaum," in *Leading Lives That Matter: What We Should Do and Who We Should Be*, ed. Mark R. Schwehn and Dorothy C. Bass (Grand Rapids, MI: Eerdmans, 2006), 309. The perception that there are difficult decisions to make where both would be wrong is also echoed in the theory of double effect; but this theory still assumes a choice is possible, namely, that in situations where both outcomes are considered wrong, the choice is for the lesser of two evils. Nussbaum is of the view that often a choice is impossible, and in such circumstances would lead to a permanently troubled conscience, though she does not use the language of conscience in her interview. See also Martha Nussbaum, *The Fragility of Goodness* (Cambridge: Cambridge University Press, 1986).

important decisions about their chosen path of research do so in an academic community that has its own ethos and implicit or explicit values that shape what options are most likely to come to the surface in individual judgments of conscience. The particular institutional pressure on individuals to make choices in given directions may be either intentional or unintentional, and researchers need to be aware of this influence. In many institutions, academic programs and institutes are dedicated to explicit issues of social justice and compassion for the most vulnerable members of society in a global context.

Preliminary Conclusions: Prudence, Action, and Responsibility

One of the key distinguishing marks of prudence is that it includes *action*, and in this respect, it is distinguished from conscience, which may or may not be "obeyed" and lead to practical outcomes. Prudence, therefore, necessitates a *putting into practice* and a testing out that are highly relevant across a wide range of disciplines, both theoretical and applied. I suggest that this aspect of prudence is particularly important for choices of research focus across a wide range of disciplines, since different options can be "tried out" in educational and research contexts as part of the experience of learning.

Developing prudence can also be linked with encouraging a sense of responsibility—both for individuals and for the communities of which they are part. For those researchers who understand God to be the cause of their commitment to scientific discovery or other types of research, there will be a resonance with Frederick Buechner's claim that "the place God calls you to is the place where your deep gladness and the world's deep hunger meet."[37] For researchers who do not share these assumptions, a wider sense of moral and social responsibility is often present; what they perceive as good may often be shared with those who take a more specifically theological perspective. Hence, learning the art of being a responsible chemist, biologist, or engineer may not differ very much whatever the religious background or perception of the individual. Developing as a researcher in both secular and religious cases is not simply transactional—that is, not simply a matter of how one functions in a society and the role that one plays, as if it were a matter of a linear logical deduction. Rather, there are likely to be *transcendent* elements in any sense of keen responsibility for others, whether these are acknowledged or not.

The task of the researcher and educator is to discern what *kind* of responsibilities are the most appropriate as goals in the light of the particular decision to

---

[37] Frederick Buechner, *Wishful Thinking: A Theological ABC* (New York: HarperCollins, 1973), 95.

be made. The classical tradition, drawing on Aristotelian philosophy, stressed human flourishing as that which oriented particular decisions and served to build morally responsible agents.

Both practical wisdom and conscience work together in the life of individuals and communities to help them discern what might be the best available choice at a particular moment. The epistemic issue of how one might come to *know* the most appropriate choice to make is confounded by the possibility of misinterpreting the direction in which to go or being deceived. Practical wisdom and conscience are, in some respects, building on that insight, as well as taking into account the communal aspects of decision-making. Decisions of practical wisdom will never have the kind of certainty of mind that might be true for other aspects of life, and in this respect the strategic direction for research initiatives will participate in that uncertainty. Both practical wisdom and conscience help navigate the increasingly complex factors that come into play as researchers face new responsibilities. In this respect, practical wisdom and conscience are implemented through particular decisions, even as they are formed in the process of that implementation. Knowing what good research will be when there is a range of possible options presupposes imagination and confidence, in that knowing is developed through time, the particular expression of which will be unique for each individual as situated in a particular social network. A research community, in this sense, can only hope to be a midwife, nurturing research to go in one direction rather than an alternative.

Contributors

Stefan Alkier
Professor of New Testament Theology, Goethe-University of Frankfurt

Rüdiger Bittner
Professor of Philosophy, the University of Bielefeld

Celia Deane-Drummond
Senior Research Fellow in Theology and Director of the Laudato Si' Research Institute, Campion Hall, the University of Oxford; Honorary Visiting Professor in Theology and Science, the University of Durham, UK; and Adjunct Professor of Theology, the University of Notre Dame

Bernold Fiedler
Professor and Director, Institute for Mathematics, the Free University of Berlin

Andreas Glaeser
Professor of Sociology, the University of Chicago

Gary S. Hauk
University Historian, Emeritus, and former Vice President, Emory University

Jörg Hüfner
Professor and Director, Institute for Theoretical Physics, the University of Heidelberg

Michael Kirschfink
Professor and Director, Institute of Immunology and Serology, the University of Heidelberg

Andreas Schüle
Professor of Old Testament Theology, the University of Leipzig

William Schweiker
Edward L. Ryerson Distinguished Service Professor of Theological Ethics, the University of Chicago

Michael Welker
Senior Professor of Systematic Theology and Director of FIIT, the Research Center International and Interdisciplinary Theology, the University of Heidelberg

John Witte Jr.
Robert W. Woodruff Professor of Law, McDonald Distinguished Professor of Religion, and Director of the Center for the Study of Law and Religion, Emory University School of Law

Forthcoming

John Witte | Michael Welker | Stephen Pickard (Eds.)
The Impact of the Family
on Character Formation, Ethical Education, and the Communication
of Values in Late Modern Pluralistic Societies
approx. 2021

Stephen Pickard | Michael Welker | John Witte (Eds.)
The Impact of Education
on Character Formation, Ethics, and the Communication
of Values in Late Modern Pluralistic Societies
approx. 2021

The Impact of Military/Defense
on Character Formation, Ethical Education, and the Communication
of Values in Late Modern Pluralistic Societies
approx. 2022

The Impact of Media
on Character Formation, Ethical Education, and the Communication
of Values in Late Modern Pluralistic Societies
approx. 2022

The Impact of Healthcare
on Character Formation, Ethical Education, and the Communication
of Values in Late Modern Pluralistic Societies
approx. 2023

The Impact of Politics
on Character Formation, Ethical Education, and the Communicatio
of Values in Late Modern Pluralistic Societies
approx. 2023

Tel +49 (0) 341/ 7 11 41 -44   shop@eva-leipzig.de

Jürgen von Hagen | Michael Welker
John Witte | Stephen Pickard (Eds.)
The Impact of the Market
on Character Formation, Ethical Education,
and the Communication of Values
in Late Modern Pluralistic Societies

300 pages | paperback | 15,5 x 23 cm
ISBN 978-3-374-06406-9
EUR 30,00 [D]

Pluralism has become the defining characteristic of modern societies. Individuals with differing values clamor for equality. Some see in this clash of principles and aims the potential for a more just human community, while others fear the erosion of enduring culture. Yet beneath this welter stand powerful and pervasive institutions, whose distinctive norms profoundly shape our moral commitments and character—notably the family, the market, the media, and systems of law, religion, politics, research, education, health care, and defense. Globalization carries the shifting dynamic between individuals and institutions into every part of the globe.

Drawing on scholarship from five continents, many disciplines, and diverse religious perspectives, this series examines the impact of these various institutions. The contributors hope that this conversation will help address the increasing challenges confronting our pluralist societies and our world.

In the theoretical, empirical, and historical contributions to this volume, theologians, economists and market practitioners discuss the many tensions between market economics, ethics and the Christian religion, thus adding to the fruitful and much needed dialogue between economics and theology.

EVANGELISCHE VERLAGSANSTALT
Leipzig   www.eva-leipzig.de

Tel +49 (0) 341/ 7 11 41 -44   shop@eva-leipzig.de

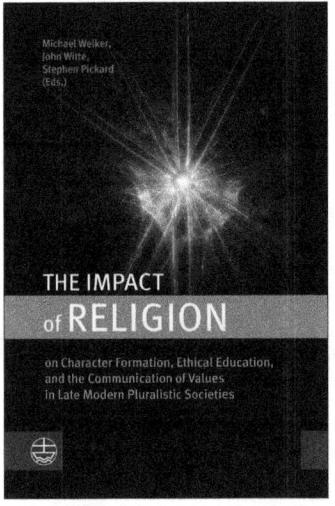

Michael Welker | John Witte
Stephen Pickard (Eds.)
The Impact of Religion
on Character Formation, Ethical Education,
and the Communication of Values
in Late Modern Pluralistic Societies

288 pages | paperback | 15,5 x 23 cm
ISBN 978-3-374-06410-6
EUR 30,00 [D]

Pluralism has become the defining characteristic of modern societies. Individuals with differing values clamor for equality. Organizations and groups assert particular interests. Social movements flourish and fade. Some see in this clash of principles and aims the potential for a more just human community, while others fear the erosion of enduring culture. Yet beneath this welter stand powerful and pervasive institutions, whose distinctive norms profoundly shape our moral commitments and character—notably the family, the market, the media, and systems of law, religion, politics, research, education, health care, and defense.

Drawing on scholarship from five continents, many disciplines, and diverse religious perspectives, this series examines the impact of these various institutions on moral education, character, and values. As globalization carries the shifting dynamic between individuals and institutions into every part of the globe, the contributors hope that this conversation will help address the increasing challenges confronting our pluralist societies and our world.

The overwhelming majority of the contributions in this volume deal with the Christian religion, as pluralistic societies today thrive substantially in Christian environments.

EVANGELISCHE VERLAGSANSTALT
Leipzig   www.eva-leipzig.de

John Witte | Michael Welker (Eds.)
The Impact of the Law
on Character Formation, Ethical Education,
and the Communication of Values
in Late Modern Pluralistic Societies

288 pages | paperback | 15,5 x 23 cm
ISBN 978-3-374-06801-2
EUR 30,00 [D]

This volume addresses whether, how, and where laws (variously defined) teach values and shape moral character in late modern liberal societies. Each author recognizes the essential value of state law in fostering peace, security, health, education, charity, trade, democracy, constitutionalism, justice, and human rights, among many other moral goods. Each author also recognizes, however, the grave betrayals of law in supporting fascism, slavery, apartheid, genocide, persecution, violence, racism, and other forms of immorality and injustice. They thus call for state laws that set a basic civil morality of duty for society and for robust freedoms that protect private individuals and private groups to cultivate a higher morality of aspiration.

EVANGELISCHE VERLAGSANSTALT
Leipzig   www.eva-leipzig.de

Tel +49 (0) 341/ 7 11 41 -44   shop@eva-leipzig.de

www.ingramcontent.com/pod-product-compliance
Lightning Source LLC
Chambersburg PA
CBHW071441150426
43191CB00008B/1192